THE
WAR
ON
NORMAL
PEOPLE

THE TRUTH ABOUT AMERICA'S
DISAPPEARING JOBS AND
WHY UNIVERSAL BASIC INCOME
IS OUR FUTURE

ANDREW YANG

NEW YORK   BOSTON

Hachette Books
Hachette Book Group
1290 Avenue of the Americas
New York, NY 10104
hachettebooks.com
twitter.com/hachettebooks

First Edition: April 2018

Hachette Books is a division of Hachette Book Group, Inc.
The Hachette Books name and logo are trademarks of Hachette Book Group, Inc.

The publisher is not responsible for websites (or their content) that are not owned by the publisher.

The Hachette Speakers Bureau provides a wide range of authors for speaking events. To find out more, go to www.hachettespeakersbureau.com or call (866) 376-6591.

Library of Congress Control Number: 2017918606

ISBNs: 978-0-316-41424-1 (hardcover), 978-0-316-41425-8 (ebook)

Printed in the United States of America

LSC-H

10 9 8 7 6 5 4 3 2 1

To everyone who helped build Venture for America over the years.

You made me believe in people.

CONTENTS

CONTENTS

We are at the most dangerous moment in the development of humanity… the rise of artificial intelligence is likely to extend job destruction deep into the middle classes, with only the most caring, creative or supervisory roles remaining.

—STEPHEN HAWKING

Human beings are also animals, to manage one million animals gives me a headache.

—TERRY GOU, FOUNDER OF FOXCONN

INTRODUCTION

THE GREAT DISPLACEMENT

I am writing from inside the tech bubble to let you know that we are coming for your jobs.

I recently met a pair of old friends for drinks in Manhattan. One is an executive who works at a software company in New York. They replace call center workers with artificial intelligence software. I asked her whether she believed her work would result in job losses. She responded matter-of-factly, "We are getting better and better at things that will make large numbers of workers extraneous. And we will succeed. There needs to be a dramatic reskilling of the workforce, but that's not going to be practical for a lot of people. It's impossible to avoid a lost generation of workers." Her confidence in this assessment was total. The conversation then quickly shifted to more pleasant topics.

I later met with a friend who's a Boston-based venture capitalist. He told me he felt "a little uneasy" about investing in software and robotics companies that, if successful, would eliminate large numbers of jobs. "But they're good opportunities," he noted, estimating that 70 percent of the startups he's seeing will contribute to job losses in other parts of the economy.

In San Francisco, I had breakfast with an operations manager for a large tech company. He told me, "I just helped set up a factory that had 70 percent fewer workers than one even a few years ago would have had, and most of them are high-end technicians on laptops. I have no idea what normal people are going to do in a few years."

Normal people. Seventy percent of Americans consider themselves part of the middle class. Chances are, you do, too. Right now some of the smartest people in the country are trying to figure out how to replace you with an overseas worker, a cheaper version of you, or, increasingly, a widget, software program, or robot. There's no malice in it. The market rewards business leaders for making things more efficient. Efficiency doesn't love normal people. It loves getting things done in the most cost-effective way possible.

A wave of automation and job loss is no longer a dystopian vision of the future—it's well under way. The numbers have been telling a story for a while now that we have been ignoring. More and more people of prime working age have been dropping out of the workforce. There's a growing mass of the permanently displaced. Automation is accelerating to a point where it will soon threaten our social fabric and way of life.

Experts and researchers project an unprecedented wave of job destruction coming with the development of artificial intelligence, robotics, software, and automation. The Obama White House published a report in December 2016 that predicted 83 percent of jobs where people make less than $20 per hour will be subject to automation or replacement. Between 2.2 and 3.1 million car, bus, and truck driving jobs in the United States will be eliminated by the advent of self-driving vehicles.

Read that last sentence again: we are confident that between 2 and 3 million Americans who drive vehicles for a living will lose their jobs in the next 10 to 15 years. Driving a truck is the most common occupation in 29 states. Self-driving vehicles are one of the most obvious job-destroying technologies, but there are similar innovations ahead that will displace cashiers, fast food workers, customer service representatives, administrative assistants, and even well-paid white-collar jobs like wealth managers, lawyers, and insurance agents, all within the span of a few short years. Suddenly out of work, millions will struggle to find a new job, particularly those at the lower end of the skill ladder.

Automation has already eliminated about 4 million manufacturing jobs in the United States since 2000. Instead of finding new jobs, a lot of those people left the workforce and didn't come back. The U.S. labor force participation rate is now at only 62.9 percent, a rate below that of nearly all other industrialized economies and about the same as that of El Salvador and the Ukraine. Some of this is driven by an aging population, which presents its own set of problems, but much of it is driven by automation and a lower demand for labor.

Each 1 percent decline in the labor participation rate equates to approximately 2.5 million Americans dropping out. The number

Labor Force Participation Rate (1950-2017)

Source: U.S. Bureau of Labor Statistics.

of working-age Americans who aren't in the workforce has surged to a record 95 million. Ten years into the nation's recovery from the financial crisis and 95 million working-age Americans not in the workforce—I've taken to calling this phenomenon the Great Displacement.

The lack of mobility and growth has created a breeding ground for political hostility and social ills. High rates of unemployment and underemployment are linked to an array of social problems, including substance abuse, domestic violence, child abuse, and depression. Today 40 percent of American children are born outside of married households, due in large part to the crumbling marriage rate among working-class adults, and overdoses and suicides have overtaken auto accidents as leading causes of death. More than half of American households already rely on the government for direct income in some form. In some parts of the United States, 20 percent of working-age adults are now on disability, with increasing numbers citing mood disorders. What Americans who cannot find jobs find instead is despair. If you care about communities and our way of life, you care about people having jobs.

This is the most pressing economic and social issue of our time; our economy is evolving in ways that will make it more and more difficult for people with lower levels of education to find jobs and support themselves. Soon, these difficulties will afflict the white-collar world. It's a boiling pot getting hotter one degree at a time. And we're the frog.

In my role as founder of Venture for America, I spent the past six years working with hundreds of startups across the country in cities like Detroit, New Orleans, Cincinnati, Providence, Cleveland, Baltimore, Philadelphia, St. Louis, Birmingham, Columbus, Pittsburgh,

San Antonio, Charlotte, Miami, Nashville, Atlanta, and Denver. Some of these places were bustling industrial centers in the late 19th and 20th centuries, only to find themselves faced with population loss and economic transition as the 20th century wound down. Venture for America trains young aspiring entrepreneurs to work at startups in cities like these to generate job growth. We've had many successes. But the kinds of jobs created tend to be very specific; every business I worked with will hire the very best people it can find—particularly startups. When entrepreneurs start companies and expand, they generally aren't hiring a down-on-his-or-her-luck worker in need of a break. They are hiring the strongest contributors with the right mix of qualities to help an early-stage company succeed. Most jobs in a startup essentially require a college degree. That excludes 68 percent of the population right there. And some of these companies are lifting further inefficiencies out of the system—reducing jobs in other places even while hiring their own new workers.

There's a scene in Ben Horowitz's book *The Hard Things about Hard Things* in which he depicts the CEO of a company meeting with his two lieutenants. The CEO says to one of them, "You're going to do everything in your power to make this deal work." Then he turns to the other and says, "Even if he does everything right, it's probably not going to work. Your job is to fix it." That's where we're at with the American economy. Unprecedented advances are accelerating in real time and wreaking havoc on lives and communities around the country, particularly on those least able to adapt and adjust.

We must do all we can to reduce the worst effects of the Great Displacement—it should be the driving priority of corporations, government, and nonprofits for the foreseeable future. We should invest in education, job training and placement, apprenticeships, relocation, entrepreneurship, and tax incentives—anything to help make hiring and retaining workers appealing. And then we should acknowledge that, for millions of people, it's not going to work.

In the United States we want to believe that the market will resolve most situations. In this case, the market will not solve the problem—quite the opposite. The market is driven to reduce costs. It will look to find the cheapest way to perform tasks. The market doesn't want to provide for unemployed truck drivers or cashiers. Uber is going to get rid of its drivers as soon as it can. Its job isn't to hire lots of people—its job is to move customers around as efficiently as possible. The market will continue to throw millions of people out of the labor force as automation and technology improve. In order for society to continue to function and thrive when tens of millions of Americans don't have jobs, we will need to rethink the relationship between work and being able to pay for basic needs. And then, we will have to determine ways to convey the psychic and social benefits of work in other ways.

There is really only one entity—the federal government—that can realistically reformat society in ways that will prevent large swaths of the country from becoming jobless zones of derelict buildings and broken people. Nonprofits will be at the front lines of fighting the decline, but most of their activities will be like bandages on top of an infected wound. State governments are generally hamstrung with balanced budget requirements and limited resources.

Even if they don't talk about it in public, many technologists themselves fear a backlash. My friends in Silicon Valley want to be positive, but many are buying bunkers and escape hatches just in case. One reason that solutions are daunting to even my most optimistic friends is that, while their part of the American economy is flourishing, little effort is being made to distribute the gains from automation and reverse the decline in opportunities. To do so would require an active, stable, invigorated, unified federal government willing to make large bets. This, unfortunately, is not what we have. We have an indebted state rife with infighting, dysfunction, and outdated ideas and bureaucracies from bygone eras, along with a populace that cannot agree on basic facts like vote totals or climate change. Our politicians offer half-hearted solutions that will at best nibble at the edges of the problem. The budget for research and development in the Department of Labor is only $4 million. We have a 1960s-era government that has few solutions to the problems of 2018.

This must change if our way of life is to continue. We need a revitalized, dynamic government to rise to the challenge posed by the largest economic transformation in the history of mankind.

The above may sound like science fiction to you. But you're reading this with a supercomputer in your pocket (or reading it on the supercomputer itself) and Donald Trump was elected president. Doctors can fix your eyes with lasers, but your local mall just closed. We are living in unprecedented times. The future without jobs will come to resemble either the cultivated benevolence of *Star Trek* or the desperate scramble for resources of *Mad Max*. Unless there is a dramatic course correction, I fear we are heading toward the latter.

As Bismarck said, "If revolution there is to be, let us rather undertake it not undergo it." Society will change either before or after the revolution. I choose before.

I'm a serial entrepreneur who started out as a lawyer. Before launching Venture for America, I co-founded an Internet company, worked at a health care software startup, and ran a national education company that was acquired in 2009. I've worked in startups and economic development for 17 years. I know how companies operate and how jobs are created and reduced. I'm also both an ardent capitalist and completely certain that our system needs to change in order to continue our way of life.

Our society has already been shaped by large-scale changes in the economy due to technological advances. It turns out that Americans have been dealing with the lack of meaningful opportunities by getting married less and becoming less and less functional. The fundamental message is that we are already on the edge of dystopia with hundreds of thousands of families and communities being pushed into oblivion.

Education and retraining won't address the gaps; the goalposts are now moving and many affected workers are well past their prime. We need to establish an updated form of capitalism—I call it Human-Centered Capitalism, or Human Capitalism for short—to amend our current version of institutional capitalism that will lead us toward ever-increasing automation accompanied by social ruin. We must make the market serve humanity rather than have humanity continue to serve the market. We must simultaneously become more dynamic and more empathetic as a society. We must change and grow faster than most think possible.

When the next downturn hits, hundreds of thousands of people will wake up to do their jobs only to be told that they're no longer needed. Their factory or retail store or office or mall or business or truck stop or agency will close. They will look for another job and, this time, they will not find one. They will try to keep up a brave face, but the days and weeks will pass and they will become more and more defeated. They will almost always blame themselves for their lot. They will say things like, "I wish I'd applied myself more in school," or "I should have picked another job." They'll burn through their meager savings. Their family lives and communities will suffer. Some will turn to substance abuse or watch too much TV. Their health will slip—the ailments they've been working through will seem twice as painful. Their marriages will fail. They will lose their sense of self-worth. Their physical environments will decay around them and their loved ones will become reminders of their failure.

For every displaced worker, there will be two or three others who have their shifts and hours reduced, their benefits cut, and their already precarious financial lives pushed to the brink. They will try to consider themselves lucky even as their hopes for the future dim.

Meanwhile, in Manhattan and Silicon Valley and Washington, DC, my friends and I will be busier than ever fighting to stay current and climb within our own hypercompetitive environments. We will read articles with concern about the future and think about how to redirect our children to more fertile professions and livelihoods. We will retweet something and contribute here and there. We will occasionally reflect on the fates of others and shake our heads, determined to be among the winners in whatever the new economy brings.

The logic of the meritocracy is leading us to ruin, because we are collectively primed to ignore the voices of the millions getting pushed into economic distress by the grinding wheels of automation and innovation. We figure they're complaining or suffering because they're losers.

We need to break free of this logic of the marketplace before it's too late.

We must reshape and accelerate society to bring us all to higher ground. We must find new ways to organize ourselves independent of the values that the marketplace assigns to each and every one of us.

We are more than the numbers on our paychecks—and we are going to have to prove it very quickly.

PART ONE:

WHAT'S HAPPENING TO JOBS

ONE

MY JOURNEY

I grew up a skinny Asian kid in upstate New York who was often ignored or picked on—like one of the kids from *Stranger Things* but nerdier and with fewer friends. It stuck with me. I've never forgotten what it felt like to be young. To be gnawed at by doubts and fears so deep that they inflict physical pain, a sense of nausea deep in your stomach. To feel like an alien, to be ignored or ridiculed. I didn't think it was possible to forget all that. But it turns out that most of us do. In movies, they show children going through

formative experiences at home. The protagonists go back where they came from later to make it better. In real life, none of us goes back.

My parents valued education deeply. My father, who immigrated from Taiwan, worked in the research labs of GE and IBM. He got his PhD in physics from Berkeley and generated 69 patents over his career. He met my mom, also from Taiwan, while in grad school. She has a master's in statistics and worked as a computer services administrator at our local university before becoming an artist. My brother became a professor, which is kind of the family business. Being the first generation born in this country gave me both a fierce love for the United States and a deep sense of what it means to struggle to fit in.

I was one of the only Asians in my local public school. That didn't go unnoticed. Classmates offered frequent reminders as to my identity:

"What's up, chink."

"Hey…you…wanna fight?" said with mouth moving but no sound coming out, to imitate a kung fu movie with bad dubbing.

"Ching chong ching chong."

"Hey, you know what Chinese use for blindfolds? Dental floss!"

"You see that?" Demonstrates a blank face. "That's the way the gook laughs."

"Hey, Yang, you hungry? You want a gook-ie?"

"Hey, Yang. I see where you're looking. No interracial dating."

"Hey, Yang, what's it like having such a small dick? Everyone knows Chinese guys have small dicks. Do you need tweezers to masturbate?"

Most of this was in middle school. I had a few natural responses: I became quite self-conscious. I started wondering if I did indeed have a small dick. Last, I became very, very angry.

Perhaps as a result, I've always taken pride in relating to the underdog or little guy or gal. As I grew up, I tried to stick up for whoever seemed excluded or marginalized. I became a Mets fan. I'd go to a party and find the person who seemed the most alone or uncomfortable and strike up a conversation. I worked out a little too much in college.

I grew up and found that my zeal extended into my professional life. I love small companies and helping them grow. After five months as a corporate lawyer, I co-founded an Internet company when I was 25, back in 2000. After it went bust, I worked at a medical records software company, and then helped a friend, Zeke Vanderhoek, with his GMAT prep company when he was starting out as a solo tutor in a Starbucks. He eventually asked me to take over as CEO. Between the two of us and our team, we grew the company to become number one in the country.

By 2010 I was riding high. Our company, Manhattan Prep, had been acquired by the Washington Post Company's Kaplan division for millions of dollars. I was 35 years old, the head of a national education company that I loved, living in New York City among family and friends, and engaged to marry my fiancée the following year. I was on top of the world.

And yet, something bothered me that I couldn't let go. I'd trained hundreds of young people—as CEO of Manhattan Prep I'd taught the analyst classes at Goldman Sachs, McKinsey, J.P. Morgan, Morgan Stanley, and many other companies. These college graduates often seemed disenchanted with their careers; they were looking to go to business school to take a break and find the next step. Many of them hailed from other parts of the country—Michigan, Ohio, Georgia— and had come to Wall Street for better opportunities. When I talked to them after class, they seemed to be searching for some higher purpose that had eluded them. They reminded me of myself a decade earlier, when I had started my career as an unhappy corporate lawyer.

I thought, "Wow, we have a ton of smart people doing the same few things in the same few places." I imagined what the best use of their talent would be. One weekend I was back on campus at Brown and met an entrepreneur in Providence, Charlie Kroll, who had started a local company with 100 employees instead of heading to Wall Street. I arrived at a vision: an army of smart, enterprising graduates building businesses in Detroit, New Orleans, Providence, Baltimore, Cleveland, St. Louis, and other communities that could use a boost. New companies have accounted for all domestic job growth the past 20 years. More people building things in areas of need would inject vitality, create opportunities, and help regional economies become more dynamic. Cities like Detroit and New Orleans seemed to me to be the ultimate underdogs.

I knew building a new company was a very tall order for any recent graduate. But I had learned a lot from working with more experienced CEOs and teams; I believed this apprenticeship model was the best way to develop, since that's the way that I'd learned throughout my twenties. Win or lose, they'd get stronger. They'd also likely reflect a different set of values after having worked in a startup in an emerging city for a few years.

I became fixated on the idea of training hundreds of enterprising college grads and sending them to startup companies in other U.S. cities to promote job growth and innovation in regions across the country. We would provide an accelerator and seed fund to help them start businesses after two years. Our goal would be to help create 100,000 new U.S. jobs by 2025. I called the organization Venture for America. People loved the idea. Many said they would have done something like Venture for America if it had existed when they had graduated from college.

I took my first trip to Detroit in 2010 to see if there were businesses there that could use talent to help them grow. The city was just beginning its descent into bankruptcy—I remember the cold, empty streets feeling abandoned. I joked with a friend, "I felt like running red lights as soon as I got here, it's so empty." The city has come a long way since those low points. I met with several local entrepreneurs who said they'd jump at the chance to hire energetic recent grads who wanted to get their hands dirty. The same was true in Providence, New Orleans, and Cincinnati. Meeting with the entrepreneurs in these cities convinced me that I was on the right track.

In 2011 I donated $120K and quit my job to start Venture for America, with the mission of revitalizing American cities and communities through entrepreneurship. That first year our budget was about $200K.

In 2018, our budget is more than 25 times higher and we've recruited and trained hundreds of young up-and-coming aspiring entrepreneurs from around the country out of thousands of applicants. Supporters include CEOs, celebrities, entrepreneurs, major companies, foundations, and even the state of Ohio. Our efforts have helped create over 2,500 jobs in 18 cities and our alums have started dozens of companies. Out of our last class, 43 percent were women and 25 percent were black or Latino. I wrote a well-received book, and a documentary, *Generation Startup*, followed six of our entrepreneurs as they started businesses in Detroit.

I've seen dozens of idealistic 22-year-olds evolve into founders and CEOs of scrappy young companies that touch thousands of lives. I've seen and helped hundreds of little startups grow into mature companies with hundreds of employees. I've seen neighborhoods on the edge of desolation become filled with people and new businesses. I've worked with some of the most idealistic and noble people in the country making great things happen in unlikely places. My work with Venture for America opened new doors, and people sought out my advice on innovation and entrepreneurship. Here's me explaining Venture for America to President Obama in 2012:

I was riding high. My personal life progressed as well in these years. My wife and I got married, and we now have two sons who occupy many of our waking hours. Being a parent is much harder than I ever thought it would be but brings its own sense of fulfillment.

And yet in 2016 something started bothering me—a feeling I couldn't seem to shake. As I crisscrossed the country, I often found places that seemed to be in the midst of long-term decay. I ate in diners where I was one of very few customers they'd see all day, drove past boarded up businesses and FOR SALE signs, walked into derelict buildings and factories, saw the looks of resignation on people's faces. The overall feeling was one of defeat and downtroddenness. The entrepreneurship messages of "take risks" and "it's okay to fail" seemed ridiculous and misplaced in many of these contexts. It felt like the metaphorical water level in many places had risen and overtaken whole communities. I would often fly back to Manhattan or Silicon Valley after a trip and think, "I can't believe I'm still in the same country." I'd sit down for dinner with my friends and feel like a character in a play about people who ate well while the world burned, struggling to understand and share what I'd seen.

It was less the buildings and surroundings and more the people. They seemed despondent and depressed, like their horizons had been lowered to simply scraping by.

As for me, I had gone from being an underdog to one of the guys with the answers, from finding the most marginalized or excluded person in the room to finding the richest person and making him or her feel special. The mechanics of growing a nonprofit made me into the head of an establishment, which in turn made me more responsive to resource-rich institutions and people. I spent a lot of time with people who had already won, which was not what I'd envisioned.

I began to see the limitations of what was then happening in the entrepreneurship, nonprofit, and government sectors. I would be invited to high-level conferences or design sessions, only to have colleagues—even people who were considered the most successful in the field—confide to me that they didn't believe they were meaningfully addressing the problems they set out to solve, that they would need 10 or 100 or 1,000 times the resources to have a chance to do so. People were clapping us on the back, congratulating us on our accomplishments, and we were thinking to ourselves, *What are you congratulating us for? The problems are just getting worse.*

This sense of unease plagued me, and I became consumed by two fundamental and uncomfortable questions: "What the heck is happening to the United States?" and "Why am I becoming such a tool?" I began to feel that my life more closely resembles a dream life in a bubble than the experience of the average American, and that too much of our human and financial capital is flowing to just a handful of places doing things that are speeding the machine up rather than fixing what is going wrong. I was also morphing from the guy who wanted to fix the machine into an add-on to the machine. I love Venture for America. It was the culmination of my life's work. But it needed to be much, much bigger to stem the tide.

I started digging into research about trends in the labor market and talking to friends to better understand the long-term shifts happening in the American economy. I wanted to know what the challenges were. Donald Trump's election in late 2016 heightened my sense of urgency; it felt like a cry for help.

What I found shocked me and verified my experiences on the road. America is starting 100,000 fewer businesses per year than it was only 12 years ago, and is in the midst of shedding millions of jobs due primarily to technological advances. Our economic engine is stalling out in many places, and automation is eliminating livelihoods for hundreds of thousands of the most vulnerable Americans in regions across the country. New jobs are less numerous, are most often created in towns located far from those most hard hit, and require far different skills than the ones that are being lost. Technology is about to reach a point where it won't just be folks in the interior that are threatened, but many white-collar and educated workers as well.

I remember the moment it finally sank in completely. I was reading a CNN article that detailed how automation had eliminated millions of manufacturing jobs between 2000 and 2015, four times more than globalization. I had walked through many of the cities that had previously been home to those jobs—Cleveland, Cincinnati, Indianapolis, Detroit, Pittsburgh, St. Louis, Baltimore, and their surrounding areas. I knew what my friends were working on and what was coming down the road. As I felt the pieces fall into place, my heart sank and my mind raced. Nothing will stop us. We had decimated the economies and cultures of these regions and were set to do the same to many others.

In response, American lives and families are falling apart. Rampant financial stress is the new normal. We are in the third or fourth inning of the greatest economic shift in the history of mankind, and no one seems to be talking about it or doing anything in response.

I spent the past six years trying to address these problems by helping growth companies create jobs in different regions and training entrepreneurs. It has been my job for the past six years to create jobs. I'm about to lose—we're all about to lose—on an epic scale. I'm now certain that the wave—the Great Displacement—is already here and is having effects bigger and faster than most anyone believes. The most pernicious thing about this wave is that you can't really tell who it has hit as it grinds up people and communities.

I've switched gears. My goal now is to give everyone a sense of what's coming and then prepare us to fight for the version of the future that we want. It will be a massive challenge. It's up to us; the market will not help us. Indeed, it is about to turn on us. The solutions aren't beyond us yet, but it's getting late in the day and time is running short. I need you to see what I see.

TWO

HOW WE GOT HERE

The Great Displacement didn't arrive overnight. It has been building for decades as the economy and labor market changed in response to improving technology, financialization, changing corporate norms, and globalization.

In the 1970s, when my parents worked at GE and Blue Cross Blue Shield in upstate New York, their companies provided generous pensions and expected them to stay for decades. Community banks were boring businesses that lent money to local companies for a modest return. Over 20 percent of workers were unionized. Some economic problems existed—growth was uneven and inflation periodically high. But income inequality was low, jobs provided benefits, and Main Street businesses were the drivers of the economy. There were only three television networks, and in my house we watched them on a TV with an antenna that we fiddled with to make the picture clearer.

That all seems awfully quaint today. Pensions disappeared for private-sector employees years ago. Most community banks were gobbled up by one of the mega-banks in the 1990s—today five banks control 50 percent of the commercial banking industry, which itself mushroomed to the point where finance enjoys about 25 percent of all corporate profits. Union membership fell by 50 percent.

Ninety-four percent of the jobs created between 2005 and 2015 were temp or contractor jobs without benefits; people working multiple gigs to make ends meet is increasingly the norm. Real wages have been flat or even declining. The chances that an American born in 1990 will earn more than their parents are down to 50 percent; for Americans born in 1940 the same figure was 92 percent.

Thanks to Milton Friedman, Jack Welch, and other corporate titans, the goals of large companies began to change in the 1970s and early 1980s. The notion they espoused—that a company exists only to maximize its share price—became gospel in business schools and boardrooms around the country. Companies were pushed to adopt shareholder value as their sole measuring stick. Hostile takeovers, shareholder lawsuits, and later activist hedge funds served as prompts to ensure that managers were committed to profitability at all costs. On the flip side, CEOs were granted stock options for the first time that wedded their individual gain to the company's share price. The ratio of CEO to worker pay rose from 20 to 1 in 1965 to 271 to 1 in 2016. Benefits were streamlined and reduced and the relationship between company and employee weakened to become more transactional.

Simultaneously, the major banks grew and evolved as Depression-era regulations separating consumer lending and investment banking were abolished. Financial deregulation started under Ronald Reagan in 1980 and culminated in the Financial Services Modernization Act of 1999 under Bill Clinton that really set the banks loose. The securities industry grew 500 percent as a share of GDP between 1980 and the 2000s while ordinary bank deposits shrank from 70 percent to 50 percent. Financial products multiplied as even Main Street companies were driven to pursue financial engineering to manage their affairs. GE, my dad's old company and once a beacon of manufacturing, became the fifth biggest financial institution in the country by 2007.

With improved technology and new access to global markets,

American companies realized they could outsource manufacturing, information technology, and customer service to Chinese and Mexican factories and Indian programmers and call centers. U.S. companies outsourced and offshored 14 million jobs by 2013, many of which would have previously been filled by domestic workers at higher wages. This resulted in lower prices, higher efficiencies, and some new opportunities but also increased pressures on American workers who now had to compete with a global labor pool.

Automation started out on farms earlier in the century with tractors and then migrated to factories in the 1970s. Manufacturing employment began to slip around 1978 as wage growth began to fall. Median wages used to go up in lockstep with productivity and GDP growth before diverging sharply in the 1970s. Since 1973, productivity has skyrocketed relative to the hourly compensation of the average wage earner:

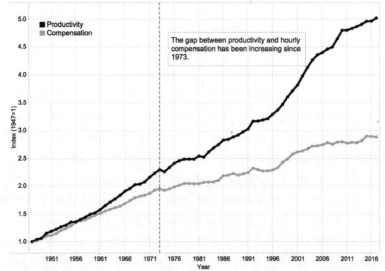

Productivity and Hourly Compensation Growth (1949-2017)

The gap between productivity and hourly compensation has been increasing since 1973.

Source: U.S. Bureau of Labor Statistics, Business Sector: Real Compensation per Hour and Real Output per Hour of All Persons, retrieved from FRED, Federal Reserve Bank of St. Louis.

How workers are compensated and how their companies perform stopped being aligned over the same period. Even as corporate profitability has soared to record highs, workers are earning less. The share of GDP going to wages has fallen from almost 54 percent in 1970 to 44 percent in 2013, while the share going to corporate profits went from about 4 percent to 11 percent. Being a shareholder has been great for your bottom line. Being a worker, not so much.

Today, inequality has surged to historic levels, with benefits flowing increasingly to the top 1 percent and 20 percent of earners due to an aggregation of capital at the top and increased winner-take-all economics. The top 1 percent have accrued 52 percent of the real income growth in America since 2009. Technology is a big part of this story, as it tends to lead to a small handful of winners. Studies have shown that everyone is less happy in an unequal society—even

Cumulative Growth in Average After-Tax Income, by Income Group (1979-2007)

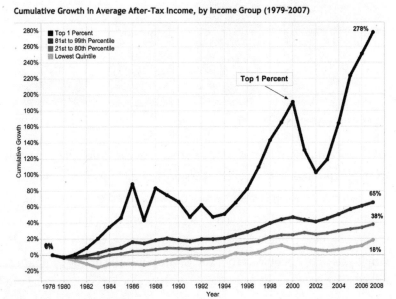

Source: Congressional Budget Office.

those at the top. The wealthy experience higher levels of depression and suspicion in unequal societies; apparently, being high status is easier when you don't feel bad about it.

JOBS DON'T GROW LIKE THEY USED TO

Companies can now prosper, grow, and mint record profits without hiring many people or increasing wages. Both job creation and wage growth have been weaker than the top-line economic growth would suggest since the 1970s. In each of the last several decades, the economy has created lower percentages of new jobs, including no new net jobs between 2000 and 2010 due to the Great Recession.

Jobs Added to the U.S. Economy (1976-2015)

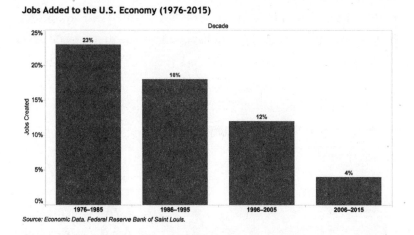

Source: Economic Data. Federal Reserve Bank of Saint Louis.

The changing role of labor can be seen in the time it has taken to recover from the past several recessions. The United States has suffered several major recessions since 1980. Each recession has stripped out more jobs and taken longer to recover from than the last.

When new companies do prosper and grow, they don't tend to employ as many people as they did in the past. The major companies of today employ many fewer workers than the major enterprises of yesteryear.

Number of Employees at Major Companies: Present Day versus Past Years

Company	Number of Employees in 2017	Company	Number of Employees (Year)
Amazon	341,400	Walmart	1,600,000 (2017)
Apple	80,000	GM	660,977 (1964)
Google	57,100	AT&T	758,611 (1964)
Microsoft	114,000	IBM	434,246 (2012)
Facebook	20,658	GE	262,056 (1964)
Snap	1,859	Kodak	145,000 (1989)
Airbnb	3,100	Hilton Hotels	169,000 (2016)

The companies of the future simply don't need as many people as the companies of earlier eras, and more of their employees have specialized skills.

If one looks at the numbers they clearly show an economy that is having a harder time creating new jobs at previous levels. They also show stagnant median wages, high corporate profitability, low returns on labor, and high inequality, all of which one would expect if technology and automation were already transforming the economy in fundamental ways. As MIT professor Eryk Brynjolfsson puts it: "People are falling behind because technology is advancing so fast and our skills and our organizations aren't keeping up."

The winner-take-all economy has set us up for what's coming. But rather than recognize the extent to which economic value is diverging more and more from human time and labor, we essentially keep pretending it's the 1970s. We've been able to get away with this pretense for a few decades by loading up on debt and cheap money and putting off future obligations. That has run its course just as technology is really set to take off and render more of our labor obsolete, particularly for normal Americans.

You might be wondering at my choice of terminology in "normal Americans"—we'll explore that next.

THREE

WHO IS NORMAL IN AMERICA

The future is already here—it's just unevenly distributed.
—William Gibson

Some of my friends didn't like the title of this book when I shared it with them. The word "normal" has become freighted, meant to signify a certain perspective or way of life.

When I say "normal," I mean the average. As in, if you lined up Americans by some quality or trait or classification—education, income, savings, proximity to living in a city, and so on—the person in the middle would be normal. So having a PhD is not normal, but neither is being a junior high dropout.

When I was traveling in New Orleans last year, I had a conversation with my Uber driver that stuck with me. Laurie was a pleasant woman in her late forties who looked like a typical suburban mom. When she found out that I worked in entrepreneurship she exclaimed, "That's great—I'm an entrepreneur, too!" She had started a kitchen remodeling business a few years earlier. As we talked, it emerged that her business had dried up and that she was driving an Uber to make ends meet. She had two sons, one of whom had special needs, and she teared up talking about trying to find the right

school for him. She and her family got by on a partial disability pay-
ment that she received on behalf of her husband who had died a few
years earlier. "I don't know what we'd do without that—we're barely
scraping by as it is," she said, her voice cracking. By the end of the
ride, she had composed herself but seemed a little embarrassed as
we said our goodbyes.

I was a little embarrassed, too, for a different reason. I thought,
Man, my problems are total nonsense compared to her problems. My
circles didn't include many people in her position who were stressed
about paying next month's bills. But the single mom I chatted with
in New Orleans driving a car to make ends meet was pretty normal.
The Iraq vet working as a security guard in Detroit who talked sports
with me is normal; he came home having seen a couple friends die
and felt lucky to have found a secure job. The bartender in Cleveland
I spoke to who's trying to save up to go to nursing school is normal.
She was taking time off from school to save money.

I've found conversations with Americans like these enlighten-
ing. Most of my friends and peers in New York and San Francisco
have little reason to visit cities in the middle of the country. And
even cities like New Orleans, Detroit, Cleveland, Pittsburgh, Birmingham, Baltimore, St. Louis, and Cincinnati are relative pillars of
commerce, education, and prosperity compared to their surrounding areas and most of the country.

Most of us live around people like ourselves. What feels normal
to each of us is based on our context. Knowing what's truly normal
or average in a big country like America requires some work. Take
education for instance—if you are reading this, you are probably a
college graduate or student and most of the people you know also
graduated from college. That puts you, your friends, and your family in approximately the top third of the U.S. population. If you have
a graduate or professional degree, you are in the top 12 percent of

the population by educational attainment. The average American achieves something between one credit of college and an associate's degree; 60.25 percent of Americans 25 years and older have attended some college and 43.51 percent have at least an associate's degree. These numbers trend slightly upward among younger people. However, it would be entirely accurate to say that the average American is not a college graduate.

Think of your five best friends. The odds of them all being college graduates if you took a random sampling of Americans would be about one-third of 1 percent, or 0.0036. The likelihood of four or more of them being college graduates would be only about 4 percent. If that described you, you're among the educated class (even without necessarily knowing it; in your context, you're perfectly normal).

Educational Attainment of People (25 Years and Over) by Sex & Race (2016)

Characteristic	High school graduate or more	Some college or more	Associate's degree or more	Bachelor's degree or more	Advanced degree
Sex					
Male	88%	58%	41%	32%	12%
Female	89%	60%	43%	33%	12%
Race					
White alone	89%	59%	43%	33%	12%
Non-Hispanic White alone	93%	64%	47%	36%	14%
Black alone	87%	53%	32%	23%	8%
Asian alone	89%	70%	60%	54%	21%
Hispanic (of any race)	67%	37%	23%	16%	5%

Source: U.S. Census Bureau, 2016 Current Population Survey.

That's what's normal in education. How about wealth and income?

The median household income was $59,309 in 2016. Each

household typically consists of multiple family members, however. The median personal income in the U.S. was $31,099 in 2016 and the mean was $46,550. The relevant statistic for seeing how most people live and work is the median, as the mean gets dragged up by the handful of people making millions at the top. The median is the midpoint if you lined everyone up by income. Half of Americans make less than $31,099 and half make more, with 70 percent of individuals making $50K or less.

Here is the median income sorted by education level:

Median Personal Income by Educational Attainment (2015)

Level of Education Attainment	Median income
Less than 9th grade	$16,267
9th to 12th grade, no diploma	$17,116
High school graduate	$25,785
Some college, no degree	$30,932
Associate degree	$35,072
Bachelor's degree or more	$55,071
Bachelor's degree	$49,804
Master's degree	$61,655
Professional degree	$91,538
Doctorate degree	$79,231

Source: U.S. Census Bureau, Current Population Survey, 2016 Annual Social and Economic Supplement.

Again, if you're reading this it's unlikely that 70 percent of the people you know make $50K or less. Among the college graduate crowd, the average is $55K, with higher averages of $61K and $91K for those with a master's or professional degree, respectively.

The Bureau of Labor Statistics places the median hourly wage at $17.40, which would mean about 35 hours of paid work per week over 50 weeks. This is consistent with the average of 34.4 hours reported by the OECD. So the average American worker has less than an associate's degree and makes about $17 per hour.

The last U.S. census mapped 80.1 percent of American people in urban areas and 19.9 percent in rural areas. This is misleading, though; the census classified anything in a metro area, even the most far-flung suburb, as urban. A recent national survey from the online real estate site Trulia found that only 26 percent of people identified their neighborhood as urban, while 53 percent described it as suburban and 21 percent as rural. The consensus view is that about half of Americans live in the suburbs, and that this still represents the most common type of home for most Americans.

Per capita income varies by state and district. In 2016, the District of Columbia had the highest per capita income at $50,567, while Mississippi had the lowest at $22,694. The 25th and 26th ranked states were Ohio and Maine, with an average income of $29,604 and $29,164, respectively. It's telling that our national capital has the highest income.

You might have seen some of the stories about financial insecurity in the United States. A Bankrate survey in 2017 found that 59 percent of Americans don't have the savings to pay an unexpected expense of $500 and would need to put it on a credit card, ask for help, or cut back for several months to manage it. A similar Federal Reserve report in 2015 said that 75 percent of Americans could not pay a $400 emergency expense out of their checking or savings accounts.

For average Americans with high school diplomas or some college, the median net worth hovers around $36,000, including home
equity—63.7 percent of Americans own their home, down from a
high of 69 percent in 2004. However, their net worth goes down
to only $9,000–$12,000 if you don't include home equity, and only
$4,000–7,000 if you remove the value of their car.

Median Value of Assets for Households, by Age & Educational Attainment (2013)

Characteristic	Net Worth	Assets at Financial Institutions	Stocks and Mutual Fund Shares	Net Worth Excluding Own Home
Age				
Less than 35 years	$ 6,936	$ 2,330	$ 8,000	$ 4,138
35 to 44 years	$ 45,740	$ 2,800	$ 16,000	$ 18,197
45 to 54 years	$ 100,404	$ 3,500	$ 28,000	$ 38,626
55 to 64 years	$ 164,498	$ 4,650	$ 50,000	$ 66,547
65 years and over	$ 202,950	$ 8,934	$ 73,300	$ 57,800
65 to 69 years	$ 193,833	$ 6,749	$ 62,000	$ 66,168
70 to 74 years	$ 225,390	$ 9,817	$ 75,000	$ 68,716
75 and over	$ 197,758	$ 10,001	$ 78,575	$ 46,936
Educational Attainment				
No high school	$ 5,038	$ 560	$ 28,153	$ 1,800
High school only	$ 36,795	$ 1,500	$ 20,200	$ 9,380
Some college	$ 36,729	$ 1,800	$ 20,500	$ 12,119
Associate's degree	$ 66,943	$ 3,000	$ 21,000	$ 22,905
Bachelor's degree	$ 147,578	$ 6,900	$ 30,000	$ 70,300
Graduate degree	$ 325,400	$ 15,500	$ 50,000	$ 200,071

Source: U.S. Census Bureau, Survey of Income and Program Participation, 2014 Panel. Wave 1
(available online June 2017).

Unfortunately, the racial disparities are dramatic, with black
and Latino households holding dramatically lower assets across the
board and whites and Asians literally having 8 to 12 times higher
levels of assets on average while owning homes at dramatically

higher rates (75 percent and 59 percent for whites and Asians versus 48 percent and 46 percent for Hispanics and blacks).

Median Value of Assets for Households, by Type of Asset Owned & Race (2013)

Race	Net Worth	Assets at Financial Institutions	Stocks and Mutual Fund Shares	Net Worth Excluding Own Home
White alone	$ 103,963	$ 4,600	$ 35,000	$ 34,755
White alone, not Hispanic	$ 132,483	$ 5,500	$ 37,500	$ 51,096
Black alone	$ 9,211	$ 1,000	$ 9,000	$ 2,725
Asian alone	$ 112,250	$ 7,600	$ 25,000	$ 41,507
Other	$ 13,703	$ 1,300	$ 15,000	$ 4,270
Hispanic origin (any race)	$ 12,460	$ 1,380	$ 10,000	$ 5,839
Not of Hispanic origin	$ 99,394	$ 4,500	$ 34,000	$ 33,699

Source: U.S. Census Bureau, Survey of Income and Program Participation, 2014 Panel. Wave 1 (available online June 2017).

The racial statistics make my head and heart hurt.

There are also consistent differences between men and women. Women-led households have 12 percent less wealth than male-led households, and women on average make 20 percent less than men. This is also painful. However, women are pulling ahead of men on the education front—much more on this later.

We tend to use the stock market's performance as a shorthand indicator of national well-being. However, the median level of stock market investment is close to zero. Only 52 percent of Americans own any stock through a stock mutual fund or a self-directed 401(k) or IRA, and the bottom 80 percent of Americans own only 8 percent of all stocks. Yes, the top 20 percent own 92 percent of stock market holdings. This means that the average American benefits minimally from a rising stock market beyond the wealth effect, which is that the rich people around them spend more money and the economy is more buoyant.

So what's normal? The normal American did not graduate from college and doesn't have an associate's degree. He or she perhaps attended college for one year or graduated from high school. She or he has a net worth of approximately $36K—about $6K excluding home and vehicle equity—and lives paycheck to paycheck. She or he has less than $500 in flexible savings and minimal assets invested in the stock market. These are median statistics, with 50 percent of Americans below these levels.

If you're reading this, this probably doesn't describe your life or those of your friends and family. It may be shocking to you that this is statistically totally normal. It's only somewhat less surprising to me because of my travel and work these past years.

When jobs start to disappear in large numbers due to technological advances, the normal American won't have much to fall back on.

FOUR

WHAT WE DO FOR A LIVING

I recently emailed a friend, David, to schedule a meeting. When David replied, he copied in another recipient, Amy Ingram, who I assumed was his assistant. Here is the email I got from Amy:

> **Amy Ingram <amy@x.ai>**   **Jan. 12**
>
> Hi Andrew,
>
> Happy to get something on David's calendar.
>
> Does **Tuesday, Jan 17 at 8:30 AM EST** work? Alternatively, David is available Tuesday, Jan 17 at 2:00 PM EST or Wednesday, Jan 18 at 10:30 AM.
>
> David likes Brooklyn Roasting Company, 25 Jay St, Brooklyn, NY 11201, USA, for coffee.
>
> > Amy
> > Amy Ingram | Personal Assistant to David
> >
> > x.ai—an artificially intelligent assistant that schedules meetings

I responded and then got a calendar invite. Only days later did I register that "Amy Ingram" was a chatbot and that x.ai was a tech company. Laughing, David told me that he'd once scheduled a meeting with someone else who was using the same service. The two bots emailed each other repeatedly to hash out a time.

Of course, assistants do more than schedule meetings. They draft correspondence, conduct research, remind you of deadlines, sit in on calls and meetings, and do many other tasks. But increasingly all of these tasks are going to be the domain of cloud-based artificial intelligence.

The rise of the machine that makes human work obsolete has long been thought to be science fiction. Today, this is the reality we face. Although the seriousness of the situation has not reached the mainstream yet, the average American is in deep trouble. Many Americans are in danger of losing their jobs right now due to automation. Not in 10 or 15 years. Right now.

Here are the standard sectors Americans work in:

Largest Occupational Groups in United States (2016)

Occupational Group	Total Number Employees	Percentage of Workforce	Mean Hourly Wage	Median Hourly Wage
All	140,400,040	100.00%	$23.86	$17.81
Office and Administrative Support	22,026,080	15.69%	$17.91	$16.37
Sales and Retail	14,536,530	10.35%	$19.50	$12.78
Food Preparation and Serving	12,981,720	9.25%	$11.47	$10.01
Transportation and Material Moving	9,731,790	6.93%	$17.34	$14.78
Production	9,105,650	6.49%	$17.88	$15.93

Source: Bureau of Labor Statistics, Department of Labor, Occupational Employment Statistics (OES) Survey, May 2016.

Sixty-eight million Americans out of a workforce of 140 million (48.5 percent) work in one of these five sectors. Each of these labor groups is being replaced right now.

CLERICAL AND ADMINISTRATIVE STAFF

This is the most common occupational group. McKinsey suggests that between 64 and 69 percent of data collecting and processing tasks common in administrative settings are automatable. Google, Apple, and Amazon are investing billions in artificial intelligence (AI) administrative assistants that can replace these jobs. Many of the settings for these jobs are large corporates that, during the next downturn, will replace headcount with a combination of software, bots, and AI.

Consider that 2.5 million of the jobs in the clerical and administrative category are customer service representatives. They are typically high school graduates making $15.53 an hour or $32,000 a year in call centers.

We've all had crummy experiences with voice recognition software and pounded our phone keys until we got a human on the line. But the AI experience is about to improve to a point where we're not going to be able to tell the difference. Several companies right now employ a hybrid approach where voice recordings are combined with a human in the Philippines tapping buttons so that a Filipino can "call" you but you think you're talking to a native speaker because you're hearing a prerecorded voice. This is called accent-erasing software. Soon, it will be an AI hitting the buttons and our ability to distinguish between a call from a bot and a person will disappear.

Rob LoCascio, the founder and CEO of LivePerson, which manages customer service for thousands of businesses, is one of the leading authorities on call centers as the inventor of web chat technology. LivePerson just started rolling out "hybrid bots" for clients like Royal Bank of Scotland; a customer can be passed between a bot and a human and back again depending on the set of issues. Rob estimates that 40–50 percent of tasks performed in customer care are ripe for automation today based on existing technology. He foresees an "automation tsunami" that will leave "tens of millions of workers stranded, with curtailed employment prospects...a hereditary shockwave of economic hardship that could be felt for generations." He notes that most of the affected people are "likely to be in lower income brackets without the luxury of time to re-train...and without the savings to invest in re-education." When the CEO of a company called LivePerson says that about the prospects of human workers in his industry, that's a pretty terrible sign.

I met with a technologist who works with one of the major financial institutions. He estimated that 30 percent of the bank's home office workers—more than 30,000 employees—were engaged in clerical tasks transferring information from one system to another, and he believed that their roles would be automated within the next five years. I had a similar conversation with a friend at another bank who told me that many of the people in the San Francisco homeless shelter he volunteers at used to work in clerical roles that are no longer necessary, and that his bank was similarly downsizing back office and clerical workers in large numbers.

Some argue that it will be possible to automate only a portion of each person's job. But if you have a department of 100 clerical workers and you find that 50 percent of their work can be automated, you fire half of them and tell the remaining workers to adjust. And then you do it again the next year. Clerical tasks are almost always cost centers, not growth drivers. Office and administrative support jobs are going to disappear by the tens of thousands into the cloud as offices become increasingly more automated and efficient.

SALES AND RETAIL

We've all gone to our local CVS to be greeted by a self-serve scanner at the end. There's only one employee, the troubleshooter, where there used to be two or three cashiers. This is the case where local stores still exist—a lot of them are closing outright.

About 1 in 10 American workers work in retail and sales, with 8.8 million working as retail sales workers. They have an average income of $11 per hour, or $22,900 per year. Many have not graduated from high school, yet their median age is 39. Sixty percent of department store workers are female.

The year 2017 marked the beginning of what is being called the "Retail Apocalypse." One hundred thousand department store workers were laid off between October 2016 and May 2017—more than all of the people employed in the coal industry combined. Said the *New York Times* in April 2017, "The job losses in retail could have unexpected social and political consequences, as huge numbers of low-wage retail employees become economically unhinged, just as manufacturing workers did in recent decades."

Wall Street analysts have deemed the entire sector borderline uninvestable. Dozens and soon hundreds of malls are closing as their anchor stores—JCPenney, Sears (soon to be bankrupt), and Macy's—close dozens of locations. Among the chains that have declared bankruptcy recently are Payless (4,496 stores), BCBG (175 stores), Aeropostale (800 stores), Bebe (180 stores), and the Limited (250 stores). As of 2017, those in danger of default include Claire's (2,867 stores), Gymboree (1,200 stores), Nine West (800 stores), True Religion (900 stores), and other fixtures that may be bankrupt or defunct by the time you read this. Credit Suisse estimated that 8,640 major retail locations will close in 2017, the highest number in history, exceeding the 2008 peak during the financial crisis. Credit Suisse also estimated that as many as 147 million square feet of retail space will close in 2017, another all-time high. For reference, the Mall of America is the biggest mall in the country, at 2.8 million square feet. The equivalent of 52 Malls of America are closing in 2017, or one per week.

CoStar, a commercial real estate firm, estimated in 2017 that roughly 310 out of the nation's 1,300 shopping malls are at high risk of losing an anchor store, which typically begins a mall's steep decline. Another retail analyst predicted that 400 malls will fail in the next few years and that 650 of the remaining 900 malls will struggle to stay open. Here's a map of scheduled Macy's, Sears, and Kmart closures as of 2017:

I grew up going to my local mall in Yorktown Heights, New York. It represented the height of many things to me at the time— commerce, culture, freedom, status. I would stake out a few clothing items and wait for them to go on sale. Buying a thing or two would give me joy. I would run into classmates at the mall, for good or ill. That time is gone for good in much of the country.

When a mall closes or gets written down, there are many bad things that happen to the local community. First, many people lose their jobs. Each shuttered mall reflects about one thousand lost jobs. At an average income of $22K, that's about $22 million in lost wages for a community. An additional 300 jobs are generally lost at local businesses that either supply the mall or sell to the workers.

It gets worse. The local mall is one of the pillars of the regional budget. The sales tax goes straight to the county and the state. And so does the property tax. When the property gets written down, the community loses a big chunk of tax revenue. This means shrunken municipal budgets, cuts to school budgets, and job reductions in local government offices. On average, a single Macy's store generates about $36 million a year. At current sales tax and property tax rates, that store, if closed, would leave a budget hole of several million dollars for the state and county to deal with.

If you've ever been to a dead or dying mall, you know that it's both depressing and eerie. It's a sign that a community can't support a commercial center and that it may be time to leave. It's not just you. Dying malls become havens for crime. One declining Memphis-area mall reported 890 crime incidents over several years. "Cars are keyed randomly in mall parking lots, and there is not enough security to provide the level of safety a family wants while they are at the mall," said one local resident. In Akron, a dying mall was the site of a man's electrocution death when he was trying to steal copper wire, while a homeless man was sentenced to prison for living inside a vacant store. The mayor of Akron eventually instructed residents to "stay clear of the area" before the mall was targeted for demolition.

Ghost malls are an example of what I call negative infrastructure. The physical structure of a mall has immense value if there is commerce and activity within. If there isn't, it can very quickly become a blight on a community. It reminds me of when I first visited Detroit and its surrounding suburbs at the bottom of their decline. You could see all the hallmarks of people leading lives in a once-thriving economy—hair salons, day care centers, coffee shops, and so on—but as the economy decayed, people left and businesses closed. The value of all of those buildings, storefronts, and homes went from hugely positive to hugely negative. Unused infrastructure decays quickly and gives an environment a bleak, dystopian atmosphere, like a zombie movie set. I'm glad to say that Detroit has gotten a lot better since 2011.

There have been heroic efforts to repurpose malls in innovative ways—churches, office parks, recreation centers, medical offices, experiential retail, even public art spaces. There's a giant mall outside San Antonio that the web hosting company Rackspace has turned into its corporate headquarters; it's amazing to visit. But for every successful adaptation, there are going to be 10 others that lie vacant in disuse and become crime-ridden shells that reduce property value for miles around.

Why are so many malls and stores closing? Developers may have built too many of them. But the main cause is the rise of e-commerce. Particularly Amazon. Amazon now controls 43 percent of total e-commerce in the United States. It has a market capitalization of $435 billion. Overall, e-commerce has been rising by $40 billion a year since 2015, which is now pushing traditional retail into extinction. Amazon just bought Whole Foods to expedite their move into grocery delivery. Most everyone I know buys a lot of stuff on Amazon. It is virtually impossible for any brick and mortar retailer to compete against Amazon on price. This is because Amazon doesn't have to invest in storefronts and can focus on building an efficient delivery system at the highest volumes.

Here's their other advantage—Amazon doesn't even need to make money. In its 20 years as a public company, Amazon often has not turned a profit. A number of years ago, some financial types noticed and shorted the stock, saying, "Amazon doesn't make money." In response, Amazon founder Jeff Bezos stopped investing in anything new for a year and ramped up profitability. The people betting against the stock were burned badly. Now, no one bets against Amazon, and its stock price is over $900 per share, making Jeff one of the richest people in the world. Jeff is dedicating $1 billion of his personal wealth to his space exploration company, Blue Origin, each year. A friend of his joked to me that "we'll get Jeff to care about what happens on this planet one of these days."

Amazon is known for its competitive—some might even say ruthless—practices. In 2009, they were trying to push Diapers.com to the negotiating table, so they discounted diapers to a point where no one was making money. It worked and they bought Diapers.com for $545 million a little while later.

I don't think Jeff Bezos has it out for local malls, per se. But there will nonetheless be hundreds of thousands of people who suffer from the demise of retail, driven by e-commerce giants like Amazon: the mall workers, the people who liked shopping at the mall, the county workers who needed the mall's property tax to pay for their jobs, the property owners near the mall, and so on. Hundreds of our communities are going to have giant holes blasted in them by progress that will disrupt thousands of lives and livelihoods in each. And the victims are likely to be among the weakest in the labor market—retail workers are paid less than workers in most other industries and typically lack a college degree. Where are they going to go?

It's not just the malls—little shops and restaurants everywhere are closing. You're probably seeing empty storefronts around where you live and work right now.

A *New York Times* op-ed by the economic historian Louis Hyman detailed the plight of towns in upstate New York and other places that have seen their retail sectors decline and offered some recommendations for how workers could readjust to the new economic reality:

> Main Street…exists, but only as a luxury consumer experience…If the answer to rural downward mobility is to turn everyone into software engineers, there is no hope… Today, for the first time, thanks to the internet, small-town America can pull back money from Wall Street (and big cities more generally). Through global freelancing platforms like Upwork, for example, rural and small-town Americans can find jobs anywhere in the world, using abilities and talents they already have. A receptionist can welcome office visitors in San Francisco from her home in New York's Finger Lakes. Through an e-commerce website like Etsy, an Appalachian woodworker can create custom pieces and sell them anywhere in the world.

This op-ed is a great summary of the general constructive thinking. It recognizes that the retail sector will shrink and happily debunks the ridiculous "let's turn everyone into coders" idea, which is realistic for only a tiny proportion of displaced workers. If you dig into the author's alternative suggestions for workers though, they're equally unrealistic and could only be offered by someone who hadn't tried any of them. Upwork primarily finds work for developers, designers, and creatives on a global scale. Asking a retail worker from small-town America to log on and get work assumes they have a skill to offer. These global platforms have people offering their services from abroad, who can price their time at as little as $4 an hour even for a college graduate. Getting work on these platforms is highly competitive, doesn't pay very well, and carries no benefits.

Offices in San Francisco have either iPads or human beings as receptionists. They don't have avatars staffed by human beings in small towns hundreds of miles away. Selling woodwork on Etsy is the kind of thing that would work for a handful of humans and is unlikely to feed your family. On average, sellers' income from Etsy contributes only 13 percent to their household income and is intended as a supplement to traditional work. Forty-one percent of Etsy sellers who focus on their business full-time get their health care through a spouse or partner, and 39 percent are on Medicare or Medicaid or another state-sponsored program.

It's possible that some workers in towns with dying retail stores could find menial jobs on their computers as telemarketers, phone sex operators, English tutors to Chinese kids, or image classifiers to help train AI. That's not exactly an appealing future though—and long-distance low-skilled jobs are the ones most subject to automation and a race to the lowest-cost provider. Most retail workers at least had the gratification of leaving home, conversation with colleagues and customers, getting a store discount, and generally being a member of society.

The reason that even well-meaning commentators suggest increasingly unlikely and tenuous ways for people to make a living is that they are trapped in the conventional thinking that people must trade their time, energy, and labor for money as the only way to survive. You stretch for answers because, in reality, there are none. The subsistence and scarcity model is grinding more and more people up. Preserving it is the thing we must give up first.

FOOD PREPARATION AND SERVICE

For the number three job in America, the median hourly wage is $10 an hour with an annual average wage of $23,850. Most of these workers have not attended college. Food service and food prep workers are not in immediate danger of replacement to the same degree as are call center workers and retail workers. Mom-and-pop restaurants are not changing their practices anytime soon, and food service workers are generally so inexpensive that the incentives to replace them are modest. The restaurant industry is facing headwinds due to lower foot traffic in many places, more lunches eaten at desks (the "lunch depression"), high levels of competition, the decline of mid-price restaurants, and the rise of eat-at-home delivery services like Blue Apron, but people anticipate restaurants holding up better than traditional retail.

Still, change is brewing. I had brunch with a venture capitalist friend in San Francisco. She told me an important story: "A company came to me with a software product that helps fast food workers get scheduled for shifts more efficiently among multiple locations. Any given worker could be optimally assigned a shift across several nearby stores. It seemed like a good idea. But when I went to a couple fast food companies and I asked them if they would use this kind of software, their response was, 'We're not trying to schedule our workers more efficiently. We're trying to replace them altogether.' So I didn't invest in that company. Instead, I invested in a couple companies that make smoothies and pizza with robots and delivery."

She's not alone. There is now a mechanized barista in a lobby in San Francisco. It's named Gordon. You can text in your order and the robot can be set up in most any location. I tried it and my Americano was delicious, for about 40 percent less than at Starbucks. Gordon provides a more efficient, cheaper, and equally high- or even higher-quality product than a human barista. In the morning, when you are running late to work and all you want is a quick cup of coffee, these pluses will be valuable. After Gordon debuted, Starbucks was forced to issue a statement saying that it didn't plan on replacing its 150,000 baristas.

Some workers will be easier to replace than others. For instance, we all like fast food drive-thru restaurants for their efficiency and do not mind the limited human interaction. In fact, 50 to 70 percent of fast food sales take place at drive-thru windows in the United States—McDonald's being the one that most of us know and (used to) love. There are 1–2 workers per location who take the order through the speaker—they wear those cool headsets. These workers will be replaced by software in many locations in the next five years. Publicly traded fast food chains will be among the most aggressive adopters of increased efficiencies because they have the scale, resources, and quarterly earnings pressures to maximize shareholder returns. McDonald's just announced an "Experience of the Future" initiative that will replace cashiers in 2,500 locations to start. The former CEO of McDonald's suggested that large-scale automation is around the corner. "It's cheaper to buy a $35,000 robotic arm than it is to hire an employee who's inefficient making $15 an hour bagging French fries," he said while defending the current prevailing fast food wage of $8.90. The robot arm is only going to get cheaper and more efficient, while the fast food wage has no place to go but up. Approximately 4 million workers work in fast food.

If you've been through an airport recently, you might have noticed restaurants that have replaced servers with iPads. Eatsa, a recently opened restaurant chain, has a whole row of iPads for you to enter the order, and then a series of lockers where your food appears. They've gotten rid of all of the front-of-house workers. Eatsa was recently named one of the most influential brands in the restaurant industry, and it's here to stay. All it takes is a few chains to bite the bullet and enjoy labor-free efficiencies and the others will follow quickly. McKinsey estimates that 73 percent of food prep and service activities are automatable.

On the production end, you can now use a 3D printer to make hot pizza in five minutes that can be customized to particular orders. BeeHex's bot, called the Chef 3D, will appear at select theme parks and sports arenas starting later this year. Just like the robot barista, Chef 3D is faster, cleaner, and more reliable than human workers. Only one person is needed to work the machine, which can mix the composition and lay down the sauce and the toppings in one minute. Apparently it tastes great. No more person in the back making pizzas by the oven. There are companies now launching that are essentially pizzerias on wheels, where they make the pizza in special trucks on their way to you in anticipation of your order.

For the last mile, there are now food delivery robots being used in Washington DC, and San Francisco. They are essentially coolers on wheels that deliver food to your door for around a dollar. One company called Starship Technologies has 20 or so robots deployed that are already learning their local terrain in Washington, DC, which has officially made self-driving robots legal on its sidewalks. These robots will eliminate the need for many deliverypeople.

A friend of mine, Jeff Zurofsky, ran a chain of sandwich shops for a number of years. He said to me, "Our biggest operational issue is that sometimes people just don't show up to work. We pay significantly over the minimum wage, but employee reliability is a recurring problem."

Food prep and service jobs are going to remain numerous for a while to come because of low costs and industry fragmentation. But fundamentally, most of the tasks are highly repetitive and automatable. Companies with resources are going to continue to experiment with new ways to reduce costs and we will see fewer and fewer workers in many restaurants over time. Also, as regional economies weaken, restaurants in those regions will struggle and close.

FIVE

FACTORY WORKERS AND TRUCK DRIVERS

Y ou would have to have been asleep these past years not to have noticed that manufacturing jobs have been disappearing in large numbers. In 2000 there were still 17.5 million manufacturing workers in the United States. Then, the numbers fell off a cliff, plummeting to fewer than 12 million before rebounding slightly starting in 2011.

More than 5 million manufacturing workers lost their jobs after 2000. More than 80 percent of the jobs lost—or 4 million jobs—were

U.S. Employment in Manufacturing (1970-2017)

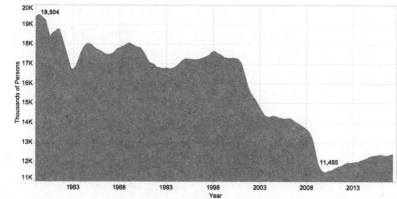

Source: Economic Research. The Federal Reserve Bank of St. Louis.

due to automation. Men make up 73 percent of manufacturing workers, so this hit working-class men particularly hard. About one in six working-age men in America is now out of the workforce, one of the highest rates among developed countries.

What happened to these 5 million workers? A rosy economist might imagine that they found new manufacturing jobs, or were retrained and reskilled for different jobs, or maybe they moved to another state for greener pastures.

In reality, many of them left the workforce. One Department of Labor survey in 2012 found that 41 percent of displaced manufacturing workers between 2009 and 2011 were either still unemployed or dropped out of the labor market within three years of losing their jobs. Another study out of Indiana University found that 44 percent of 200,000 displaced transportation equipment and primary metals manufacturing workers in Indiana between 2003 and 2014 had no payroll record at all by 2014, and only 3 percent graduated from a public college or university in Indiana during that time period. The study noted, "Very few went back to school, and relatively few seemed to avail themselves of a lot of the government programs available to assist displaced workers."

The manufacturing jobs that still exist require more education and technical skills as factories have become more advanced and automated. Jobs in manufacturing for people with graduate degrees grew by 32 percent after 2000, even as overall employment in the sector was plummeting. Of course, as we've seen, most people don't have graduate degrees or even college or associate's degrees, and it is unrealistic for many to get them.

"The recession led to this huge wiping out of one-industry towns, particularly in those places that were heavily dependent on the industrial or manufacturing economy," says Steve Glickman, CEO of the Economic Innovation Group. "We're asking: What's around the corner for them? And we're seeing a shockingly low rate of new businesses that can become the new employers for those regions of the country."

How do the 40 percent of displaced manufacturing workers who don't find new jobs survive? The short answer is that many became destitute and applied for disability benefits. Disability rolls shot up starting in 2000, rising by 3.5 million, with the numbers increasing dramatically in Ohio, Michigan, Pennsylvania, and other manufacturing-heavy states. In Michigan, about half of the 310,000 residents who left the workforce between 2003 and 2013 went on disability. Many displaced manufacturing workers essentially entered a new underclass of government dependents who have been left behind.

Percent of Working Age Population Employed & Receiving Disability Insurance (1994-2015)

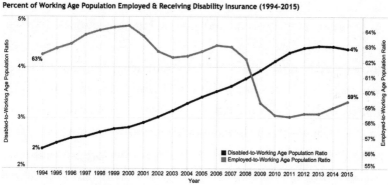

Source: U.S. Bureau of Labor and the Social Security Administration.

This is a good indicator of what will occur when truck drivers lose their jobs. The average age of truck drivers is 49, 94 percent are male, and they are typically high school graduates. Driving a truck is the most popular job in 29 states—there are 3.5 million truck drivers nationwide.

Trucks that drive themselves are already rolling out around the world. Self-driving trucks successfully made deliveries in Nevada and Colorado in 2017. Rio Tinto has 73 autonomous mining trucks hauling iron ore 24 hours a day in Australia. Europe saw its first convoys of self-driving trucks cross the continent in 2016. In 2016 Uber bought the self-driving truck company Otto for $680 million and now employs 500 engineers to perfect the technology. Google spun off its self-driving car company Waymo, which is working on self-driving trucks with the big truck manufacturers Daimler and Volvo.

Jim Scheinman, a venture capitalist at Maven Ventures who has backed startups in both autonomous trucks and cars, says that self-driving trucks will arrive significantly before cars because highway driving is so much easier. Highways, the domain of semi trucks, are much less complex than urban areas, with fewer intersections and clearer road markings. And the economic incentives around freight are much higher than with passenger cars.

Morgan Stanley estimated the savings of automated freight delivery to be a staggering $168 billion per year in saved fuel ($35 billion), reduced labor costs ($70 billion), fewer accidents ($36 billion), and increased productivity and equipment utilization ($27 billion). That's an enormously high incentive to show drivers to the door—it would actually be enough to pay the drivers their $40,000 a year salary to stay home and still save tens of billions per year.

Switching to automated drivers would not only save billions, but it also has the potential to save thousands of lives. Crashes involving large trucks killed 3,903 people in the United States in 2014, according to the National Highway Traffic Safety Administration, and a further 110,000 people were injured. More than 90 percent of the accidents were caused at least in part by driver error. Driver fatigue is a factor in roughly one out of seven fatal accidents. Most of us when we were taught to drive growing up were told to avoid trucks on the highway. There's a reason for that.

So the incentives to adopt automated truck driving are massive—tens of billions of dollars saved annually plus thousands of lives. They are so large that one could argue it is important for national competitiveness and human welfare that this happen as quickly as possible. Adding to the incentives is that many freight companies report labor shortages because they can't find enough people willing to take on the physically demanding and punishing job of spending hundreds of hours sitting in a confined space. Truck drivers spend 240 nights per year away from home staying in truck stops and motels and 11 hours per day on the road. Obesity, diabetes, smoking, inactivity, and high blood pressure are common, with one study saying 88 percent of drivers had at least one risk factor for chronic disease.

Many, however, will argue for the preservation of truck driving because they recognize just how problematic it would be for such a large number of uneducated male workers to be displaced quickly.

Taking even a fraction of the 3.5 million truckers off the road will have ripple effects far and wide. It is impossible to overstate the importance of truck drivers to regional economies around the country. As many as 7.2 million workers serve the needs of truck drivers at truck stops, diners, motels, and other businesses around the country. Over 2,000 truck stops around the country serve as dedicated hotels, restaurants, grocery stores, and entertainment hubs for truckers every day. If one assumes that each trucker spends only $5K a year on consumption on the road (about $100 per week), that's a $17.5 billion economic hit in communities around the country. Beyond the hundreds of thousands of additional job losses, many communities may risk losing a sense of purpose without thousands of truckers coming through each day. For example, in Nebraska one out of every 12 workers—63,000 workers—works in and supports the trucking industry.

Truck drivers do not see it coming. Indeed, when Bloomberg's Shift Commission in 2017 asked truck drivers about how concerned they were about their jobs being replaced by automation, they almost uniformly weren't concerned at all. Let me assure you it's coming. Elon Musk recently announced that Tesla will be offering a freight truck as of November 2017. Musk also proclaimed that by 2019, all new Teslas will be self-driving. "Your car will drop you off at work, and then it will pick other people up and make you money all day until it's time to pick you up again," Musk proclaimed. "This will 100 percent happen." It is obvious that Tesla trucks will eventually have the same self-driving capabilities as their cars. Other autonomous vehicle companies report similar timelines, with 2020 being the first year of mass adoption. And it's not just those driving trucks who are at risk. A senior official at one of the major ride-sharing companies told me that their internal projections are that half of their rides will be given by autonomous vehicles by 2022. This has the potential to affect about 300,000 Uber and Lyft drivers in the United States.

The replacement of drivers will be one of the most dramatic, visible battlegrounds between automation and the human worker. Companies can eliminate the jobs of call center workers, retail clerks, fast food workers, and the like with minimal violence and fuss. Truck drivers will be different.

Right now, the federal government has said that it will allow autonomous vehicles in any states that permit them. One industry report noted that "the [U.S.] Department of Transportation is throwing its full support behind development of autonomous vehicles as a way to improve safety on our roadways." In 2016 the trucking industry spent $9.1 million on lobbying, and the Ohio government has already committed $15 million to set up a 35-mile stretch of highway outside Columbus for testing self-driving trucks.

Arizona, California, and Nevada have begun allowing self-driving car trials in their states, and others will follow.

Will truckers and the industry fight back? Back in the 1950s, truckers were highly unionized, with the Teamsters being legendary in their aggressiveness. Today, only about 13 percent of U.S. truckers are unionized, and 90 percent of the trucking industry is made up of small businesses with 10 or fewer trucks. About 10 percent of truck drivers—350,000—are solo owner operators who own their own trucks; the trucking companies have been pushing drivers to buy or lease their own trucks to reduce overhead.

It will happen in stages. First, there will be automated trucks with a human driver as a failsafe. The technology will allow truckers to go beyond their current 11 hours per day on the road as the driver will be able to rest and do other things during long stretches. This will increase the productivity of trucks and equipment, and likely reduce the wages of truckers as the pay scale changes. The next stage will have convoys of trucks with the lead truck having a driver and the others following automatically, which lowers wind resistance and fuel costs. There will be docking stations outside urban areas where drivers will enter the trucks for the last 10 miles.

At some point, as the industry becomes more and more automated, truck drivers will realize that the combination of much more efficient trips and lower need for labor will dramatically shrink their total employment. Those who have other options will flee the field. But for many, their opportunities outside of truck driving will be minimal, and they know it. Many are ex-military; about 5 percent of Gulf War veterans—80,000—worked in transportation in 2012. They will be proud and desperate. What might happen when the 350,000 American truckers who bought or leased their own trucks are unemployed and angry? All it takes is one out of 350,000 to lead the others. It doesn't take a big leap of the imagination to imagine mass protests that could block highways, seize up the economy, and wreak havoc.

The best estimates for when this will unfold are between 2020 and 2030. That is right around the corner.

SIX

WHITE-COLLAR JOBS WILL DISAPPEAR, TOO

H ere's an article written in 2017 about an earnings report for a jam company, J.M. Smucker:

EPS ESTIMATES DOWN FOR J.M. SMUCKER IN PAST MONTH

Over the past three months, the consensus estimate has sagged from $1.25. For the fiscal year, analysts are expecting earnings of $5.75 per share. A year after being $1.37 billion, analysts expect revenue to fall 1% year-over-year to $1.35 billion for the quarter. For the year, revenue is expected to come in at $5.93 billion.

A year-over-year drop in revenue in the fourth quarter broke a three-quarter streak of revenue increases.

The company has been profitable for the last eight quarters, and for the last four, profit has risen year-over-year by an average of 16%. The biggest boost for the company came in the third quarter, when profit jumped by 32%.

Notice anything off about the piece? The prose isn't going to win any awards. But it's perfectly understandable. As it turns out, the article was written by AI.

A company called Narrative Science produces thousands of earnings previews and stock updates for *Forbes* and recaps of sports stories for fantasy sports sites in real time. The company's bots won't be winning any Pulitzers in investigative reporting, but in the coming years, the quality of AI-produced writing will go from acceptable to very good—and those journalists who write routine stories like this will find their jobs increasingly at risk.

We tend to think of automation as displacing blue-collar workers with jobs that involve basic, repetitive skills. The truth is a little bit more complicated than that. The important categories are not white collar versus blue collar or even cognitive skills versus manual skills. The real distinction is routine vs. nonroutine. Routine jobs of all stripes are those most under threat from AI and automation, and in time more categories of jobs will be affected. Doctors, lawyers, accountants, wealth advisors, traders, journalists, and even artists and psychologists who perform routine activities will be threatened by automation technologies. Some of the jobs requiring the most education are actually among the most likely to become obsolete. Some of these threatened workers, like investment advisors, may find themselves surprised to be on the chopping block after supporting the profit-growing potential of automated technologies.

A friend of mine is a radiologist at Columbia University. He told me a story about how the chair of his department was recently invited to General Electric to take part in a demonstration where humans would compete with computers to read patient films. GE invited doctors with decades of experience, the tops in their field, to see whether the doctors could more effectively diagnose tumors based on radiology films than a computer.

Guess who won?

The computer won quite easily. It turns out a software program can "see" a shade of gray on a film that is invisible to the human eye. The computer can also draw on millions of films to compare it with, a much larger reference set than even the most experienced doctor.

We are entering an age of super-intelligent computers that can take any complex data set—every legal precedent, radiology film, asset price, financial transaction, actuarial table, Facebook like, customer review, résumé bullet, facial expression, and so on—synthesize it, and then perform tasks and make decisions in ways that are as good as or better than the smartest human in the vast majority of cases. To think that this will not dramatically change the way organizations perform work and the employment of people is to ignore the way companies operate. Companies are paid to perform certain tasks, not employ lots of people. Increasingly, employing lots of people will mean that you're behind the times.

During my brief tenure as a corporate attorney when I started my career back in 1999, I practiced at Davis Polk and Wardwell, one of the top firms in the world. When we were assigned a deal, the first thing we would do was look for whatever deal precedent we had in the system that was most similar. We used to joke about how much of what we did was "finding and replacing" terms in a contract.

There is a lot of repetitive functioning in what we consider high-end professional jobs—what I call intellectual manual labor. A doctor, lawyer, accountant, dentist, or pharmacist will go through years of training and then do the same thing over and over again in slightly different variations. Much of the training is to socialize us into people who can sit still for long periods and behave and operate consistently and reliably. We wear uniforms—either white coats or business suits. We are highly rewarded by the market—paid a lot—and treated with respect and deference for accruing our expertise and practice.

Basically, we are trained and prepped to become more like machines. But we'll never be as good as the real thing.

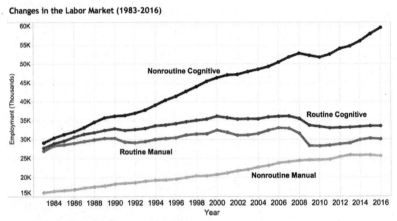

Changes in the Labor Market (1983-2016)

Source: Economic Data, The Federal Reserve Bank of Saint Louis.

The Federal Reserve categorizes about 62 million jobs as routine—or approximately 44 percent of total jobs. The Fed calls the disappearance of these middle-skill jobs "job polarization," meaning we will be left with low-end service jobs and high-end cognitive jobs and very little in between. This trend goes hand-in-hand with the disappearance of the American middle class and the startlingly high income inequality in the United States.

The vanishing jobs are due in part to the incredible development of both computing power and artificial intelligence. You might have heard of Moore's Law, which states that computing power grows exponentially, doubling every 18 months.

It's hard to understand what exponential growth means over time. Take the example of a 1971 Volkswagen Beetle's efficiency. If it had advanced according to Moore's Law, the vehicle, in 2015, would be able to go 300,000 miles per hour and get two million miles per gallon of gas. That's what's happening with computers. People didn't

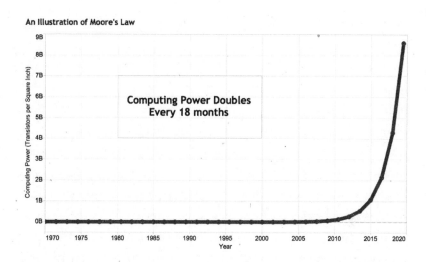

An Illustration of Moore's Law

Computing Power Doubles Every 18 months

think Moore's Law could hold for the past 50 years, but it has, and computers continue to get smarter. Intel, Microsoft, Google, and IBM are investing in quantum computers—computers that store information on subatomic particles—that would extend Moore's Law for years to come.

We are just now hitting the rapid ascent of computers that are unfathomably fast and powerful. When the IBM computer Deep Blue defeated the world's foremost chess master in 1996, people were impressed but not *that* impressed. Chess is a game where there is a very large but finite number of moves and possibilities, and if you have enough computing power you can project out all of the next possible steps.

Go is another story. Go is a 3,000-year-old Chinese game with theoretically infinite moves. In order to beat the world's best go players, an AI would need to use something resembling judgment and creativity in addition to pure computation. In 2015 Google's DeepMind beat the world's best go player and then did it again in 2017 against other world champions. Go champions looked at the

DeepMind strategies and said that it used moves and tactics no one had ever seen before.

New kinds of AI are emerging that can do much of what we now consider intelligent and creative. You might have heard the term "machine learning," which is an application of AI in which you give machines access to data and let them learn for themselves what the best methods are. Machine learning is particularly powerful because you don't have to prescribe the exact actions and routes. You set guidelines, and then the AI starts synthesizing data and making choices and recommendations. Some of the early applications of machine learning include tagging images, spam filtering, finding keywords in documents, detecting outliers for credit card fraud, recommending stock trades, and other rules-based tasks.

Machine learning is often used in conjunction with another term you've heard: big data. Because of the digital revolution, we now have access to much more information than at any point in history, and the rate of new information is growing exponentially. One estimate is that more data has been created in the past two years than in the entire history of the human race. For example, we perform 40,000 search queries every second just on Google, which adds up to 1.2 trillion searches per year, each of which represents a new piece of information. By 2020 about 1.7 megabytes of information will be created every second for every human being on the planet.

Much of this information is mundane—a catalogue of people clicking on friends' photos on Instagram and the like. But the point is that in this flood of new data, there will be very useful pieces of actionable information. The author Yuval Harari postulates a world where, based on analyzing your online data, an AI could tell you which person you should choose to marry. There is now big money pouring into trying to process all of this information—one estimate is that a typical Fortune 1000 company could make another $65 million a year by increasing its use of data by 10 percent, and that only 0.5 percent of available data is presently analyzed and used. Another estimate is that the health care system could save $300 billion per year—or $1,000 per citizen per year—with improved use of data.

Industries that utilize large amounts of data—like financial services—are already being transformed to take advantage of new capabilities. The finance industry is in many ways a natural home for automation; the tasks are highly repetitive and logical, the institutions are rich and efficiency-minded, and the culture is hypercompetitive. Founded in 2008, Betterment is an automated investment service that by 2017 had more than $9 billion under management. With lower fees and automated investment decisions, Betterment and its competitor Wealthfront largely replace the traditional financial advisor. Said the *Financial Times*, "Younger clients don't want, and can't afford, an annual meeting with an advisor talking about the relative pros and cons of emerging markets, bonds or structured products. They want simple guidance and 24-hour access…they don't want advice delivered in an office, they want an app." By 2020, global assets under management of robo-advisors is projected to skyrocket to $8.1 trillion by 2020, and 72 percent of investors under 40 said they would be comfortable working with a virtual advisor.

Fifty-five hundred floor traders once roamed the trading floor of the New York Stock Exchange. Now there are fewer than 400, as most trading jobs have been taken over by servers running trading algorithms. Those scenes you see on CNBC are not of the New York Stock Exchange but of the Chicago Mercantile Exchange, where they still have enough humans to make a good backdrop. Goldman Sachs went from 600 NYSE traders in 2000 to just two in 2017 supported by 200 computer engineers. In 2016 the president of the financial services firm State Street predicted that 20 percent of his 32,000 employees would be automated out of jobs in the next four years. A new AI for investors platform called Kensho has been adopted by the major investment banks that does the work that used to be done by investment banking analysts to write detailed reports based on global events and company data—Kensho is valued at $500 million after less than four years in business. With Kensho, a report that would have taken 40 hours for a highly educated human being paid $250,000 per year can now be done in minutes. Accordingly, Bloomberg reported that Wall Street reached "peak human" in 2016 and will now shed jobs progressively, which has been borne out by layoffs this year at most of the major banks.

The insurance industry, which employs 2.5 million Americans, revolves around processing information, which also makes it particularly ripe for automation. McKinsey predicts a massive diminution in insurance staffing across the board, particularly in their operations and sales agent departments, projecting a 25 percent total decrease in employment by 2025. That will mean hundreds of thousands fewer white-collar workers in cities around the country.

Accountants and bookkeepers are vulnerable, too. One accountant described switching from billing per hour to monthly retainers because cloud accounting software was automatically doing the bookkeeping and he suddenly wasn't spending any time on it. There are 1.7 million bookkeeping, accounting and auditing clerks in the United States and an additional 1.2 million accountants and auditors. Bookkeepers and clerks are already starting to disappear. Accountants talk bravely about shifting their time to advise clients on financial strategy. I've employed half a dozen accountants in my life, and most of the time you just want to get your taxes done and filed.

Even occupations that revolve more around words than numbers are at risk. A Deloitte report in 2016 projected that 39 percent of jobs in the legal sector will be automated and that the industry should expect "profound reforms" in the next 10 years. In particular, paralegals and legal secretaries are expected to be replaced, and overall employment in the sector is expected to shrink as many law firms will contract or consolidate. When I went to law school in the late 1990s, people regarded it as a safe career move. Today, law schools churn out many more graduates than the market requires, and the market for their services is shrinking. A friend of mine runs an AI company that is automating basic litigation tasks—routine responses, filings, and document review—for large companies, who won't need to hire as many freshly minted lawyers as a result.

I met with Cliff Dutton, the chief innovation officer of a global legal processing company, who described how human attorneys have about a 60 percent precision rate reviewing boxes of legal documents. I remember performing document review as a young associate—my eyes glazed over after a couple of hours even when I was trying hard to focus. The comparable rate for AI-enabled software is already closer to 85 percent accuracy, and it's a lot faster than a team of lawyers could ever be.

Even more than lawyers, doctors have built up their expertise, wisdom, and decision-making ability through many painstaking years of both training and practice. Yet I asked a high-end doctor friend who attended MIT and Harvard how much of medical practice he thought could be performed via automation. He said, "At least 80 percent of it is 'cookbook.' You just do what you know you're supposed to do. There's not much imagination or creativity to most of medicine."

I sat with a technologist to project which aspects of medicine were most ripe for automation. His responses were radiology (as discussed above), pathology (very similar), family medicine (a nurse practitioner or even layperson could handle most issues with the assistance of AI), dermatology (similar), and a couple other specialties. He also talked about how surgeons he knows enjoy the robot-assisted operating theatre, because it greatly enhanced their vision and ability to see things and the robot tools automatically accounted for unwanted movements and motions like a trembling hand. Also, students who were meant to train could see everything without being in the room, and the surgeon could review his procedure after the fact.

I asked if doctors could potentially perform surgeries from remote locations. He responded, "Eventually. Right now doctors want to be nearby, and the latency of long-distance data transmission still could cause delays or lags." Still, he agreed that robo-assisted surgery will soon open up the ability for a top surgeon to perform surgeries around the world. It also means that you can record surgeries and all of the micro decisions that surgeons make. With that data, eventually AI could analyze thousands of surgeries and know what to do in every situation. The first robot dental implantation—with no human intervention—just took place in China in September 2017. The robot went in and installed two new implants that had been printed by a 3D printer. Robot super surgeons might be one generation away.

Most people assume that humans will always have the advantage over AI when it comes to work that requires creativity, like painting or music, and jobs that requires nuanced, sensitive human interaction, like therapy. In fact, Google's neural network, a computer system modeled to "think" like a human, has produced art that could easily be confused for a human being's, like the work on the next page. You can also check out a symphony online that was composed by a software program, Iamus, which many listeners found indiscernible from a human composition when it was performed. Google "Adsum" by Iamus and take a listen.

You might have figured that therapy would be the last province of automation. If so, you were wrong. USC researchers funded by the Department of Defense in 2016 created an AI therapist named Ellie to treat veterans for post-traumatic stress disorder (PTSD). Ellie appears as a video avatar and provides soothing questions and responses. Ellie measures voice tone and facial expressions to try to identify whether a soldier needs to seek additional treatment with a human counselor. Early research is promising and indicates that soldiers often feel more comfortable confiding in a clearly artificial therapist than an actual human being. Ellie is meant to be a complement to human therapists—but one can easily imagine her checking in with patients in between appointments and taking on more over time.

When I was 13, I had to have four teeth pulled in preparation for wearing braces. I was actually kind of excited about it because I saw my dad's teeth and was like, "whatever it takes, let's not have those." I remember going to the dentist and wondering what kind of magic he would employ to pull the teeth. Not much—Dr. Goodman just put some pliers on the first tooth and yanked and jerked until it came out. The second one was stubborn and he had to shift positions a few times—I remember him putting his foot on my chest and yanking away.

I walked away thinking, "Wow, dentists have to be kind of strong to do what they do." Also, my jaw hurt.

I tell this story because often the boundary between what we consider intellectual and manual work will be unclear. Surgeons are among the highest-trained, most highly compensated doctors because cutting people open is a big deal. Yet their highest-value work is, for the most part, manual and mechanical. My surgeon friends often swear off activities like basketball because they are worried they'll hurt their fingers or hands.

Some jobs might not go away the instant new technology arrives that could replace them. Much of how automation unfolds in medicine is dependent upon regulations and licensing. It is presently illegal to do many things without a doctor or pharmacists' license. This is very likely to be a field where technical innovation far outstrips implementation because doctors will fight the steps, and they have a very powerful lobby. They will argue that no one is as good for a patient as a highly trained human doctor, even in the face of dramatic evidence to the contrary as AI improves. Some patients also might prefer seeing a human doctor, though I suspect this preference will fade over time.

There are many obstacles to AI truly becoming broadly intelligent—one neuroscientist described most systems today as being better than a human could ever be at one specific task and dumber than a two-year-old at anything else. Still, our conception of what is beyond the capacity of a computer is about to change. There is a lot of white-collar and creative work that can be automated. In startups, we have a saying of what to do when you're not sure what the answer is: "Throw money at the problem." Soon, the answer to everything will be "Throw AI at the problem."

If you think your job is safe from computers, you'll probably be wrong eventually. The purpose and nature of work is going to change a lot in the next 10 years. The question is what will drive this change aside from the fact that fewer of us will have jobs to go to.

SEVEN

ON HUMANITY AND WORK

've been in one significant car accident. I was 20 years old, driving at night from Providence to visit my brother in Boston. I was behind the wheel of my family's old Honda Accord. It was a rainy night. As I approached Boston, full-speed highway traffic ended with a traffic light, and I noticed only when the stopped car in front of me was way too close. I jammed the brakes and my tires screeched, but I still hit the car in front of me hard. The impact crumpled the rear third of the car in front of me and caved in the front of my old Accord, which folded up like an accordion. I jerked forward into my seat belt, stunned.

After a few seconds I got out and went to the car in front of me. "Is everyone okay?" The sight of the ruined car in front of me made me cringe. No one was hurt—there were three people in the car not much older than me. They were shaken up but fine. They weren't angry at all. I apologized several times. I felt like a grade-A jerk.

We all waited for a police car and tow trucks as cars went past us in the rain. We made small talk about how we weren't sure if our cars were salvageable. It took about 30 minutes but it felt like hours. I rode in the passenger seat of the tow truck to the garage and waited there for my brother to come and get me. The garage was closed so after the truck driver left I waited outside in the rain on the curb with my head in my hands.

I remember this night in part because I had broken up with my college girlfriend—or she had broken up with me—earlier that day. This was back when people dated in college. I was upset about it and was heading to Boston to hole up with my brother. It's safe to say that my emotional state contributed to my inattentiveness, and may even have been a key factor in my rear-ending that car.

Our humanity is what makes us unique. People are the most important aspect of all of our lives.

That said, our human qualities may not always make us ideal drivers, counselors, servers, salespeople, helpdesk workers, and so on. Drivers lose concentration. Counselors break confidences. Servers have bad days and are rude. Salespeople have biases and act inappropriately. Helpdesk workers get bored. And so on. There's a big distinction between humans as humans and humans as workers. The former are indispensable. The latter may not be.

Yuval Harari in *Homo Deus* makes the point that our cab driver can look into the sky, contemplate the meaning of life, tear up at the sounds of an opera, and generally do a million things that a robot driver cannot. But most of those things don't matter to us when we get into the back of the cab. Oftentimes, we'd prefer to be left alone rather than make conversation. I know I'm occasionally guilty of this.

One of the common themes of the new economy is that women are better equipped to excel in the growth areas and opportunities in a service economy, including nurturing and teaching other people, which are among the toughest activities to automate. Conventionally male-dominated jobs like manufacturing, warehouse shelving, and truck driving are among the easiest. I've heard women say, "Why don't men just adapt and take on more 'feminine' roles?" That's a lot easier said than done, and I'm not convinced asking people to go against type because the market demands it is the right response. The market doesn't care what's best for us—trying to reshape humanity to meet its demands may not be the answer. On other fronts, there are significant initiatives to include more women in high-paying fields like technology and finance that remain predominantly male.

I've started a few companies and enjoy nothing more than building great teams of people who are happy and engaged with their work. That said, I think that many people both overestimate the qualities that humans bring to work and underestimate the drawbacks of hiring humans. Here's a partial list of things that can make people imperfect workers and management an all-consuming role:

- People generally require a degree of training.
- We typically want more over time.
- We need to rest.
- We require health care that you sometimes must pay for and we can be very particular about.
- We get sick.
- We want to feel good about what we're doing.
- We have bad days.
- We can't do the same task precisely the same way millions of times.
- We have families who we want to spend time with.
- We are sometimes bad at our jobs and need to be fired. In which case we generally want severance pay or we will make you feel bad.
- We get bored.

- We have legal protections. We occasionally sue our employers.
- We can become demoralized and unproductive.
- We take 15–20 years of rearing to become productive and then we are unproductive and infirm for 10–15 years at the back ends of our lives. We often want you to pay us to account for both the time at the end and the cost of raising our children.
- If something bad happens to one of us, the others notice.
- We occasionally harass each other or sleep with each other.
- We sleep.
- We sometimes are dishonest and even steal.
- We occasionally quit and look for other jobs.
- We see things. We share information.
- Some of us use drugs.
- We get injured and disabled.
- We are unreliable. We sometimes change our minds.
- We sometimes take breaks when we should be working.
- We sometimes organize and negotiate for various benefits beyond what we could get on our own.
- We sometimes have bad judgment and can act in ways that will tarnish your brand.
- We have social media accounts.
- We expect time off for holidays.
- We sometimes get divorced or have relationships end which can make us sad and unproductive.
- We sometimes talk to reporters.
- You cannot sell us to another firm.
- We do not come with warranties.
- Our software often does not upgrade easily.

At the beginning of the book, I quote Terry Gou, the founder of the Taiwanese manufacturing company Foxconn, comparing humans to animals. He brought 300,000 robots into his factories to supplement his million workers making Apple products in part because 14 Foxconn workers had committed suicide in the previous two years. In contrast, robots do not experience emotions and do not get depressed.

The automation wave is coming in part because, if your sole goal is to get work done, people are much trickier to deal with than machines. Acknowledging this is not a bad thing—it is a necessary step toward finding solutions. It may push us to think more deeply about what makes humanity valuable.

It's worth considering whether humans are not actually best suited for many forms of work. Consider also the reverse: Are most forms of work ideal for humans? That is, if we're not good for work, is work good for us?

Voltaire wrote that "Work keeps at bay three great evils: boredom, vice, and need." The total absence of work is demonstrably a bad thing for most people. Long-term unemployment is presently one of the most destructive things that can happen to a person—happiness levels tank and never recover. One 2010 study by a group of German researchers suggests that it's worse over time for life satisfaction than the death of a spouse or permanent injury. "There is a loss of status, a general malaise and demoralization, which appears somatically or psychologically" with prolonged unemployment, said Ralph Catalano, a public health professor at UC Berkeley.

On the other hand, most people don't actually like their jobs. According to Gallup, only 13 percent of workers worldwide report being engaged with their jobs. The numbers are a little better in America, with 32 percent saying they were engaged with their work in 2015. Still, that means that more than two-thirds of Americans aren't exactly skipping on their way to and from the office each day.

As comedian Drew Carey put it, "Oh, you hate your job? Why

didn't you say so? There's a support group for that. It's called every-body, and they meet at the bar." Most of us struggle to find work that we're excited about, particularly if we have financial goals and pres-sures to meet. Even the successful among us have made a number of compromises and learned to more effectively adapt to them over time. When you encounter someone who really likes his or her job, you remember it because it's so rare.

The relationship between humanity and work involves money, but in something of a negative correlation. The jobs and roles that are the most human and would naturally be most attractive tend to pay nothing or close to nothing. Mother, father, artist, writer, musician, coach, teacher, storyteller, nurturer, counselor, dancer, poet, philosopher, journalist—these roles often are either unpaid or pay so little that it is difficult to survive or thrive in many environ-ments. Many of these roles have high positive social impacts that are ignored by the market.

On the other hand, the most lucrative jobs tend to be the most inorganic. Corporate lawyers, technologists, financiers, traders, management consultants, and the like assume a high degree of efficiency. The more that a person can submerge one's humanity to the logic of the marketplace, the higher the reward. Part of this understanding in America is a high level of commitment to work—educated Americans are working longer hours than they did 30 years ago, and many are expected to be available via email on nights and weekends, even as working hours have dropped in other devel-oped countries. Four in 10 Americans reported working more than 50 hours per week in a recent Gallup survey.

This wasn't always the case; Americans workweeks were actu-ally getting shorter up until 1980. John Maynard Keynes, the Brit-ish economist, famously predicted in 1930 that, given the continued growth in productivity and progress, by 2030 the Western standard of living would be four times higher and we would be working only 15 hours per week. He was right on the standard of living and very wrong on our work hours. Meanwhile, numerous studies have shown that a lot of the work we're doing isn't really adding value, and that we could cut our hours and maintain most of our productivity.

Benjamin Hunnicutt, a historian at the University of Iowa, argues that if a cashier's job were a video game, we would call it completely mindless and the worst game ever designed. But if it's called a job, politicians praise it as dignified and meaningful. Hunnicutt observes that "Purpose, meaning, identity, fulfillment, creativity, autonomy—all these things that positive psychology has shown us to be necessary for well-being are absent in the average job." Most jobs today are a means for survival. Without their structure and support, people suffer psychologically and socially, as well as financially and even physically.

Whether work is good for humans depends a bit on your point of view. We don't like it and we're almost certainly getting too much of it. But we don't know what to do with ourselves without it. Oscar Wilde wrote, "Work is the refuge of people who have nothing better to do." Unfortunately that may describe the vast majority of us.

The challenge we must overcome is that humans need work more than work needs us.

EIGHT

THE USUAL OBJECTIONS

I have had hundreds of conversations about the impact of automation on the labor market with people all over the country of various backgrounds. The most common question I hear is, "If this were happening, wouldn't we know about it?" People are uncertain and skeptical as to what's happening with the American economy. A lot of people want to believe what they see right in front of them or what they hear from partisan websites and social media that reinforce their current ideas. It's hard to believe in things that are developed hundreds of miles away on the campuses of technology companies, often behind closed doors.

Before we move on to the next part of the book and explore what the future might hold, I want to tackle a few of the common questions I hear.

"Aren't fears of disappearing jobs something that people claim periodically, like with both the agricultural and industrial revolution, and it's always wrong?"

It's true that agriculture went from 40 percent of the workforce in 1900 to 2 percent in 2017 and we nonetheless managed to both grow more food and create many wondrous new jobs during that time. It's also true that service-sector jobs multiplied in many unforeseen ways and absorbed most of the workforce after the Industrial Revolution. People sounded the alarm of automation destroying jobs in the 19th century—the Luddites destroying textile mills in England being the most famous—as well as in the 1920s and the 1960s, and they've always been wildly off the mark. Betting against new jobs has been completely ill-founded at every point in the past.

So why is this time different?

Essentially, the technology in question is more diverse and being implemented more broadly over a larger number of economic sectors at a faster pace than during any previous time. The advent of big farms, tractors, factories, assembly lines, and personal computers, while each a very big deal for the labor market, were orders of magnitude less revolutionary than advancements like artificial intelligence, machine learning, self-driving vehicles, advanced robotics, smartphones, drones, 3D printing, virtual and augmented reality, the Internet of things, genomics, digital currencies, and nanotechnology. These changes affect a multitude of industries that each employ millions of people. The speed, breadth, impact, and nature of the changes are considerably more dramatic than anything that has come before.

It is true that this would be the first time that the labor market did not meaningfully adapt and adjust. But Ben Bernanke, the former head of the Federal Reserve, said in May 2017, "You have to recognize realistically that AI is qualitatively different from an internal combustion engine in that it was always the case that human imagination, creativity, social interaction, those things were unique to humans and couldn't be replicated by machines. We are coming close to the point where not only cashiers but surgeons might be at least partially replaced by AI." Fifty-eight percent of cross-sector experts polled by Bloomberg in 2017 agreed with the statement "it is in fact different this time" and that the labor market disruptions will be severe and unprecedented. The consensus is growing.

Economists in particular seem predisposed to suggest that all will be well. People invoke the Industrial Revolution and say, "We have heard these fears before, all the way back to the Luddites. New jobs always appear." There is an almost magical embracing of ignorance cloaked in humility: "It is unknowable what the new jobs will be. It is beyond human wisdom. It would be arrogant to guess. I just know that they will be there." Oftentimes, the person who thinks all will be okay is guilty of what I call constructive institutionalism—operating from a default stance that things will work themselves out.

This is, to my mind, a disavowal of judgment and reality. History repeats itself until it doesn't. No one has an incentive to sound the alarm. To do so could make you seem uneducated and ignorant of history, and perhaps even negative and shrill.

It also would make you right in this case.

There has never been a computer smarter than humans until now. Self-driving cars are a different type of leap forward than the invention of cars themselves. Data is about to supplant human judgment. And on and on. It's like the warning you get when investing—sometimes the past is not the best indicator of the present or future.

It's important also to remember that things got quite rough during the Industrial Revolution; in America this is the period between 1870 and 1914 when factories and assembly lines absorbed millions of workers before World War I. There was considerable upheaval, and the role of the state evolved in response to unrest. Labor unions rose up in 1886 and pushed for increased worker rights, 40-hour work weeks, and defined pensions. Labor Day was inaugurated as a national holiday in 1894 in response to a railway strike that killed 30 people and caused $80 million in damages—the equivalent of $2.2 billion today. The United States instituted

universal high school; in 1910 only 19 percent of American teenagers were in a high school, and barely 9 percent of 18-year-olds graduated. By 1940, 73 percent of teenagers were in high school and the
median American graduated. The women's suffrage movement culminated in success in 1920. Socialism, communism, and anarchism
were all vital political movements. There was a constant whiff of revolution. Even if you rely solely on history, you'd expect a lot of conflict and change ahead as the labor pool shifts due to technological
advances.

"Isn't the labor market simply going to adjust to the new reality and people will move on to other jobs?"

In college, I learned about the efficient capital market hypoth-
esis: stock market prices reflect all available information, and
attempts to beat the market are going to be ineffective over time.
Now, most every investment professional believes that this is grossly
incorrect or at least incomplete given the financial crash, the rise of
behavioral economics, the success of certain hedge funds, and the
fact that trading firms are investing millions in having a faster pipe
to the exchanges to front-run other traders.

The labor market is assumed to be similarly high-functioning,
too. That is, if someone gets fired or their job gets automated, they'll
find a new job that's the right fit. A lot of our public policy is built
around this. This, too, is fundamentally incorrect thinking.

For highly qualified and talented people in robust market-
places, the labor market is pretty seamless. If you're a great Silicon
Valley programmer, you can practically just cross the street and get
another high-paying job. You'll probably also have a couple of nice
headhunters helping you in order to collect the finder's fee you come
with, perhaps 12 to 15 percent of your annual salary.

The less qualified and talented you are and the less prosperous your local economy, the dicier things get. If you are a factory worker or salesperson in a store that just closed, chances are the other factories or stores nearby aren't growing and don't have job openings. Once you leave the market, it's especially rough. People who have been unemployed for a while lose confidence and skills. Studies have shown that employers think you're a major risk if you haven't been employed for six months. Atrophy can set in quickly. Women who take a break to raise children often have a hard time ramping back up, even if they're highly educated.

The employment market is loaded with friction. We all know that in real life. Yet so much of our policy assumes a dream world where people are infinitely mobile across state lines, know what jobs are there, have the savings to wait it out, make wise decisions about school, are endlessly resilient, and encounter understanding employers who are rooting for them and can see their merits. I've hired hundreds of people over the years. For the normal person, virtually none of this is true.

"Okay, I can buy that old jobs will disappear, but won't there be new jobs we can't predict that will take their place?"

Every innovation will bring with it new opportunities, and some will be difficult to predict. Self-driving cars and trucks will bring with them a need for improved infrastructure and thus perhaps some construction jobs. The demise of retail could make drone pilots more of a need over time. The proliferation of data is already making data scientists a hot new job category.

The problem is that the new jobs are almost certain to be in different places than existing ones and will be less numerous than the ones that disappear. They will generally require higher levels of education than the displaced workers have. And it will be very unlikely for a displaced worker to move, identify the need, gain skills, and fill the new role.

Look at retail. Some might say, "It's okay that the malls and main streets are closing, because you'll still need warehouse workers and truck drivers to deliver the goods plus web designers for all of the e-commerce storefronts." Yet all of the new roles are likely to be located far from the mall and other population centers. Over time the warehouse workers will be replaced by a handful of technicians who supervise and operate warehouse robots and the delivery drivers will be replaced by a handful of logistics specialists. We can celebrate the 200 new robot supervisors in suburban California and the 100 new logistics specialists in Memphis and the 50 new web designers in Seattle and say, "Hey, we didn't know we'd need these 350 college-educated people—hooray!" Meanwhile there will be 50,000 unemployed retail employees who will be looking fruitlessly for opportunities in their shrinking communities.

When newspapers began shifting from paper-based to online publishing, people complained that "we're trading analogue dollars for digital nickels and dimes." That's what's going to happen with workers. We're going to trade 100 high school graduates for 5 or 10 college graduates someplace else.

The test is not "Will there be new jobs we haven't predicted yet that appear?" Of course there will be. The real test is "Will there be millions of new jobs for middle-aged people with low skills and levels of education near the places they currently reside?"

The closest thing to a growth opportunity for the unskilled is being a home health care aide, which isn't a good fit for most—the former truck drivers will not be excited to bathe grandma. It's also a terrible job. On average, home care aides work 34 hours a week and make an average of $22,600 a year. One in four live in households below the federal poverty line and many don't have health care themselves. The field has a high rate of turnover—some estimates put it as high as 60 percent per year. Of the 10 occupations that added the most new jobs in the past several years, personal-care aides earned less than all except for fast food workers.

"Some would call it a dead-end job," said Deane Beebe, a spokeswoman for the Paraprofessional Healthcare Institute. "These are very hard jobs. They're very physically taxing—they have one of the highest injury rates of any occupation—and they're very emotionally taxing: It's intimate work; it's isolating work."

If home health care aide is our answer to the future of jobs, we're in deep trouble.

"The government should provide education and retraining programs to help transition workers to new jobs."

In theory, this sounds great, and it makes for wonderful soundbites.

In reality, studies have shown that retraining programs, as currently practiced, tend to show few, if any benefits. The biggest recent efforts revolved around manufacturing workers over the past 15 years. One study of the Trade Adjustment Assistance (TAA) program, a federal program for displaced manufacturing workers, found that participants in the program garnered less income over a four-year time period than the control group, with older workers showing particularly little benefit. An independent analysis by Mathematica Policy Research compared TAA recipients to workers who got traditional unemployment assistance and found that TAA recipients had lower earnings than people who received regular unemployment assistance, and only 37 percent of those who were trained for specific jobs were actually working in that profession. A similar evaluation of Michigan's No Worker Left Behind program found that one-third of workers did not find any work after participation in the program, not vastly lower than the 40 percent unemployment rate that laid-off factory workers experienced generally in another study.

One laid-off Chrysler worker, Mal Stephen, commented to an interviewer after completing a $4,200 course at a private training center paid for by the government, "I still haven't got a job in my skill" a year after finishing the course, and "[Government-funded retraining is] just a way for these little cheap schools to make money, everybody's scamming the money." Stephen, 51, received a certificate in computer skills and business math after 16 weeks at public expense. Other workers describe new and for-profit schools of dubious quality offering retraining targeted to laid-off workers with little benefit. The sociologist who interviewed Stephen described him and his fellow laid-off workers as having gone through "the fiction of learning so that they could put it on their résumés and the state could write them off as retrained."

This is when one is able to access educational benefits; the No Worker Left Behind program had a waitlist of tens of thousands in Michigan in 2010 and stopped taking new applicants shortly thereafter. A study of several dozen laid-off workers in Michigan could only find one who was taking classes that were paid for through a government retraining program. The others had been denied retraining benefits because too much time had passed, the courses they were trying to take were in another state, the subject matter wasn't supported by the program, or there were pauses between classes and the program required retraining to be continuous. Others said they were unable to determine what benefits were available to them and were told to leave their name on a list, only to never hear back.

Successfully retraining large numbers of displaced workers would require a heroic number of assumptions to prove true. The government needs to be able to identify displaced workers over a range of industries and have both the resources to pay for mass retraining and the flexibility to accommodate individual situations. Each person needs to have the capacity and will to be retrained in an in-demand field. The government needs to be an effective disseminator of information to thousands of individuals in real time. The worker needs to actually learn new marketable skills from the course or school in question. Last, there need to be new employers in the region that want to hire large numbers of newly trained middle-aged workers as opposed to, say, younger workers.

All of the above will hold true for some proportion of the displaced, but not for most of them. The reality is more often displaced workers spending government funds or racking up debt at the University of Phoenix or another for-profit institution in desperate bids to stay relevant and marketable.

We should 100 percent invest in successful retraining of employees. But we should also know that we're historically very bad at it even in situations where we know displacement is happening. Expecting this to be effective over a large population over a range of industries is more wishful thinking than policy recommendation.

"If jobs are already vanishing, wouldn't it be showing up in the unemployment rate?"

Not necessarily, because the unemployment rate doesn't measure what you likely think it measures.

As of September 2017, the unemployment rate is only 4.2 percent, close to the lowest rate since the 2008 economic crisis. That sounds great, and economists are talking about the very optimistic case of "full employment," which is when an economy has as many jobs for people in the workforce as want them.

The problem is that the unemployment rate is defined as how many people in the labor force are looking for a job but cannot find one. It does not consider people who drop out of the workforce for any reason, including disability or simply giving up trying to find a job. If you get discouraged and stop looking for any reason, you no longer are considered "unemployed." The unemployment rate also doesn't take into account people who are underemployed—that is, if a college graduate takes a job as a barista or other role that doesn't require a degree. Conservative economist Nick Eberstadt says the unemployment rate "no longer serves as a reliable predictor of the numbers or proportions of people who are not working—or for that matter, for those who are working."

The unemployment rate is like checking how a party is going based on everyone who's at the party. It doesn't take into account the people who were never invited to the party or couldn't get in. It also doesn't take into account the people who are in the wrong room at the party and having a bad time.

The proportion of Americans who are no longer in the workforce and have stopped looking for work is at a multi-decade high. There are presently a record 95 million working-age Americans, a full 37 percent of adults, who are out of the workforce. In 2000, there were only 70 million. The change can be explained in part by demographics—higher numbers of students and retirees—but there are still 5 million Americans out of the workforce who would like a job right now that aren't considered in the unemployment rate. Both the historically low labor participation rate and broader measures like the "U-6" rate that include underemployment show high levels of dislocation and a less healthy labor market, particularly for younger workers. The New York Federal Reserve recently measured the underemployment rate of recent college graduates and came up with 44 percent.

The U-6 unemployment rate was 8.4 percent in May 2017, almost twice the headline number. The U-6 rate is a much more revealing measurement and has ranged between 9 percent and 16 percent for the past 10 years.

The unemployment rate is a terribly misleading number that we should stop relying on unless it's accompanied by a discussion of both the rate of underemployment and the labor force participation rate.

"If we were undergoing a technological revolution, wouldn't we be seeing it appear in increased productivity?"

You probably weren't thinking about this one. But it's a question that economists and academics have been debating. The thought is that we'd see a productivity spike if we were doing a ton more with technology and fewer people. Productivity numbers are actually lower now than they have been in quite some time, leading people to say that any automation-related job displacement concern is misplaced.

There are a few possible explanations. One is that productivity indicators are backward-looking. For example, productivity numbers will show zero indication of self-driving vehicles until tens of thousands are on the road. Yet, we can be pretty sure they're coming. We're not ostriches—we can look around and make reasonable projections of the future. Counting on the measurements to tell us what's going on is like waiting until the storm is here before battening down the hatches.

Another is that it's possible that low productivity numbers actually reflect an overabundance of labor looking for things to do. Ryan

Avent of the *Economist* poses a theory that technology has created an abundance of labor, both human and machine, and that companies when faced with both low labor costs and a low-growth environment invest less in new technology, which leads to lower productivity growth. This would suggest that we're in an environment where employers are faced with low incentives to innovate because people are quite cheap to hire.

For example, imagine if over the years I slowly invented a machine that did the work of 10 percent of American workers. Would unemployment surge by 10 percent over that time? No, because the displaced workers would have to keep working in order to feed themselves, and so would take any jobs in sight, thus depressing wages and keeping productivity low. It would also keep incentives low to automate away further labor and depress the labor participation rate. This is a pretty perfect description of where we are right now.

There is another big reason that productivity statistics do not show a massive increase in output balanced by fewer workers: We're still technically in an expansion, and employers save the toughest, most unpopular decisions for when times get hard.

When I was the CEO of my education company in the mid-2000s, we had many years of robust growth. Times were flush, which made it a lot easier to be a generous boss. We had free food a lot and regular company outings. I bought the company Knicks and Mets season tickets that we divided among the team. People got raises and bonuses very reliably.

Then, we had a month where revenue was lower than the year before. It was January 2009, so it seemed like it might be a very important sign of things to come. I went into my office and started planning for different scenarios. The contraction path had me looking at personnel and ways to make things more efficient. These included not hiring new people, outsourcing certain non-core services, scaling back on planned raises, and renegotiating with vendors. We had an exceptional team, but there were a couple recent hires that I thought we could potentially let go of if things became really rough. In flush times, I would not have given those recent hires a second thought.

February came, our revenue shot back up, and I put the contingency plan away, adopting only one item from it that seemed like a good thing to do.

Dan Gilbert once said to me, "I've always told my teams that if you have one choice, choose growth." The way management teams work is that we generally try to grow and take advantage of opportunities. We try to operate efficiently, but it's not our number one priority all of the time. We also don't walk around trying to be jerks in periods of relative prosperity.

When things get tight, however, management teams start to scrutinize everything in the name of cost discipline. People, processes, technology, vendors, suppliers, partners, leases, holiday events, you name it—it all goes on the table. If it's not nailed down, we look at ways to make it cheaper or do without it. And even if it is nailed down, we might look for a nail remover.

If you look at the histories of layoffs, they maintain a fairly normal pace until a recession hits. Then employers go wild looking for efficiencies and throwing people overboard.

The real test of the impact of automation will come in the next downturn. Companies will look to replace their call centers and customer service departments with artificial intelligence and hybrid bot-worker arrangements. Fast food CEOs will experiment with robot burger flippers. Freight companies will embrace cost savings. Large companies will question why their accounting and legal bills are so high. And on and on. Cost-cutting knives will come out,

Initial Jobless Claims (1970-2016)

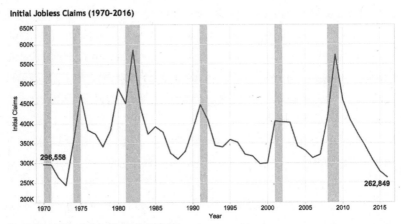

Source: Economic Research. Federal Reserve Bank of St. Louis.

turbocharged by new automated tools. Productivity will then shoot up in the worst way possible as companies accomplish the same tasks with many fewer workers. Our public sector will also be faced with dramatic new needs even as tax revenues decrease.

In the introduction, I said that we were the frog and the water's getting hotter. It might be more accurate to say that we're the frog and the grill is being preheated.

PART TWO:

WHAT'S HAPPENING TO US

NINE

LIFE IN THE BUBBLE

SIX PATHS TO SIX PLACES

We've talked a little bit about what I've termed "normal" Americans. Before starting Venture for America, I spent six years running a national test prep company that served college graduates, so I've also been highly exposed to what highly educated Americans are doing. Their paths are quite predictable and consistent. Whether they realize it consciously or not, many educated Americans have been shifting their studies and career intentions toward paths that seem more sustainable amid a narrowing job market.

We joked at Venture for America that "smart" people in the United States will do one of six things in six places: finance, consulting, law, technology, medicine, or academia in New York, San Francisco, Boston, Chicago, Los Angeles, or Washington, DC. Conventional wisdom says the "smartest" things to do today are to head to Wall Street and become a financial wizard or go to Silicon Valley and become a tech genius.

The finance and technology industries spend tens of millions each year to build massive talent recruitment pipelines. They hang out on college campuses and essentially stalk top prospects, throwing at them food, money, drinks, flights, prestige, status, training, network, peer pressure, and anything else that might be considered enticing. A friend in financial services estimated that her firm spends $50,000 per high-end hire just on sourcing and recruiting. One hedge fund paid Dartmouth students $100 each to tell them why they decided *not* to engage in its recruitment process. There is even a Goldman Sachs room at Columbia's career services office. A friend of mine at a Wall Street bank commented that he felt funny recruiting PhDs from Caltech to write trading algorithms for him. "I feel like they should be working on the mission to Mars or something." But he keeps doing it every year.

In Silicon Valley, many young people, generally from very good colleges, are making more money in a year than normal Americans will see in a decade. Even summer interns—non-engineers—at tech companies might make $7,000+ a month and get perks like free flights home to visit on weekends. Bidding wars and five- and six-digit signing bonuses are being paid out for freshly minted engineering grads; Google recruits the heck out of Stanford, Berkeley, Carnegie Mellon, MIT, and other top schools, offering six figures to start, plus bonuses. Facebook sponsors hackathons at the top schools, stays in touch with professors, and invests tons of resources in order to be the most visible and obvious employer. Average salaries are inching close to $200,000 in Silicon Valley, to say nothing of the upside of equity-based compensation (aka stock options), which can be dramatically higher.

Don't think that the smart kids haven't noticed—the proportion of Stanford students majoring in the humanities has plummeted from over 20 percent to only 7 percent in 2016, prompting panic among history and English departments, whose once-popular classes no longer have students. One administrator joked to me that Stanford is now the Stanford Institute of Technology. Here's the latest available data on what graduates of various high-end universities are doing after graduation:

Popular Job Destinations for College Graduates

School	Finance	Consulting	Tech & Eng	Grad School	Law	Med School
Harvard	18%	21%	18%	14%	13%	16%
Yale	16%	13%	15%	12%	15%	17%
Princeton	15%	9%	9%	14%	11%	12%
Stanford	11%	11%	16%	22%	6%	17%
UPenn	25%	17%	15%	12%	9%	13%
MIT	10%	11%	51%	32%	0.4%	5%
Brown	13%	10%	17%	15%	9%	17%
Dartmouth	17%	14%	8%	16%	10%	14%
Cornell	19%	16%	18%	19%	9%	17%
Columbia	23%	11%	19%	19%	12%	16%
Johns Hopkins	14%	19%	13%	28%	7%	31%
University of Chicago	27%	11%	16%	14%	11%	11%
Georgetown	23%	17%	9%	7%	20%	15%
Average	18%	14%	17%	17%	10%	15%

Sources: The Career Services Office of the colleges.

Not only do grads from national universities do the same things, they also do them in the same places. Eighty percent of graduates of Brown University, my alma mater, moved to one of four metropolitan areas after graduating in 2015: New York City, Boston, San Francisco, or Washington, DC. Similarly, more than half of the graduates in the class of 2016 at Harvard University had plans to move to New York, Massachusetts, or California. Seventy-four percent of Yale seniors in the United States reported accepting jobs in one of the following places last year: New York, California, Connecticut, Massachusetts, and Washington, DC. MIT graduates preferred to stay in Massachusetts or move to California or New York. Stanford's class of 2015 showed a strong preference for staying in California.

Our national universities are effectively a talent drain on 75 percent of the country. If you're a high achiever from, say, Wisconsin or

Most Popular States for Post-Graduation Employment

School	New York	Massachusetts	California	DC	Total
Harvard	24%	20%	15%	N/A	59%
UPenn	38%	N/A	11%	6%	55%
MIT	8%	44%	23%	N/A	75%
Stanford	7%	N/A	75%	N/A	82%
Brown	36%	20%	19%	8%	83%
Dartmouth	25%	16%	15%	6%	62%
Georgetown	30%	3%	6%	24%	63%
Yale*					74%

* 74.2% of the Yale seniors residing in the United States reported accepting jobs in one of the following states: New York, California, Connecticut, Massachusetts, and Washington, DC.

Sources: The Career Services Office of the colleges.

Vermont or New Mexico and you go to Penn or Duke or Johns Hopkins, the odds are that you'll move to New York or California or DC and your home state will never see you again.

Financial services and technology are absorbing most of our top educational products. They are like twin cannons on opposite sides of the country continuously pushing for increased profitability and efficiency. The normal American is meant to benefit through increased access to technology, capital gains, and more streamlined businesses. Unfortunately these benefits are now being counterbalanced by a dramatic reduction in opportunities. Cheap T-shirts, a booming stock market, and a wide array of apps are cold comfort when you don't own any stock and your local factory or main street closes.

Why are so many bright people doing the same things in the same places? They are driven by a desire to succeed, and there are only a few clear versions of what success looks like today thanks to the built-up recruitment pipelines. Money, status, training, a healthy dating market, peer pressure, and an elevated career trajectory all seem to lead in the same directions.

Also driving the uniformity is a pervasive anxiety and scramble that prioritizes credentialing and market success over all else, in part because failure seems to bring catastrophic economic and social consequences. Instead of seeing college as a period of intellectual exploration, many young people now see it as a mass sort or cull that determines one's future prospects and lot in life.

One reason students feel pressured to seek high-paying jobs is the record level of school debt. Student debt levels have exploded relative to other forms of debt over the past decade in particular. Educational loan totals recently surpassed $1.4 trillion in the United States, up from $550 billion in 2011 and only $90 billion in 1999. The average level of indebtedness upon graduation is $37,172 and there are 44 million student borrowers. Default rates have crept up steadily to 11.2 percent.

Cumulative Growth of Student Debt versus Other Household Debt (2003-2017)

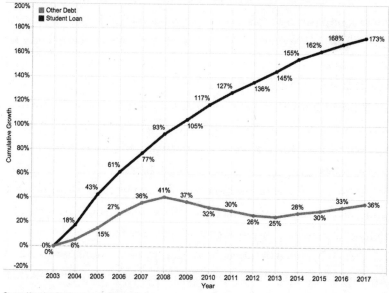

Source: New York Fed Consumer Credit Panel/Equifax.

Among children of even successful and highly educated families, there are sky-high levels of anxiety and depression. The use of prescription drugs is at an all-time high among college students, as is the use of college counseling offices, which report being overwhelmed. Demand for counseling increased at five times the rate of enrollment over the last 10 years. Waitlists to see a counselor at USC, a well-resourced private school, were reported as being 6 to 8 weeks long for non-emergency cases, and many schools had similar difficulty meeting demand. Julie Lythcott-Haims, a dean at Stanford, wrote a book in 2015 about the changing character of the students she was seeing, who had gone in one generation from independent young adults to "brittle" and "existentially impotent." In 2014, an American College Health Association survey of close to 100,000 college students reported that 86 percent felt overwhelmed by all they had to do, 54 percent felt overwhelming anxiety, and 8 percent seriously considered suicide in the last 12 months.

Relationships have changed as well. Gender imbalances on many campuses—women now outnumber men 57 percent to 43 percent in college nationally—have helped lead to a "hookup culture" that erodes a sense of connection. One in three students say that their intimate relationships have been "traumatic" or "very difficult to handle," and 10 percent say that they've been sexually coerced or assaulted in the past year. The academic Lisa Wade describes an environment where the prevailing norm is to downgrade your partner for days afterward to make sure that they don't "catch feelings." What was a couple generations ago an environment to find love and maybe even a partner is now a place where you prove yourself detached enough to ignore someone the next day.

When I applied to college in 1992, my parents were pumped that I got into Stanford and Brown, schools that had acceptance rates of 21 and 23 percent, respectively, at the time. Today, the acceptance rates at those schools are only 4.8 percent and 9.3 percent. What was once very difficult now requires planning and cultivation from birth. This competition breeds a need for constant forward momentum. "I feel this constant pressure to make something of myself," relates one Venture for America alum who now works at a startup after interning at an investment bank. "Even during celebrations, it's like we're all plotting the next competition. My friends have a ton of ambition and no clear place to channel it. I get the sense that we're all trading happiness to run a little faster, even if we're not sure where."

"If you're not the cream of the crop, why be in the crop at all," said a recent graduate of Northwestern who grew up in Westchester County.

Of course, some young people dislike the conformity and yearn for a sense of choice and exploration. One college senior at Princeton remarked to me, "Once you're here, you become awfully risk-averse. It's more about not failing than doing anything in particular." Another said, "I'm so busy here. I'd love some time to think," as if thinking and college didn't belong in the same sentence.

In his book *Excellent Sheep*, William Deresiewicz describes the current generation of strivers as "driven to achieve without knowing why." And then they become paralyzed when they're not sure how to proceed. I remember when I was growing up, I'd study for days trying to get good grades. If I got an A, I'd feel elation for about 30 seconds, and then a feeling of emptiness. I called the hang-ups associated with a drive to succeed the "achievement demons." Thousands of young people share the same thirst to achieve that I had— rising out of a combination of family pressures, alienation, and an identity that they're smart or talented or special or destined to do something significant—all on top of a dread that failure to stay in the winner's circle leads to an unimaginably dire fate.

You might be thinking, "Who cares if the coddled college kids are depressed?" One reason to care is that private company ownership is down more than 60 percent among 18- to 30-year-olds since 1989. The *Wall Street Journal* ran an article titled "Endangered Species: Young U.S. Entrepreneurs," and millennials are on track to be the least entrepreneurial generation in modern history in terms of business formation. It turns out that depressed, indebted, risk-averse young people generally don't start companies. This will have effects for decades to come.

But more profoundly, there is something deeply wrong if even the winners of the mass scramble to climb into the top of the education meritocracy are so unhappy. They are asking, "What are we striving and struggling for?" No one knows. The answer seems to be "to try to join the tribes in the coastal markets and work your ass off," even as those opportunities become harder to come by. If you don't like that answer, there are very few others.

I tried to provide a new answer when I started Venture for America in 2011. The new path would be to build businesses in diverse places around the country. I thought that would be productive and character-building. Our mission statement read in part:

To restore the culture of achievement to include value creation, risk and reward and the common good.

Upon joining Venture for America, we ask our fellows to adopt the following credo:

My career is a choice that indicates my values.

There is no courage without risk.

Value creation is how I measure achievement.

I will create opportunity for myself and others.

I will act with integrity in all things.

The credo is awfully lofty and idealistic. When I stood in front of the first class in 2012 to discuss these values, I'll admit to feeling a little bit self-conscious.

I shouldn't have worried. Venture for America's sense of purpose and community has been like water to very thirsty people. So many VFAers have developed close friendships and relationships based on shared values and trying to do difficult things together. Venture for America has filled a void in many people's lives in supporting individual paths and choices. But for every person in Venture for America, there are about 10,000 other young people who want the same things.

LIFE IN THE BUBBLE

Even as I have been working with young people from around the country these past years, I've been living in Manhattan and Silicon Valley. I call those places "the bubble." And we have strange lives and jobs in the bubble.

I recently had dinner with a friend of mine who works for a real estate investment firm. We met at a Japanese restaurant in Manhattan. After catching up for a bit, I asked him if he'd bought any fancy hotels lately—he'd gotten me a discount to one a few years ago.

He responded, "Our appetite for risk has gone down. You know what we've been buying? Trailer parks."

I became more interested. "Really? Why is that?"

He answered, "They're good investments. Tenants pay to keep their mobile home in a space with water and utilities. All we really have to do is keep the place clean and keep the water flowing."

I asked him if he ever had problems with delinquency.

"The delinquency rate is very low because first, they get a late notice on the day after their rent is due if they haven't paid. We are very diligent about monitoring and everyone knows it. Second, there's no place cheaper to live. It's really these places or the street for a lot of people. They find ways to pay. It's a nice stable investment for us."

"Fascinating. How do you grow?"

He shrugged, "We'll probably look at raising prices over time."

This has nothing to do with automation but I thought it was a pretty good illustration of what we do. We maximize market efficiencies and take tolls.

Many of my friends work in technology and know that they are automating away other people's jobs. For some of them, it's a key part of their sales pitch. Many explicitly talk about how much cost savings will be realized by having fewer workers around.

The technologists and entrepreneurs I know are generally good people. If they were given a choice to "Do your job and eliminate normal jobs" or "Do your job and create abundant opportunities," they would choose the latter. Most of them would happily even take a small hit to do so. But this isn't a choice they're given. They do their own jobs to the best of their ability and let the market do the rest. They may feel troubled at times that their success will displace hundreds or thousands of American workers, but they believe in progress and that their work is overall for the good.

You may find this objectionable. Here's the thing—it is not the innovator's job to figure out the social implications of what they do. Their job is to create and fund innovation in the market as cost-effectively as possible. This is itself a difficult job.

It is *our job* to account for society. That is, it's the job of our government and our leaders.

Unfortunately, our leaders are typically a country away from these conversations. They're trapped in cycles of warring press releases and talk show appearances and fundraising dinners. They also generally don't understand technology so they're reduced to lionizing innovators and trying to get on their good side. In turn, technologists often see government as a hindrance, to be ignored as much as possible, lobbied when necessary, and navigated around while they make things better/faster/cheaper/more automated.

This is a disaster in the making because technology is transforming society and our economy while politicians are left responding to the effects ineffectively years after the fact or, worse yet, ignoring them.

This is not to say that the people in the bubble have it all good. We are anxious about the path ahead, too. We feel stuck in place, competing at the top of the pyramid for the most resources for our children. We are constantly asked to choose between family and function, and fear that if we let up for even a little while our race will be lost. Women choose between time with their children—or having children—and keeping their job. Men choose between life on the road and being bypassed. Children get used to seeing one parent routinely, or maybe no parent at all. We talk openly with our friends about having someplace to fly to when things go south. We compare ourselves to our peers in our high-cost bubble and feel dissatisfied.

Occasionally we see people leave for a more hospitable or child-friendly environment. We envy them a little, while also patting ourselves on the back for sticking it out. Professional empathy is limited. We are fighters. Our organizations have little use or need for noncombatants. We work long hours and pride ourselves on being available and indefatigable.

In the bubble, the market governs all. Character is a set of ideas that comes up in the books we read to our children before sending them to test for the gifted and talented program, or a means of doing right by our bosses and reports, or a good way to burnish one's personal network. On some level, most of us recognize that we are servants to the tide of innovation and efficiency. As the water rises, we will protest as we clamber to higher ground. We will be sure to stay out of the way and keep ourselves pliant and marketable to the extent possible. Our specialty is light-commitment benevolence. We will do something to help but not enough to hurt us or threaten our own standing. We know better than to do that.

In the bubble, many of us came up through the meritocracy and we've internalized its lessons. The underlying logic of the meritocratic system is this: If you're successful, it's because you're smart and hardworking, and thus virtuous. If you're poor or unsuccessful, it's because you're lazy and/or stupid and of subpar character. The people at the top belong there and the people at the bottom have only themselves to blame.

I know how deeply mistaken these premises are because of my own experiences. I had very little going for me as a kid except for the fact that I had demanding parents and was very good at filling out bubbles on standardized tests. I went to the Center for Talented Youth at Johns Hopkins University because I did well on the SAT. I went to Exeter because I did well on the SSAT. I got into Stanford and Brown because I did well on the SAT. I went to law school at Columbia because I did well on the LSAT, which led directly to a six-figure job. I even became the CEO of an education company in part because I did well on the GMAT.

Being good at these tests, however, has very little to do with character, virtue, or work ethic. They just mean you are good at the tests. There were many people who studied much harder than I did who didn't do well. I remember one classmate crying when we got our test results back because she'd studied so hard for it.

We say success in America is about hard work and character. It's not really. Most of success today is about how good you are at certain tests and what kind of family background you have, with some exceptions sprinkled in to try to make it all seem fair. Intellect as narrowly defined by academics and test scores is now the proxy for human worth. Efficiency is close behind. Our system rewards specific talents more than anything. I got pushed forward for having certain capacities. Others had their horizons systematically lowered for having capacities that our academic system had no use for. I've seen countless people lose heart and feel like they should settle for less, that they don't deserve abundance.

J. D. Vance wrote in his bestselling memoir, *Hillbilly Elegy*, about growing up in Middletown, Ohio:

> The message wasn't explicit: teachers didn't tell us that we were too stupid or poor to make it. Nevertheless, it was all around us, like the air we breathed: No one in our families had gone to college... Students don't expect much from themselves, because the people around them don't do very much... There was, and still is, a sense that those who make it are of two varieties. The first are lucky: They come from wealthy families with connections, and their lives were set from the moments they were born. The second are the meritocratic: They were born with brains and couldn't fail if they tried... To the average Middletonian, hard work doesn't matter as much as raw talent.

The people of Middletown have gotten the message. The SAT came into its own during World War II as a way to identify smart kids and keep them from going to the front lines. Now, every year is wartime.

One of my sons was diagnosed as being on the autism spectrum a couple years ago. He has a particularly mild, high-functioning form and will, I believe, lead an amazing and fulfilling life. We are in a fortunate position to be able to provide a lot for our son at the right time. There are families around the country who are not as fortunate.

The meritocracy was never intended to be a real thing—it started out as a parody in a British satire in 1958 by Michael Young. At the time, a world where "intelligence fully determined who thrived and languished was understood to be predatory, pathological and far-fetched," observes journalist David Freedman. Today, we've made it real and embraced and exalted it. The logic of the marketplace is seductive to all of us. It gives everything a tinge of justice. It makes the suffering of the marginalized more palatable, in that there's a sense that they deserve it. Perhaps the most remarkable thing is that they often agree—they think they deserve it, too.

They're wrong. Intelligence and character aren't the same things at all. Pretending that they are will lead us to ruin. The market is about to turn on many of us with little care for what separates us from each other.

I've worked with and grown up alongside hundreds of very highly educated people for the past several decades, and trust me when I say that they are not uniformly awesome. People in the bubble think that the world is more orderly than it is. They overplan. They mistake smarts for judgment. They mistake smarts for character. They overvalue credentials. Head not heart. They need status and reassurance. They see risk as a bad thing. They optimize for the wrong things. They think in two years, not 20. They need other bubble people around. They get pissed off when others succeed. They think their smarts should determine their place in the world. They think ideas supersede action. They get agitated if they're not making clear progress. They're unhappy. They fear being wrong and looking silly. They don't like to sell. They talk themselves out of having guts. They worship the market. They worry too much. Bubble people have their pluses and minuses like anyone else.

When I was a kid I just wanted to belong. As a smart person I was taught to leave others behind. We have to snap out of it and start remembering our own humanity. We're all the same people we were before we got sorted and socialized. We're all mothers, fathers, sisters, and brothers above all who want the same things for ourselves and our families.

We're running out of time. In coming years it's going to be even harder to forge a sense of common identity across different walks of life. A lot of people who now live in the bubble grew up in other parts of the country. They still visit their families for holidays and special occasions. They were brought up middle-class in normal suburbs like I was and retain a deep familiarity with the experiences of different types of people. They loved the mall, too.

In another generation this will become less and less true. There will be an army of slender, highly cultivated products of Mountain View and the Upper East Side and Bethesda heading to elite schools that has been groomed since birth in the most competitive and rarefied environments with very limited exposure to the rest of the country.

When I was growing up, there was something of an inverse relationship between being smart and being good-looking. The smart kids were bookish and awkward and the social kids were attractive and popular. Rarely were the two sets of qualities found together in the same people. The nerd camps I went to looked the part.

Today, thanks to assortative mating in a handful of cities, intellect, attractiveness, education, and wealth are all converging in the same families and neighborhoods. I look at my friends' children, and many of them resemble unicorns: brilliant, beautiful, socially precocious creatures who have gotten the best of all possible resources since the day they were born. I imagine them in 10 or 15 years traveling to other parts of the country, and I know that they are going to feel like, and be received as, strangers in a strange land. They will have thriving online lives and not even remember a car that didn't drive itself. They may feel they have nothing in common with the people before them. Their ties to the greater national fabric will be minimal. Their empathy and desire to subsidize and address the distress of the general public will likely be lower and lower.

Yuval Harari, the Israeli scholar, suggests that "the way we treat stupid people in the future will be the way we treat animals today." If we're going to fix things to keep his vision from coming true, now is the time.

TEN

MINDSETS OF SCARCITY AND ABUNDANCE

spoke at a high school in Cleveland a while back about entrepreneurship. Many parents were there, and one father asked me, "What made you think that *you* were capable of starting a company?"

I thought for a second and responded, "When I was a kid my parents hammered into me that I could do anything anyone else could do. I met some people who had started companies, so I figured that I could, too."

I started my first company when I was 25, in 2000—Stargiving .com, a fundraising site for celebrity-affiliated causes. It was much harder than I thought it would be. We raised about $250,000 in increments of $25,000 over a 10-month period and launched a website. Despite some early press, we quickly lost altitude. We ran out of money as the Internet bubble burst and our investors lost interest. It became clear that our prospects were terrible, and after a year and a half we shut the company down.

This first professional failure did a number on my confidence. Everyone I knew was well aware that I'd tried to launch a company and it had tanked and gone under. I still owed $100,000 from loans I'd taken out for law school. I used to call my school loans "my mistress" because it felt like I was sending a check each month to support a family in another town. My self-esteem was low, and I had a hard time meeting people or facing my parents.

Now, looking back at my first company, I realize that I was unusually well positioned to both start a company and rebound from its failure. At the time it hurt. I was 25, had lots of school debt, and didn't really know what I was doing. But I was unusually well educated. I had a co-founder—my officemate at Davis Polk had left the firm to co-found the company with me. I had savings (which I burned through) and access to credit. I was able to get in front of enough rich people to raise a couple hundred thousand in angel investment. I had a friend I could move in with to save on rent when things got tough. I didn't have any family responsibilities—I had no kids or spouse, and my parents didn't need any financial support—I merely had to listen to them periodically question my life choices. I also had confidence I could get a job if all else failed. Enough in my life had worked out that I thought I could make starting a company work out, too. I also thought—correctly—that even if it didn't work out I'd be fine.

My story is one of relative abundance, and it should feel familiar. America was once the place where starting a business was commonplace and people were optimistic about their futures. Unfortunately, this has stopped being the case for the vast majority of Americans.

I've met and worked with hundreds of young people around the country who aspire to be entrepreneurs. Many aren't from privileged backgrounds and feel that there's an overlap between starting a company and one's personal and family resources. They believe that privilege and entrepreneurship go hand in hand, and that entrepreneurship isn't meant for "someone like them" because of their background, class, gender, race, education, or geography.

Unfortunately, for the most part, they're right.

There's a substantial correlation between one's socioeconomic background and starting a successful company. A UK study found that the most common shared trait across entrepreneurs is access to money via family, an inheritance, pedigree, and/or connections. A U.S. survey found that in 2014 over 80 percent of startups were initially self-funded—that is, the founders had money and invested directly. A recent demographic study in the United States found that the majority of high-growth entrepreneurs were white (84 percent) males (72 percent) with strong educational backgrounds and high self-esteem. One of the authors commented, "If one does not have money in the form of a family with money, the chances of becoming an entrepreneur drop quite a bit."

I've worked with hundreds of successful entrepreneurs around the country, and most came from financially comfortable backgrounds. The truth is that it's a lot easier to start a company if you have a few things going for you. In addition to resources, you have a mindset of abundance. After you make one thing work out, you kind of think you can make anything work out.

I'm not trying to minimize all that goes into being a successful entrepreneur. Building a business is super difficult no matter who you are. There are always obstacles, trials, and very long hours. It's virtually impossible to build a consequential business or organization without tons of work, persistence, and heart and soul. I admire everyone who has started a business, from the corner diner on up. It's also not the case that entrepreneurs uniformly had easy lives. Many were marginalized, bullied, or made to feel like they didn't belong as kids—Elon Musk related this as his immigrant experience. Some had family traumas that gave them a chip on their shoulder and drove them to achieve. Barbara Corcoran and Daymond John both described growing up dyslexic and being told that school wasn't going to be their route to success. Immigrants have higher rates of starting businesses because some feel that they don't have much of a choice.

But the mechanics of entrepreneurship make it a lot more accessible to people who can realistically gather meaningful resources, defer money, and take on risk. The startup community nationally is very unrepresentative of the American population. Though women will soon make up nearly 60 percent of college graduates and the country will be majority nonwhite in the next 27 years, tech is dominated by (in my view, mostly good-natured) white men, most of whom are well educated. For a woman or person of color trying to start a growth business, every step is harder—lower personal savings, lower access to capital, dismissive or creepy investors, fewer professional role models and mentors, potentially more personal obligations, and so on. Venture for America is trying to help address this—our last class was 43 percent women and 25 percent black and Latino.

Entrepreneurs have among the most powerful mindsets of abundance of anyone. Silicon Valley, TED, the Aspen Institute—they're uplifting places because the people in attendance believe that all things are possible, often because they've made unlikely things happen for themselves. You can say something about starting a new company or organization, and people simply nod at you and think, "Of course." It's like there's more oxygen for ideas, along with more money.

I attended TED last year, perhaps the most exclusive conference in the world. I got invited through a friend and paid $8,500 for admission, not including travel expenses. When I got there, there was a meditation tent. My friend wanted to try it, so we sat down and each listened to a peaceful podcast. As I sat down, the attendant gave each of us a small black envelope. Within was a $150 gift card to Lululemon, the tent's sponsor. My mood improved significantly, and I wasn't sure if it was because I'd meditated or because someone gave me a $150 gift card right as I sat down.

That's an environment of abundance. Money comes to you and good things happen to you seemingly for no reason, though the real reason is where you happen to be sitting.

SCARCITY MAKES YOU THINK DIFFERENTLY

Contrast the above with the lived experience of normal Americans, who operate in a perpetual state of scarcity. The average American lurches from paycheck to paycheck with no financial cushion, spending significant bandwidth scrambling to stay one step ahead of their bills and borrowing from Peter to pay Paul.

Their paychecks are not only modest but highly variable due to unpredictable shifts and being paid cash fees for hourly work like manual labor and babysitting. A study of tens of thousands of JPMorgan Chase customers saw average monthly income volatility of 30–40 percent per month for customers with annual incomes of $35,000 and even higher swings for people making less than that. They might make $2,000 one month, $3,000 the next, $1,800 the one after that, and so on. "Since the 1970s, steady work that pays a predictable and living wage has become increasingly difficult to find," said Jonathan Morduch, a director of the U.S. Financial Diaries project, an in-depth study of 235 low- and moderate-income households. "This shift has left many more families vulnerable to income volatility." The JPMorgan Chase study showed that roughly 80 percent of customers had insufficient cash to manage the differences in monthly income and expenses, and any unexpected expense like health care or car repairs would wreck the family's picture for the year. They observed the income level at which point income volatility stopped being a problem at about $105,000 per year, a level far out of reach for most families.

Often people are unable to plan or budget effectively because they don't know how many hours they will receive at their store, restaurant, or construction site. Forty-one percent of hourly workers say they are not given more than a week's notice of their schedule, and many say that if they turn down a shift it will mean fewer hours the following month. They thus live in a perpetual state of both scheduling and income uncertainty. The average worker dreads schedule volatility so much that they're willing to sacrifice 20 percent of their income for predictability, according to one study.

Scarcity has a profound impact on one's worldview. Eldar Shafir, a Princeton psychologist, and Sendhil Mullainathan, a Harvard economist, conducted a series of studies on the effects of various forms of scarcity on the poor. They found that poor people and well-off people perform very similarly on tests of fluid intelligence, a generalized measurement that corresponds to IQ. But if each group was forced to consider how to pay an unexpected car repair bill of $3,000 just before taking the test, the poor group would underperform by the equivalent of 13 IQ points, almost one full standard deviation. Just having to think about how to pay a hypothetical expense was enough to derail their performance on a general IQ test and send them from "superior" to "average" or from "average" to "borderline deficient." Activating scarcity through a hypothetical expense was also found to reduce correct responses on a self-control test from 83 to 63 percent among the less well-off participants, with no effect on the well-off.

A mindset of scarcity is more than just "stress"—it actually makes one less rational and more impulsive by consuming bandwidth. In another study, Shafir and Mullainathan asked two groups to memorize either a two-digit number or an eight-digit number. They then presented the groups with both cake and fruit. The people who were preoccupied trying to memorize the eight-digit number ate cake much more often. When an ethnic person served the study participants a repulsive traditional dish, the preoccupied group was more likely to be rude or make a racially insensitive comment. The group with the easy mental task had the bandwidth to restrain their reaction and maintain decorum.

We all respond poorly to scarcity. Imagine yourself sitting peacefully at your desk in your office. Someone rushes in to tell you that you forgot about a meeting that starts in five minutes and you'll have to hurry across town to get there. All of a sudden you burst into action. You hurriedly think about what, if anything, you have to prepare. You might be prone to forget your keys or some other belonging on the way out the door. Getting detailed directions to where you're going seems like it will take too much time, so you just head off in the general direction. You frantically text or email the person: "On my way, will be a bit late." Some part of you wonders how you forgot about this meeting and if it's someone else's fault. You may become agitated and need to settle yourself down before you actually enter the meeting, taking a couple deep breaths to try to compose yourself to make yourself presentable.

Or imagine a particularly busy day when you are forced to skip lunch. By the afternoon you are fiending for something to eat, but you're in back-to-back meetings. Pretty soon you are distracted and just thinking about whether anyone has a granola bar or if there's a vending machine nearby instead of listening to what people are saying. Studies show that people on a diet are continuously distracted and fare worse on various mental tasks. The same goes for sleep-deprived people, lonely people, people with their phone on the table in front of them, and poor people who are asked to think about money.

Different forms of scarcity are often tied together. For example, if someone lacks the ability to pay for their car repair, they may have to figure out another way to get to work via public transportation, and then figure out if they will make it back in time to pick up their child from school, and whether that means they'll need to arrange child care, and so forth. When you're poor, these many choices define your waking hours and become almost existential and all-consuming. Any money you choose to spend means that you'll have less money to spend elsewhere, making every decision and calculation both important and taxing.

Shafir, the Princeton psychologist, observed, "There's a very large proportion of Americans who are concerned and struggling financially and therefore possibly lacking in bandwidth. Each time new issues raise their ugly heads, we lose cognitive abilities elsewhere. These findings may even suggest that after the...financial crisis, America may have lost a lot of fluid intelligence...they don't have room for things on the periphery."

One of the things that has struck me about the age of the Internet is that having the world's information at our disposal does not seem to have made us any smarter. If anything, it's kind of the opposite. Most of us find ourselves struggling with scarcity of time, money, empathy, attention, or bandwidth in some combination. It is one of the great perversions of automation that just when advancing technology should be creating more of a feeling of abundance for us all, it is instead activating economic insecurity in most of the population. It's quite plausible that as steady and predictable work and income become more and more rare, our culture is becoming dumber, more impulsive, and even more racist and misogynist due to an increased bandwidth tax as people jump from island to island trying to stay one step ahead of the economic tide. One could argue that it is essential for any democracy to do all it can to keep its population free of a mindset of scarcity in order to make better decisions.

A culture of scarcity is a culture of negativity. People think about what can go wrong. They attack each other. Tribalism and divisiveness go way up. Reason starts to lose ground. Decision-making gets systematically worse. Acts of sustained optimism—getting married, starting a business, moving for a new job—all go down. If this seems familiar, this is exactly what we're seeing by the numbers here in America. We are quickly transitioning from the land of plenty to the land of "you get yours, I get mine."

A mindset of abundance or scarcity is tied closely to what part of the country you live in. Different regions are now experiencing such different levels of economic dynamism that they often have utterly different notions of what the future holds. One's way of life is largely a product of where you happen to live.

ELEVEN

GEOGRAPHY IS DESTINY

WHERE JOBS DISAPPEAR

When jobs leave a city or region, things go downhill pretty fast.

Youngstown, Ohio, immortalized in the Bruce Springsteen song, is a poster child for postindustrial cities hit by job loss. The city rose to prominence as a hub of steel manufacturing in the early to mid-twentieth century. Youngstown Sheet and Tube, US Steel, and Republic Steel each built major steel mills in the city that supported thousands of workers. The population of the city grew from 33,000 in 1890 to 170,000 in 1930 as the industry boomed. Good jobs were so abundant that Youngstown had one of the highest median incomes in the country and was fifth in the nation in its rate of home ownership—it was known as the "city of homes." The city's steel industry was considered pivotal to national security; when union workers threatened to strike during the Korean War in 1952, President Truman ordered the Youngstown Sheet and Tube mills in Chicago and Youngstown seized by the government to keep production high.

For most of the twentieth century, Youngstown's culture was proud and vibrant. Two major department stores occupied downtown, as did four upscale movie theatres that showed the latest films. There was also a public library, an art museum, and two large, elaborate public auditoriums. The city organized an annual "community chest" to help the needy. Steelwork was central to the city's identity—a local church featured an image of a mill worker with the quote "The voice of the Lord is mighty in operation."

The steel industry began to face global competition throughout the 1960s and 1970s. Youngstown Sheet and Tube merged with Lykes Corporation, a steamship company based in New Orleans, in 1969. The mills were not reinvested in as corporate ownership left the city—the workers knew that their mills were not state-of-the-art and continuously agitated for more investment. Then, on "Black Monday," September 19, 1977, Youngstown Sheet and Tube announced that it was closing its large local mill. Republic Steel and US Steel followed suit. Within five years, the city lost 50,000 jobs and $1.3 billion in manufacturing wages. Economists coined the term "regional depression" to describe what occurred in Youngstown and the surrounding area.

Local church and union leaders organized in response to the mill closings, forming a coalition that included national outreach, a legislative agenda, and occupying corporate headquarters in protest. They succeeded in prompting Congress to pass a law saying that plant shutdowns should have more notice. They tried to engineer a worker takeover of one of the mills. Government loan programs made it possible for some ex-steelworkers to attend Youngstown State University to retrain.

These efforts were largely futile at preserving residents' way of life. The mills stayed closed and local unemployment surged to Depression-era levels of 24.9 percent by 1983. A record number of bankruptcies and foreclosures followed, as property values plummeted. Arson became commonplace, with an average of two houses per day lit on fire through the early 1980s, in part by homeowners trying to collect on insurance policies. The city was transformed by a psychological and cultural breakdown. Depression, child and spousal abuse, drug and alcohol abuse, divorces, and suicide all became much more prevalent; the caseload of the area's mental health center tripled within a decade. During the 1990s, Youngstown's murder rate was eight times the national average, six times higher than New York's, four and a half times that of Los Angeles, and twice as high as Chicago's.

Through the 1990s, local political and business leaders kept seeking new opportunities for economic development. First it was warehouses. Then telemarketing. Then minor league sports. Then prisons—four were built in the region, which added 1,600 jobs but brought other issues. Many residents were concerned about the perception of Youngstown as a "penal colony." One prison run by a private corporation was so lax that six prisoners, including five convicted murderers, escaped at midday in July 1998 and the officials didn't notice until notified by other inmates. National press descended on Youngstown, and the prison company apologized and paid the city $1 million to account for police overtime capturing the escapees. Another prison run by the county was forced to release several hundred prisoners early in 1999 because of inadequate staffing and budget shortfalls. In 1999, a 20-year investigation convicted over 70 local officials of corruption, including the chief of police, the sheriff, the county engineer, and a U.S. congressman.

In 2011, the Brookings Institution found that Youngstown had the highest percentage of its citizens living in concentrated poverty out of the top 100 metropolitan areas in the country. In 2002, the city unveiled the "Youngstown 2010" plan. The 2010 plan was an attempt at "smart shrinkage" through targeted investment and relocating people from low-occupancy areas to more viable neighborhoods. The national media touted the 2010 plan as a blueprint for postindustrial cities, and the mayor toured the country to promote it. I love the realism behind the 2010 plan. Yet, it proved to be hard to execute—the city did not succeed in meaningfully relocating citizens from low-occupancy areas and failed to complete its demolition plan.

Youngstown has been the fastest-shrinking city in the U.S. on a percentage basis since 1980. The population was down to 82,000 in 2000. Today it's about 64,000. Its largest employer now is the local university. "Youngstown's story is America's story, because it shows that when jobs go away, the cultural cohesion of a place is destroyed. The cultural breakdown matters even more than the economic breakdown," said John Russo, professor of labor studies at Youngstown State University. Echoed journalist Chris Hedges in 2010, "Youngstown, like many postindustrial pockets in America, is a deserted wreck plagued by crime and the attendant psychological and criminal problems that come when communities physically break down."

Many young people left Youngstown to look for better opportunities elsewhere. One of those who stayed around, Dawn Griffin, single mother of three, struggles to find employment. Although attached to her hometown, she is also planning on moving away in the next couple of years, because there are no opportunities for her and her children in the area. Nostalgic, she remembers the better years of her childhood when her father was working at the steel mills: "I thought we were rich." She still wonders what is going to happen to her hometown: "There is nothing but concrete left here."

The patterns one sees in Youngstown with the decimation of jobs—increased social disintegration, criminality, public corruption, desperate attempts at economic development, human capital flight—are not unique. They apply in other cities that have seen similar loss of industry.

Gary, Indiana, is another steel town that lost jobs when the mills closed. It was the hometown of Michael Jackson and Janet Jackson back in the 1960s and many locals describe growing up there as ideal. After its decline, it became known as a murder capital, reaching number one in per capita homicide rate in the United States in 1993. In 1992, 20 local police officers were indicted on federal charges of racketeering and drug distribution. In 1996, in a bid for new jobs, the city welcomed two casino boats and legalized gambling on the shore of Lake Michigan. In 2003, the city invested $45 million in a minor league baseball stadium meant to revitalize the economy, to disappointing results. In 2014, a serial killer confessed to killing at least seven people in Gary and depositing bodies in abandoned houses. Today almost 40 percent of residents live in poverty, and more than 25 percent of the city's 40,000 homes are abandoned. The city lacks the money to demolish derelict properties and is considering cutting off services to many neighborhoods. Its population peaked at 173,320 in 1960 and is down to about 77,000 as of 2016.

Ruben Roy, an 85-year-old former steelworker, recalled how beautiful Gary used to be and how easy it was to get a job when he started. "I started off working with a shovel and pick, shoveling and picking at things, but those jobs are gone. They got machines to shovel and pick now. The world has changed. Back in my day you needed a strong back and a weak mind to get a job. Now you need a weak back and a strong mind. I would tell the kids to leave. Go get an education and go to where the jobs and opportunities are. They are not here in Gary any more."

Said Imani Powell, a 23-year-old server at the local Buffalo Wild Wings who returned to Gary after one year in college in Arizona to be close to her mom and sister, "I really would like to move someplace more beautiful, where you don't have to worry about abandoned buildings. There are just so many here. It scares me to walk by them; I don't want to end up a body lost in one of them. It is complicated for people who live in Gary. They don't want to move because this is what they are used to. Do you want to go and do your own thing, or be with your family? They say places are what you make of them, but it's hard to make something beautiful when it is shit."

The city of Camden, New Jersey, is another example of what happens when industry declines. Camden companies employed thousands of manufacturing workers in shipbuilding and manufacturing in the 1950s. Camden is also the home of Campbell Soup, which was founded in 1869. After reaching a peak of 43,267 manufacturing jobs in 1950, Camden's employment base declined to only 10,200 manufacturing jobs by 1982. To respond, Camden opened a prison in 1985 and a massive trash-to-steam incinerator in 1989. Three Camden mayors were jailed for corruption between 1981 and 2000. As of 2006, 52 percent of the city's residents lived in poverty and the city had a median household income of only $18,007, making it America's poorest city. In 2011, Camden's unemployment rate was 19.6 percent. Camden had the highest crime rate in the United States in 2012, with 2,566 violent crimes for every 100,000 people, 6.6 times the national average. The population declined from 102,551 in 1970 to 74,420 in 2016. "Between 1950 and 1980...patterns of social pathology emerged [in Camden] as real elements of everyday life," wrote Howard Gillette Jr., a history professor at Rutgers. "Camden and the great majority of its citizens remain, after the fall, strivers for that illusive urban renewal that invests as much in human lives as it does in monetary return."

Matt Taibbi in *Rolling Stone* described Camden as "a major metropolitan area run by armed teenagers with no access to jobs or healthy food" in 2013, noting that 30 percent of the population was

18 or younger. Between 2010 and 2013, the state of New Jersey cut back on subsidies that supported many of the services in Camden, resulting in a surge in violent crime. The crime rate "put us somewhere between Honduras and Somalia," said Police Chief J. Scott Thomson.

The county took over policing later in 2013 and installed a $4.5 million security center as well as 121 security cameras and 35 microphones to detect gunshots and other incidents, which has brought some degree of stability and a decline in violence.

These brief descriptions are by no means full histories of these communities. For example, they gloss over the racial dynamics that each city experienced, as each underwent "white flight" during their declines. They also pay short shrift to the many heroic efforts to improve matters on the ground on a daily basis—I naturally root for the people who stuck around.

The central point is this: In places where jobs disappear, society falls apart. The public sector and civic institutions are poorly equipped to do much about it. When a community truly disintegrates, knitting it back together becomes a herculean, perhaps impossible task. Virtue, trust, and cohesion—the stuff of civilization—are difficult to restore. If anything, it's striking how public corruption seems to often arrive hand-in-hand with economic hardship.

Many entrepreneurs have experienced the difference between being part of a growing company and being part of one that is shrinking and failing. In a growing organization, people are more optimistic, imaginative, courageous, and generous. In a contracting environment, people can become negative, political, self-serving, and corrupt. You see the lesser side of human nature in most start-ups that fail. The same is true for communities, only amplified.

One of the great myths in American life is that everything

self-corrects. If it goes down, it will come back up. If it gets too high, it will come back down to earth. Sometimes things just go up or down and stay that way, particularly if many people leave a place. It's understandable—no parent wants to stick around the murder capital if they can simply move.

Youngstown, Gary, and Camden are all extreme cases. It's unlikely that their situations will be replicated in cities around the country. But they are useful as glimpses into what a future without jobs can do to a community without something dramatic filling the void.

CHANGE CAN BE A FOUR-LETTER WORD

One of the first times I visited Ohio, a friendly woman commented to me, "You know, change is a four-letter word around here. The only change we've seen the last 20 years has been bad." I didn't really understand what she meant. I couldn't fathom how someone could have such a negative outlook.

Months later, I was chatting with a venture capitalist in San Francisco, Jared Hyatt, about helping the Midwest. He said, "I was raised in Ohio. No one from my family is still there—all of us left." We mentioned another friend from Cleveland whom I went to Exeter with. He went to Yale and now works at Facebook in Silicon Valley.

There's a truism in startup world: When things start going very badly for a company, the strongest people generally leave first. They have the highest standards for their own opportunities and the most confidence that they can thrive in a new environment. Their skills are in demand, and they feel little need to stick around.

The people who are left behind tend to be less confident and adaptable. It's one reason why companies go into death spirals—the best people leave when they see the writing on the wall and the company's decline accelerates.

The same is often true for a community.

When jobs and prosperity start deserting a town, the first people to leave are the folks who have the best opportunities elsewhere. Relocating is a significant life change—moving away from friends and family requires significant courage, adaptability, and optimism.

Imagine living somewhere where your best people always leave, where the purpose of excelling seems to be to head off to greener pastures. Over time it would be easy to develop a negative outlook. You might double down on pride and insularity. The economist Tyler Cowen observed that since 1970 the difference between the most and least educated U.S. cities has doubled in terms of average level of education—that is, more and more educated people are congregating in the same cities and leaving others.

Business dynamism is now vastly unevenly distributed. Fifty-nine percent of American counties saw more businesses close than open between 2010 and 2014. During the same period, only five metro areas—New York, Los Angeles, Miami, Houston, and Dallas—accounted for as many new businesses as the rest of the nation combined. California, New York, and Massachusetts accounted for 75 percent of venture capital in 2016, leaving 47 states to compete for the remaining 25 percent. Historically, virtually all American cities had more businesses open than close in a given year, even during recessions. After 2008, that basic measurement of dynamism collapsed. A majority of cities had more businesses close than open, and this has continued to be the case for seven years after the financial crisis. The tide of businesses is no longer coming in, but going out in the majority of metro areas.

In part because regions have been diverging so sharply, the U.S. economy has become dramatically less dynamic the last 40 years. The rate of new business formation has declined precipitously during this period.

Number of Net New Businesses (1977-2013)

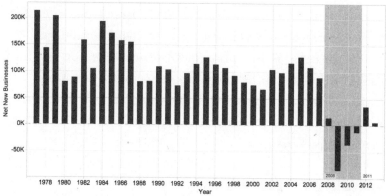

Source: The Atlas, "Net Annual Change in the Number of New Firms (US)."

Compounding the problem is that Americans now move across state lines and change jobs at lower rates than at any point in the last several decades. The annual rate of interstate relocation dropped from about 3.5 percent of the population in 1970 to about 1.6 percent in 2015. The surge in regional inequality has coincided with a surge not in people moving, but of people staying put.

A series of studies by the economists Raj Chetty and Nathaniel Hendren showed how important where you grow up is to your future prospects. Low-income children who grew up in certain counties— Mecklenburg County, North Carolina; Hillsborough County, Florida; Baltimore City County, Maryland; Cook County, Illinois—grew up to earn 25 to 35 percent less than other low-income children who grew up in better areas. The best areas for income mobility—San Francisco; San Diego; Salt Lake City; Las Vegas; Providence, Rhode Island—have elementary schools with higher test scores; a higher share of two-parent families; greater levels of involvement in civic and religious groups; and more residential integration of affluent, middle-class, and poor families. If a child from a low-mobility area moved to a better-performing area, each year produced positive effects on his or her future earnings. They were also more likely to attend college, less likely to become single parents, and more likely to earn more with each year spent in the better environment.

It may come as a surprise that Americans are now less likely to start a business, move to another region of the country, or even switch jobs now than at any time in modern history. The most apt description of our economy is the opposite of dynamic—it's stagnant and declining.

MANY DIFFERENT ECONOMIES

During my travels, I've been blown away by the disparities between America's regions and their economic prospects. At the high end, you have the major hubs and coastal cities that are vibrant, competitive, expensive, and dominated by a shifting host of name-brand firms. Here, you see continuous construction, incoming college graduates, and a sense of cultural vitality. People of color and immigrants are abundant. Growth rates are high and new businesses commonplace.

You also see high prices. In Manhattan, apartments sell for more than $1,500 per square foot, so a 2,000-square-foot apartment might cost about $3 million. The median value of a home in the United States is $200,000, and the average list price of homes currently for sale is about $250,000. So a 2,000-square-foot apartment in Manhattan might cost 12 to 15 times what a home would cost someplace else. The premium prices extend to the grocery store, where a single-serving yogurt might run you $2. It costs $15 in tolls just to drive into the city. Movie tickets are $16.50. Parking the family Subaru in the local garage costs $500 a month, which is what many people elsewhere might pay in rent. You see lots of people wearing sweatpants and sweatshirts with the names of where they went to school: Yale, University of Pennsylvania, Middlebury.

In San Francisco and Silicon Valley, they don't advertise where they went to school but the prices are just as exorbitant. Very normal-looking houses go for $2 million plus in Palo Alto and Atherton. The corporate headquarters of Google, Facebook, Airbnb, and Apple are insider tourist attractions. For the average tech worker, you wake up and drive from a leafy suburb to a grounded spaceship and stay there to eat the subsidized gourmet dinner. Or maybe you bike to your downtown office or take the dark-windowed company bus from San Francisco and tap out emails with headphones on. You think about money and housing a lot but don't talk about it. Most people are transplants.

The atmosphere is quite different in mid-sized cities like Cincinnati or Baltimore, which are typically anchored by a handful of national institutions—Procter and Gamble, Macy's, and Kroger in Cincinnati; or Johns Hopkins, T. Rowe Price, and Under Armour in Baltimore. These regions are generally in a state of equilibrium, with the anchor institutions investing in community growth while organizations rise and fall around them. Costs are average. When new construction appears, everyone knows what it is because there have been tons of news stories about it. Occasionally one of the major companies in the region starts to stumble, and the locals start to freak out. People move to these cities to work at one of the big companies, but a high proportion of residents and workers were born in the region. If you grew up in Cincinnati or Baltimore and go to college, you'll likely think long and hard about leaving. The vibe in these cities is pleasantly gritty—a blend of normalcy, functionality, and affordability.

Then there are the former industrial towns that have hit hard times. Detroit, St. Louis, Buffalo, Cleveland, Hartford, Syracuse, and many other cities fall into this category. They often feel frozen in time, as they were built up during the middle of the 20th century and then turned to managing various challenges. There are large buildings and parts of town that have been abandoned as their populations have diminished progressively. Detroit, the most famous example, today has 680,000 people in a city that once housed 1.7 million.

The postindustrial cities have a world of potential, but the mood in many is quite tough. There's a lot of negativity and a lack of confidence. Many people apologize for their own city and mock it, often because they're comparing it to other places or its own past. A friend of mine moved to Missouri from California, and he said that people asked him over and over again, "Why would you ever do that?" A Cleveland transplant from DC made the same observation and said, "People here need to stop apologizing or making jokes."

The positive manifestation is to develop a chip on their shoulder, like "Detroit Hustles Harder." I tend to like places that adopt an attitude.

One thing that has surprised me is that many of these places— Baltimore, St. Louis, New Orleans, Detroit, Cleveland—have a casino smack dab in the middle of their downtown. I've visited some of them on a weeknight and they are not encouraging places. Most of the people there do not seem like they should be gambling.

Once when I was on the road in the Midwest I ate lunch in a Chinese restaurant that had seen better days. In the bathroom, one of the urinals was broken and covered with duct tape. I thought to myself, "They should really fix that." Then I reflected on the owners' thought process. They probably have razor-thin margins. If they spent a couple hundred dollars on fixing the urinal, it may not make any difference to their flow of customers. I imagined for a second that they became really optimistic and spent a couple thousand dollars sprucing up the place. The local area was clearly losing population and there was no guarantee a revamp would generate new business. I realized that, if you're managing in a contracting environment, it's possible that leaving the urinal duct-taped might be a perfectly reasonable way to go. Optimism could be stupid. When you're used to losing people and resources, you make different choices.

Finally, there are the small towns on the periphery, places that feel like they have truly been left behind. The ambient economic activity is low. There's a rawness to them, where you sense that human beings are closer to a state of nature. They have their heads down and are just doing whatever it takes to get by.

David Brooks described such towns vividly in a *New York Times* op-ed:

Today these places are no longer frontier towns, but many of them still exist on the same knife's edge between traditionalist order and extreme dissolution...Many people in these places tend to see their communities...as an unvarnished struggle for resources—as a tough world, a no-illusions world, a world where conflict is built into the fabric of reality...The sins that can cause the most trouble are not the social sins—injustice, incivility, etc. They are the personal sins—laziness, self-indulgence, drinking, sleeping around. Then as now, chaos is always washing up against the door...the forces of social disruption are visible on every street: the slackers taking advantage of the disability programs, the people popping out babies, the drug users, the spouse abusers.

The folks in New York and San Francisco and Washington, DC, are people who have had layers and layers of extra socialization and institutional training. We are the financiers and technologists and policy professionals who traffic in abstraction. We argue about ideas. Our rents are high and our eyes are set on the next hurdle to climb. We have the luxury of focusing on injustice and incivility.

In small towns and postindustrial communities around the country, they experience humanity in its purer form. Their very family lives have been transformed by automation and the lack of opportunity. Their future will soon be ours.

TWELVE

MEN, WOMEN, AND CHILDREN

A utomation and the changing economy have already transformed millions of families and relationships across the country—and not for the better.

Five million manufacturing jobs were lost in the United States between 2000 and 2014. Almost three-quarters of manufacturing workers are male, so these changes disproportionately hit men without college degrees. The decline in opportunities for men has made working-class men less likely to marry. A study by MIT poverty researcher David Autor showed that when manufacturing work becomes less available, the proportion of men who get married in an affected community declines. Average male wages have declined since 1990 in real terms. A Pew research study showed that many men are foregoing or delaying marriage because they do not feel financially secure. The same study said that, for women, having a steady job was the single biggest factor they were looking for in a spouse.

Getting married is an act of optimism, stability, and prosperity. It also can be expensive. If you don't have a stable job all of the above becomes more difficult. Marriage has declined for all classes in the past 40 years, with the decline being most extreme among the non–college educated. The proportion of working-class adults who get married has plummeted from 70 percent in 1970 to only 45 percent today. The decline really accelerated in 2000, around the same time as manufacturing jobs started to disappear.

Percent of Married Individuals 18 and Older, by Education Attainment (1970-2015)

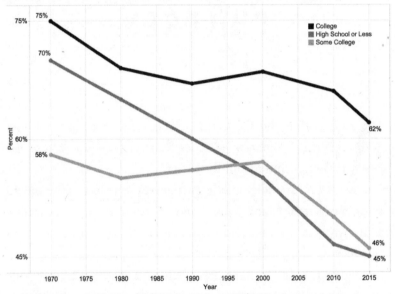

Sources: The Pew Research Center analysis of 1970–2000 decennial census and 2006–2015 American Community Survey.

There are a host of reasons for the decline of marriage. Some cite increased labor force participation and more options for women, who are now less reliant on men. Others discuss it in light of shifting cultural norms. However, the reduction in opportunities for working-class men is doubtless contributing to fewer people getting married. The problems among men have been well documented. An *Atlantic* article in 2016 called "The Missing Men" noted that one in six men in America of prime age (25–54) are either unemployed or out of the workforce—10 million men in total.

What are these men missing from the workforce doing all day?

They tend to play a lot of video games. Young men without college degrees have replaced 75 percent of the time they used to spend working with time on the computer, mostly playing video games, according to a recent study based on the Census Bureau's time-use surveys.

Women are now the clear majority of college graduates—in 2017 women comprise 57 percent of college graduates, and the trend is expected to continue in the coming years. By the time you read this, nearly three women will graduate from college for every two men. Women also go on to get a majority of master's and other graduate degrees. This is an international phenomenon: women are the majority of college graduates in most developed countries.

Fewer men in the workforce means fewer men who are considered marriageable. A working-class woman asked about marriage by journalist Alana Semuels said, "I haven't run into someone I'd consider doing that with." For women who don't have college educations, their male counterparts can't find jobs and don't seem like stable partners.

Lower rates of marriage mean that the proportion of children raised by a single parent is rising dramatically; though fertility is declining, people don't stop having children just because they don't get married. The share of children born to unmarried mothers more than doubled between 1980 and 2015, from 18 to 40 percent.

Single mothers outnumber fathers more than four to one. Of the 11 million families with children under age 18 and no spouse present, 8.5 million are single mothers. Most of the time, *single parent* means *single mother*. If you send uneducated men to the sidelines and turn them into nonproviders, you wind up forming many difficult family situations and parents who then are hard-pressed to raise their kids. "We see a decline in fertility, a decline in marriage, but a rise in the fraction of births that are disadvantaged, and as a

Percent of Babies Born to Unmarried Women (1940-2015)

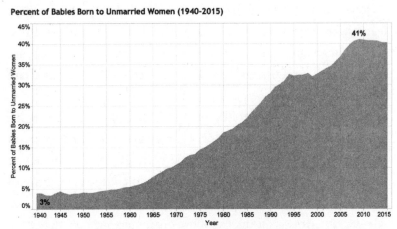

Source: Centers for Disease Control and Prevention, Table 1-17. Number and Percent of Births to Unmarried Women, by Race and Hispanic Origin: United States.

consequence the kids are living in pretty tough circumstances," said poverty researcher David Autor, commenting on a study on how the decline of manufacturing affected men and women.

Boys raised in single-parent households seem to suffer more than girls. A study showed that growing up with stably married parents makes one more likely to succeed at school, but that an absent father had a bigger impact on boys. Boys without fathers are more likely to get in trouble from elementary school onward, and appear to be "more responsive to parental inputs (or the absence thereof) than are girls." As the authors of one study put it, "As more boys grow up without their father in the home, and as women (especially in…working-class communities) are viewed as the more stable achievers, boys and girls alike come to see males as having a lower achievement orientation and less aptitude for higher education… college becomes something that many girls, but only some boys, do—the opposite of the earlier cultural norm."

J. D. Vance made the same observation about school being something boys were supposed to ignore: "As a child, I associated accomplishments in school with femininity. Manliness meant strength, courage, a willingness to fight, and later, success with girls. Boys who got good grades were 'sissies'...studies now show that working-class boys like me do much worse in school because they view schoolwork as a feminine endeavor."

I have two young boys at home, and I'm not surprised that it's boys who get less attention as children struggle. ADHD is two to three times more common among young boys than girls, with one 2015 U.S. Centers for Disease Control study finding that as many as 14 percent of boys received a diagnosis. Whereas some of my friends' daughters seem like little adults, my boys do not. Boys and girls mature differently, with the latter doing so faster and earlier. There is significant evidence that their relative maturity leads girls to be better at school. In 2012, 70 percent of U.S. high school valedictorians were girls, and girls attend college at higher rates in most developed countries.

At the high end of the spectrum, college-educated women don't like to marry non-college-educated men, quite understandably. As the gender ratio of college graduates becomes nearly three women for every two men, this means that almost one in three college-educated women will not find a male partner to marry if they want one, even assuming ideal matching. Thus, among educated women, an increasing number of women will either raise children without a partner or won't have them. I see this in my social circles; I know many successful professional women in New York City who either don't have families or are raising children as single moms. Many of them are brilliant, beautiful, amazing women. In a way it's fine, but in a way it's far less than ideal. One mom who attended Harvard Business School confided in me that she constantly feels guilty that her daughter will be an only child, but she can't imagine trying to raise more than one child on her own.

I understand: having and raising children has been the hardest experience of our lives for both my wife and me. I was cocky going into it; I thought to myself, *People have had children since the dawn of time. How hard could it be?* Now, I try to caution new parents that whatever they go through it's perfectly normal and to expect to have their lives changed and their spirits stretched. Having children has tested my wife and me as individuals and as a marriage. Both of us agree that we have no idea how any single mom or dad can make it happen unless they have incredibly supportive family members around.

Data bears this out—outcomes for children raised in single-parent households are significantly more adverse in every dimension: education, income, rate of marriage, rate of divorce, health, and so on, even controlling for income of the parent. It also explains partially why 50 percent of Americans live within 18 miles of their mothers—after you have a child you scramble for family.

Frederick Douglass wrote that "It is easier to build strong children than to repair broken men." What he left out is that it's also very hard to build strong children. I thought starting a company was hard, but being a parent is as hard or harder. I realized that there are many similarities between being a parent and being an entrepreneur. Here is a partial list:

- Everyone's got an opinion. But no one knows what they're doing.
- The first two years are brutal.
- No one cares as much as you do.
- On its best days it fills you with meaning and purpose.
- People lie about it all the time.
- Choose your partner wisely.
- Heart is more important than money. But money helps.

- It is very, very hard to outsource.
- You find out who your friends are. And you make some new ones.
- Occasionally the responsibility blows your mind.
- If you knew what it entailed you might not get started. But you're glad you did.
- There will be a thousand small tasks you never imagined.
- How you spend your time is more important than what you say.
- Everything costs more than you thought it would.
- Most of the work is dirty, thankless, and gritty.
- You learn a lot about yourself. You get tested in ways that you can't imagine.
- When you find someone who can really help you're incredibly grateful.
- You have to try to make time for yourself or it won't happen.
- Whatever your weaknesses are, they will come out.
- You think it's fragile. But it will surprise you.
- You sometimes do things you weren't sure you were capable of.
- When it does something great, there's nothing like it.
- You start out all-important. Yet the goal is to make yourself irrelevant.
- People sometimes give you too much credit.
- There is a lot of noise out there, but at the end of the day it's your call.
- It gives your life a different dimension. You grow new parts of yourself.
- It's harder than anyone expects. It's the best thing ever.

Entrepreneurship is defined as pursuing an opportunity without regard for resources currently under your control. Every parent pursues the best possible opportunities for his or her child while climbing over obstacles and limitations each day. So in a way, all parents are entrepreneurs.

My mind almost broke trying to build Venture for America and raise children (and stay married) simultaneously, despite my wife doing most of the hardest work. You never rest. Basically, being a parent is a ton of freaking work, and doing it alone seems inconceivably difficult. That's what we're setting up more and more people, most of them women, to face alone. At a time when raising and educating children and forming our human capital is of the utmost importance, we're heading in the other direction.

THIRTEEN

THE PERMANENT SHADOW CLASS: WHAT DISPLACEMENT LOOKS LIKE

n 2015, husband-and-wife economic researchers Anne Case and Angus Deaton found that mortality rates had increased sharply and steadily for middle-aged white Americans after 1999, going up 0.5 percent per year. They figured they must have made a mistake—it's more or less unheard of in a developed country to have life expectancy go down for any group for more than a momentary blip. Said Deaton: "[W]e thought it must be wrong...we just couldn't believe that this could have happened, or that if it had, someone else must have already noticed."

As it turns out, yes, it had happened, and yes, no one had noticed.

As Case and Deaton found, suicides were way up. Overdoses from prescription drugs were much higher. Alcoholic liver disease was commonplace. Historically, African Americans have had higher mortality rates and shorter life expectancies than whites.

Now, whites with a high school degree or less have the same mortality rates as African Americans with the same levels of education. What was behind the disturbing trends?

Case and Deaton point the finger at jobs. Deaton explained, "[J]obs have slowly crumbled away and many more men are finding themselves in a much more hostile labor market with lower wages, lower quality and less permanent jobs. That's made it harder for them to get married. They don't get to know their own kids. There's a lot of social dysfunction building up over time. There's a sense that these people have lost this sense of status and belonging...these are classic preconditions for suicide." They noted that the higher mortality rates and deaths of despair applied equally to middle-aged men and women in their study, though men experience these at much higher levels.

Deaths of Despair (Suicide, Drugs, & Alcohol) by Race among People Ages 50-54 (1999-2015)

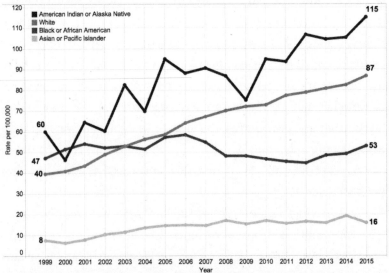

Source: Centers for Disease Control and Prevention, National Center for Health Statistics. Underlying Cause of Death 1999-2015 on CDC WONDER Online Database, released December, 2016. Data are from the Multiple Cause of Death Files, 1999-2015, as compiled from data provided by the 57 vital statistics jurisdictions through the Vital Statistics Cooperative Program.

Many of the deaths are from opiate overdoses. Approximately 59,000 Americans died of drug overdoses in 2016, up 19 percent from the then-record 52,404 reported in 2015. For the first time, drug overdoses have surpassed car accidents as the leading cause of accidental death in the United States. Coroners' offices in Ohio have reported being overwhelmed as the number of overdose victims has tripled in two years in some areas—they now call nearby funeral homes for help with storage.

The five states with the highest rates of death linked to drug overdoses in 2016 were West Virginia, New Hampshire, Kentucky, Ohio, and Rhode Island. Over 2 million Americans are estimated to be dependent on opioids, and an additional 95 million used prescription painkillers in the past year, according to the latest government report—more than used tobacco. In 12 states there are more opioid prescriptions than there are people. Addiction is so widespread that in Cincinnati hospitals now require universal drug testing for pregnant mothers because 5.4 percent of mothers had a positive drug test in past years. "Opioids are what we worry about most," explained Dr. Scott Wexelblatt, a neonatologist at Cincinnati Children's Hospital Perinatal Institute.

People often think of opioid addiction as originating with prescription painkiller use. OxyContin hit the market in 1996 as a "wonder drug," and Purdue Pharma, which was fined $635 million in 2007 for misbranding the drug and downplaying the possibility of addiction, sold $1.1 billion worth of painkillers in 2000—a sum that climbed to a staggering $3 billion in 2010. The company spent $200 million in marketing in 2001 alone, including hiring 671 sales reps who received success bonuses of up to almost a quarter million dollars for hitting sales goals. An army of drug dealers in suits marketed addictive opioids to doctors, getting paid hundreds of thousands to do it. Regarding OxyContin, CDC director Dr. Tom

Frieden noted that "we know of no other medication routinely used for a nonfatal condition that kills patients so frequently." A study showed that one out of every 550 patients started on opioid therapy died of opioid-related causes a median of 2.6 years after their first opioid prescription.

Now many opioid users have graduated to heroin. One common pattern of addiction is that people use prescription painkillers for pain relief or recreationally as a party drug—they grind up pills and sniff them for a euphoric high that lasts for hours. Then they later switch to heroin, which opioid users cited as more easily obtainable. A study conducted by the *New England Journal of Medicine* showed that 66 percent of those surveyed switched to other opioids after using OxyContin.

The majority of heroin users used to be men. However, because women are prescribed opioids at higher rates, today the gender balance of heroin users is about 50-50. Ninety percent of heroin users are white.

"We are seeing an unbelievably sad and extensive heroin epidemic, and there is no end in sight," says Daniel Ciccarone, a medical doctor at the University of California at San Francisco who studies the heroin market. "We are not, in 2017, anywhere close to the top of this thing. Heroin has a life force of its own." Drug cartels have begun to sell heroin laced with fentanyl, a synthetic opioid that increases both the high and the addiction level and is cheaper than heroin, and carfentanil, an elephant tranquilizer so powerful that simply touching it can cause an overdose when it is absorbed through the skin.

Our drug companies and medical system have produced hundreds of thousands of opioid addicts who are now heroin users buying from dealers. Heroin dealers have become ubiquitous—Ohio police say they've seen dealers text their customers to advertise two-for-one Sunday specials and offer free samples set up on car hoods in a local park. Some dealers have scheduled business hours. Others throw "testers" wrapped in paper slips printed with their phone number into passing cars, hoping to hook new business. Said Detective Brandon Connley after arresting a low-level dealer in Ohio, "Everybody and their mom sells drugs these days. There's always somebody right there to pick back up." Many dealers are addicts themselves trying to keep a steady supply.

This opioid plague will be with us for years in part because treatment is so difficult. Heroin and opioids are notoriously difficult addictions to break. Withdrawal symptoms include cravings, nausea, vomiting, depression, anxiety, insomnia, and fever. Most people relapse several times on their way to recovery, and many are forced to use opiate substitutes like methadone to manage their addiction. Only about 10 percent of people that had a drug abuse disorder received appropriate treatment, according to a 2014 study. Most people can't break the habit on their own and require extended rehabilitation. Sally Satel, a doctor and professor who has treated heroin users for years, said, "I speak from long experience when I say that few heavy users can simply take a medication and embark on a path to recovery. It often requires a healthy dose of benign paternalism and, in some cases, involuntary care through civil commitment." Treatment centers cost between $12,000 and $60,000 for 30- to 90-day inpatient care, with outpatient 30-day programs starting around $5,000, with no assurance of success.

Hand-in-hand with the spike in suicides and addiction has been the incredible increase in applications to Social Security disability programs. Almost 9 million working-age Americans receive disability benefits. That's more than the entire population of New Jersey or Virginia. The percentage of working-age Americans who received disability benefits was 5.2 percent in 2017, up from only 2.5 percent in 1980. Disability applications started surging in 2000, the same year that manufacturing employment started to plummet. The average benefit size in June 2017 was $1,172 per month, at a total cost of about $143 billion per year. The age of the disabled has gone down—in 2014, 15 percent of men and 16.2 percent of women in their 30s or early 40s were on disability, up from 6.6 percent and 6.4 percent in the 1960s.

Rates of disability track areas of joblessness, forming "disability belts" in Appalachia, the Deep South, and other regions. In a couple of counties in Virginia, fully 20 percent of working adults ages 18–64 are now receiving disability benefits. West Virginia, Alabama, Arkansas, Kentucky, and Mississippi are the top five states for disability beneficiaries, with 7.9–8.9 percent of the workforce receiving income replacement. Disability payments received by beneficiaries in these five states exceed $1 billion per month. In these areas, disability benefits are so widespread that the day that checks arrive is like a monthly holiday. Said one West Virginian who processed disability claims, "They're a vital part of our economy. A lot of people depend on them to survive. [On the days checks arrive] you avoid the pharmacy. You avoid Wal-Mart. You avoid, you know, restaurants… Everybody's received their benefits. Let's go shopping."

Some of the increasing rates of disability reflect an aging population and changing demographics. But many of them represent what one expert called "economic disability." The biggest growth categories of disability category are "mental disorders" and "musculoskeletal and connective tissue," which together now comprise about 50 percent of disability claims, nearly double what they were 20 years ago. These diagnoses are also the hardest to independently verify for a doctor.

The number of people who applied for disability benefits in 2014 was 2,485,077. On any given business day, there are 9,500 applicants. There are 1,500 disability judges around the country who administer the decisions, often without seeing the claimants. The waiting period to get a hearing is now more than 18 months in most states. To apply for disability, applicants must gather evidence from medical professionals. They compile notes from doctors, send in the information, and wait to hear back. No lawyer representing the government cross-examines them. No government doctor examines them. About 40 percent of claims are ultimately approved, either initially or on appeal. The lifetime value of a disability award is about $300K for the average recipient.

Because the stakes are so high, representing claimants has become a big business. Law firms regularly advertise for clients on late-night television to help them navigate the process and collect a fee, typically a percentage of the award. Eighty percent of appealing claimants are represented by counsel, up from less than 20 percent in the 1970s. One law firm generated $70 million in revenue in one year alone from representing disability claimants.

After someone is on disability, there's a massive disincentive to work, because if you work and show that you're able-bodied, you lose benefits. As a result, virtually no one recovers from disability. The churn rate nationally is less than 1 percent. David Autor asserts that Social Security Disability Insurance today essentially serves as unemployment insurance around the country. It's not designed for this, but that's what it is for hundreds of thousands of Americans.

One judge who administers disability decisions said that "if the American public knew what was going on in our system, half would be outraged and the other half would apply for benefits."

I spoke to a friend, Tony, about his experience applying for disability. He and I grew up together playing Dungeons and Dragons on the same street. Tony is a house painter who worked previously as a musician and sound technician. He was married briefly but is now divorced. Tony finished his college degree a few years ago at a public university. He went most of his childhood without health insurance—his father was a contractor and self-employed. In 2011, he moved to western Massachusetts and received health insurance for the first time—it was free under "Romneycare" because he was considered low income.

A couple years ago, after not being able to work for a few months due to health problems, Tony was told by his therapist, "You should try to get disability." Tony at first thought that he wouldn't qualify because his injuries were mostly brain-related: multiple traumatic brain injuries from childhood accidents (a fall on concrete when he was nine and a crashed scooter when he was 11) and concussions from playing high school football led to impaired cognition and mood swings. He also suffered from chronic fatigue, muscle pain, depression, and chronic Lyme disease.

Tony took the therapist's advice and went on the Social Security Disability Insurance (SSDI) website to apply. He submitted notes from his therapist, nurse prescriber, supervising psychiatrist, primary care physician, a specialist in holistic medicine, and a specialist in infectious disease. "I had a lot of stuff that had built up in my body over the years. I sometimes think that if I'd had proper treatment as a kid I might not be disabled today." Tony submitted the paperwork in March 2016 and was notified that he was denied benefits five months later. About 75 percent of initial claims get denied nationally. He then went online and found a local attorney who specializes in disability appeals. The lawyer worked through the appeals process on Tony's behalf. Two months later, Tony was approved and began receiving approximately $1,200 a month. "After the lawyer took over, that was it. The money showed up in my account." The lawyer collected about $2,700 for handling the appeal—25 percent of the disability payments that were retroactive to when Tony was deemed disabled.

Tony is currently on disability, and his first review will be after two years. "Thank God for disability. If not for disability I would have worked myself to death and died." Tony is 42. He volunteers at a local church. "I live in western Massachusetts, which is not someplace that people think of as struggling. But it's crazy how many people come in to church who are living in tents and on the street. People just do what they have to do to get by."

I'm personally very glad that disability was there for Tony. For him, disability was literally a lifesaver.

J. D. Vance writes of how the people in Ohio became angry that they were working hard and scraping by while others were doing nothing and living off of government checks. He cites this resentment toward government handouts as an explanation for why regions like Ohio have become more Republican.

The numbers have grown to a point where more Americans are currently on disability than work in construction. In 2013, 56.5 percent of prime-age men 25–54 who were not in the workforce reported receiving disability payments. Though the numbers have stabilized as more people in this age group have moved into Social Security retirement, they are already way beyond what anyone intended. The fund for disability insurance recently ran out and was combined with the greater Social Security fund, which is itself scheduled to run out of money in 2034.

The fact that a program designed for a relatively small number of Americans has now become such a major lifeline for people and communities is part of the Great Displacement. We pretend that our economy is doing all right while millions of people give up and "get on the draw" or "get on the check." It's a $143 billion per year shock absorber for the unemployed or unemployable, whose ranks are growing all of the time. After one gets on disability, one enters a permanent shadow class of beneficiaries. Even if you start feeling better, you're not going to risk a lifetime of benefits for a tenuous job that could disappear at any moment. And it's likely easier to think of yourself as genuinely disabled than as someone cheating society for a monthly draw.

Many Americans, disabled or not, have some degree of health problems. If you've got a good job, you might ignore your hurt back or, if your job offers health insurance, have access to an affordable way to treat it and continue working. If you don't have a job and the stress starts to mount, you can easily start to feel more infirm. This is doubly true in environments where work is mostly manual and involves a lot of wear and tear. For many, the chain of circumstances is to go from former manufacturing worker to disability recipient. The other major refuge has been retail jobs. After these jobs disappear, the ranks of the disabled will swell.

Disability illustrates the challenges of mandating the government to administer such a large-scale program. It's essentially the worst of all worlds, as the truly disabled and needy may find themselves shut out by red tape, while the process rewards those who lawyer up and the lawyers themselves. It sends a pervasive message of "game the system and get money" and "think of yourself as incompetent and incapable of work." It's subject to fraud. And once you're on, you never leave.

FOURTEEN

VIDEO GAMES AND THE (MALE) MEANING OF LIFE

Virtual worlds give back what has been scooped out of modern life... it gives us back community, a feeling of competence, and a sense of being an important person whom people depend on.

—JONATHAN GOTTSCHALL

When I was seven, my parents bought me and my brother an Atari 2600, the first mass game console. The game it came with was Asteroids. We played that game an awful lot. One night, we snuck down in the middle of the night only to discover my Dad already playing.

My brother and I loved going to local arcades and to try to make a few quarters last as long as possible. It was the perfect set of incentives: You win, you keep playing. You lose, you're forced to stand there and watch others play, hoping that someone is forced to leave their game in the middle so you can jump in. We became very good at video games. My favorite was Street Fighter II. I memorized the Mortal Kombat fatalities to inflict graphic harm on defeated enemies. On the PC, I was hooked the first time I played Ancient Art of War when I was nine. As I got older, real-time strategy games like Warcraft and Starcraft arrived to combine efficiently building armies and settlements with defeating live opponents. My friends and I would sit next to each other in a house with several networked computers taking on strangers and talking trash.

The amount of time I spent on video games dropped dramatically after I graduated from college. I wanted to go on dates, and playing video games wasn't helping. I developed a notion that virtual world building and real-life world building were at odds with each other. I started reading books on investing and financial statement analysis, which seemed to me to be the real-world analogue to becoming good at video games. By the time I started dabbling in games again and asked my brother-in-law to school me in Defense of the Ancients ("Dota") over the holidays, they had leapt forward to a point where I felt old and slow. Memorizing key commands seemed beyond me.

That said, I still understand and appreciate video games on a visceral level. I even imagine that I could get into them again. They speak to a primal set of basic impulses—to world creating, skill building, achievement, violence, leadership, teamwork, speed, efficiency, status, decision making, and accomplishment. They fall into a whole suite of things that appeal to young men in particular—to me the list would go something like gaming, the stock market, fantasy sports, gambling, basketball, science fiction/geek movies, and cryptocurrencies, most of which involve a blend of numbers and optimization. It's a need for mastery, progress, competition, and risk.

As of last year, 22 percent of men between the ages of 21 and 30 with less than a bachelor's degree reported not working at all in the previous year—up from only 9.5 percent in 2000. And there's evidence that video games are a big reason why. According to a recent study based on the Census Bureau's time-use surveys, young men without college degrees have replaced 75 percent of the time they used to spend working with time on the computer, mostly playing video games. From 2004 to 2007, young, unemployed men without college degrees were spending 3.4 hours per week playing video games. By 2011 to 2014, the average time spent per week had more than doubled to 8.6 hours.

The economists conducting the study, led by the University of Chicago's Erik Hurst, strained to figure out whether men who were already detached were playing video games to pass the time, or whether video games were actually causing them to drop out. Evidence pointed to the latter. Their research indicated that improved technological entertainment options, primarily video games, are responsible for between 20 and 33 percent of reduced work hours. The trends are different for women, who have not seen the same increase in gaming at the expense of work hours and are more likely to return to school when out of work. For many men, however, games have gotten so good that they have made dropping out of work a more appealing option.

"When I play a game, I know if I have a few hours I will be rewarded," said one 22-year-old who lives with his parents in Silver Spring, Maryland. "With a job, it's always been up in the air with the amount of work I put in and the reward." Jacob Barry, a 21-year-old in Michigan, finds it easier to get excited about playing games than his part-time job making sandwiches at a local Jimmy John's, particularly given the sense of community he finds online. He plays up to 40 hours a week, the equivalent of a full-time job.

How exactly are these game-playing men getting by? They live with their parents. In 2000, just 35 percent of lower-skilled young men lived with family. Now, more than 50 percent of lower-skilled young men live with their parents, and as many as 67 percent of those who are unemployed do so. More U.S. men aged 18–34 are now living with their parents than with romantic partners, according to the Pew Research Center.

Video games function as extremely inexpensive entertainment on a time-use basis. After one invests in a console or computer, the marginal cost is near zero. Gamers can log hundreds or thousands of hours for the cost of one game or rental subscription. Time spent gaming is what's known in economic terms as an "inferior good"—the poorer you are, the more of it you consume. Recent studies found that households making between $25,000 and $35,000 a year spent 92 more minutes per week online than households making $100,000 plus a year.

The image of legions of men in their parents' basements playing video games for hours on end may seem pathetic or sad. But their satisfaction level is high. "Happiness has gone up for this group," says Hurst, despite the high rate of unemployment. Hurst describes his findings as "staggering" and observes of his own 12-year-old son: "If it were up to him, I have no doubt he would play video games 23½ hours per day. He told me so. If we didn't ration video games, I am not sure he would ever eat. I am positive he wouldn't shower."

Video games are fun and communal. Nowadays they're also so well designed that many almost simulate jobs if a job's progress were measured in minutes and hours instead of weeks and months. In many games, you perform a variety of mundane, repetitive tasks in order to build points or currencies or accrue items. You then use these items to make yourself more capable. You complete quests with your friends or against the computer. You experience a continuous feeling of progress and accomplishment.

As one can imagine, the problems come later. Playing video games as a pseudo-job that doesn't pay can be fun, social, and even cool in your teens and 20s. By the time you're in your 30s, your friends may have moved on and you become the loser shut-in who lurks around the local GameStop. "There is some evidence that these young, lower-skilled men who are happy in their 20s become much less happy in their 30s or 40s," says Hurst. Their work skills and prospects will be limited, and competing in the workforce will be harder and harder. To the extent they ever wanted to go out and start a family, it may seem more and more unrealistic and out of reach. They are likely to stay detached, and may drift from video games to gambling, drugs, and alcohol.

Indeed, the most recent General Social Survey showed that 31 percent of working-age men who are out of the workforce admitted to illegal drug use in the past 12 months. The Annual Time Use survey in 2014 indicated high levels of time spent "attending gambling establishments," "tobacco and drug use," "listening to the radio," and "arts and crafts as a hobby," with over 8 hours per day spent on "socializing, relaxing and leisure." The same surveys showed lower likelihood of volunteering or attending religious services than for men in the workforce, despite having considerably more time.

"Every society has a 'bad men' problem," says Tyler Cowen, the economist and author of *Average Is Over*. He projects a future where a relative handful of high-productivity individuals create most of the value, while low-skilled people become preoccupied with cheap digital entertainment to stay happy and organize their lives.

Games have come a long way since I was a kid, and they're about to take yet another leap forward. Virtual reality headsets are creating experiences that will take simulations to a whole new level. Digital entertainments will get better and better. The analogue and the real world will become less and less appealing. Before long, video games, virtual reality, and pornography will merge into new forms of immersive experiences that will be more and more compelling. On a pure enjoyment basis, it's going to be hard to beat.

Imagine a 21-year-old college dropout who is not excited to make sandwiches at Jimmy John's and prefers his gaming community.

You could say to him, "Hey, this Jimmy John's job could go places. Sure you make $8 an hour now. But maybe if you stick with it for a few years you could become a manager. Eventually, you could make $35,000 or so if you really excel and are willing to work long and hard hours, including waking up at 5 a.m. to slice up tomatoes and cucumbers every morning, and commit to it."

The above is possibly true. Or, the retail district around his Jimmy John's could shrink and a management job might never open up. Or Jimmy John's could bring in an automated system that gets rid of cashiers and front-of-house staff two years from now. Or his manager could just choose someone else.

I can't really say that the food service job is more intellectually stimulating or social than playing video games. The main virtues seem to be that it pays money, imposes discipline, involves face-to-face contact with other real humans, and might lead somewhere. In previous eras of growth, it really might have.

I sympathize with this kid in part because I feel like the trade-offs are more difficult than most people realize. If I was given the choice between a dead-end low-end job for months on end or hanging with my friends playing video games, it would be very easy to choose the latter. The consequences are somewhat vague and "down the road." Men imagine themselves to be kings, warriors, CEOs, athletes, ladies' men, geniuses, soldiers, workers, achievers, and part of a band of brothers. All of these things are possible online.

Of course I believe that people should go out into the real world, get a good job, fall in love, get married, become a homeowner, have a child, be a good parent, leave the world a better place, and so on. I've tried to do it myself. It's the substance of life and humanity. It requires a degree of evolution and positive social reinforcement—particularly trying to be a good parent.

But this version of achievement is not going to be sustainable for more and more Americans. The jobs are going to lead nowhere and then disappear. There will be very limited social reinforcement. The incentives to stay immersed in the virtual world will rise as the world outside gets harder and less welcoming. Billions of dollars will be spent facilitating their immersion.

A number of my guy friends have gotten divorced in their thirties and forties. Others have become detached from society. Male dysfunction tends to take on an air of nihilism and dropping out. The world and relationships take work. You gird yourself for the workplace in a suit of armor. If you ever take it off and stop working, you get swept away.

Many men have within us the man-child who's still in that basement. The fortunate among us have left him behind, but we understand his appeal all too well. He's still there waiting—ready to take over in case our lives fall apart.

FIFTEEN

THE SHAPE WE'RE IN/ DISINTEGRATION

The progress of a few fortunate decades can too easily be swept away by a few years of trouble.

—RYAN AVENT

The challenges of job loss and technological unemployment are among the most significant faced by our society in history. They are even more daunting than any external enemy because both the enemy and the victims are hard to identify. When a few hundred workers get replaced or a plant closes, the people around them notice and the community suffers. But to the rest of us, each closing is seen as part of economic progress.

The challenges are magnified because American society is not in great shape right now. There are a number of trends that are going to make managing the transition to a new economy all the more difficult:

- We are getting older.
- We don't have adequate retirement savings.
- We are financially insecure.
- We use a lot of drugs.

- We are not starting new businesses.
- We're depressed.
- We owe a lot of money, public and private.
- Our education system underperforms.
- Our economy is consolidating around a few mega-powerful firms in our most important industries.
- Our media is fragmented.
- Our social capital is lower.
- We don't trust institutions anymore.

This last one makes everything harder—and it reminds me of my relationship with the Knicks.

I was 15 years old when I became a huge fan of the New York Knicks. I watched the Ewing-led Knicks go up 2-0 on Michael Jordan's Bulls only to lose the series 4–2. I felt the pain alongside my friends and craved revenge. The Knicks became a part of my life's fabric, with their deep playoff runs in 1994 and 1999 high-water marks. I would watch every game I could and even listened to games on the radio from my college dorm room. When I moved to New York, I stood in line each year to get nosebleed $10 and $20 seats. After the Knicks became uncompetitive, I gritted my teeth through the Isiah Thomas era and tracked the potential of draftees like Frank Williams and Mike Sweetney.

My love affair turned sour after successive years of turmoil. Not the losing—I totally don't mind rooting for a team that's developing young guys and losing competitively. But an endless series of bad behavior and bad decisions began to sour me. What started out as a wholesome sports allegiance felt more and more like an abusive relationship. I couldn't follow the Knicks anymore. Their leadership was corrupt. Their figures were unsympathetic and incompetent. I swore off the Knicks in 2014 and never looked back.

That's essentially how many Americans feel about most institutions nowadays. Their love and trust have been taken for granted and abused. Public faith in the medical system, the media, public schools, and government are all at record lows compared to past eras.

Confidence in U.S. Institutions (1970s versus 2017)

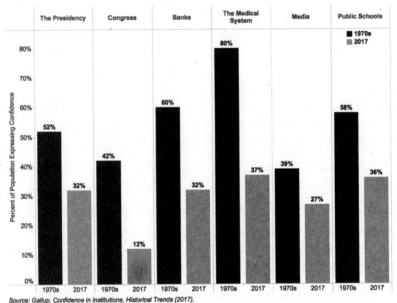

Source: Gallup. *Confidence in Institutions, Historical Trends (2017)*.

We have entered an age of transparency where we can see our institutions and leaders for all of their flaws. Trust is for the gullible. Everything now will be a fight. Appealing to common interests will be all the more difficult.

In the musical *Hamilton*, the protagonist refers to the newly formed United States as "young, scrappy, and hungry." That hasn't been us for quite a while. Membership in organizations like the PTA, the Red Cross, labor unions, and recreational leagues has declined by between 25 and 50 percent since the 1960s. Even time spent on informal socializing and visiting is down by a similar level.

Our social capital has been declining for a long time, and there is no sign of a reversal.

All of these things make addressing technological unemployment harder. We no longer believe we're capable of turning things around without something dramatic changing. Among the things being questioned is our capitalist system. Among young people, polls show a very high degree of sympathy for other types of economies, in part because they've witnessed capitalism's failures and excesses these past years.

I love capitalism—anyone who has a smartphone in their pocket has to appreciate the power of markets to drive value and innovation. We all have capitalism to thank for most of what we enjoy. It has elevated the standard of living of billions of people and defined our society for the better.

That said, capitalism, with the assistance of technology, is about to turn on normal people. Capital and efficiency will prefer robots, software, AI, and machines to people more and more. Capitalism is like our mentor and guiding light, to whom we've listened for years. He helped us make great decisions for a long time. But at some point he got older, teamed up with his friend technology, and together they became more extreme. They started saying things like, "Ah, let's automate everything" and "If the market doesn't like it, get rid of it," which made reasonable people increasingly nervous.

Even the most hard-nosed businessperson should recognize that the gains and losses from unprecedented technological advances will have dramatic sets of human winners and losers, and that the system needs to account for that in order to continue. Capitalism doesn't work that well if people don't have any money to buy things or if communities are degenerating into scarcity, anger, and despair.

The question is, what is to be done?

If we do nothing, society will become dramatically bifurcated on levels we can scarcely imagine. There will be a shrinking number of affluent people in a handful of megacities and those who cut their hair and take care of their children. There will also be enormous numbers of increasingly destitute and displaced people in decaying towns around the country that the trucks drive past without stopping. Some of my friends project a violent revolution if this picture comes to pass. History would suggest that this is exactly what will happen.

America has been getting less violent in most measurable ways—violent crimes and protests are all less common than in the past, even though it doesn't seem like it. For example, there were approximately 2,500 leftist bombings in America between 1971 and 1972, which would seem unfathomable today. It's possible that we may already be too defeated and opiated by the market to mount a revolution. We might just settle for making hateful comments online and watching endless YouTube videos with only the occasional flare-up of violence amid many quiet suicides.

Yet, it's almost certain that increasing levels of desperation will lead to destabilization. One can imagine a single well-publicized kidnapping or random heinous act against a child of the privileged class leading to bodyguards, bulletproof cars, embedded safety chips in children, and other measures. The rich people I know tend to be somewhat paranoid about their own safety and that of their families. To me, without dramatic change, the best-case scenario is a hyper-stratified society like something out of *The Hunger Games* or Guatemala with an occasional mass shooting. The worst case is widespread despair, violence, and the utter collapse of our society and economy.

This viewpoint may strike some as extreme. Consider, though, that trucking protests were common in the final days of the Soviet

Union, a large unemployed group of working-age men is a common feature in Middle Eastern countries that experience political upheaval, and there are approximately 270 to 310 million firearms in the United States, almost one per human being. We are the most heavily armed society in the history of mankind—disintegration is unlikely to be gentle. The unemployment rate at the height of the Great Depression was about 25 percent. Society experiences fractures well before all the jobs disappear.

In his book *Ages of Discord*, the scholar Peter Turchin proposes a structural-demographic theory of political instability based on societies throughout history. He suggests that there are three main preconditions to revolution: (1) elite oversupply and disunity, (2) popular misery based on falling living standards, and (3) a state in fiscal crisis. He uses a host of variables to measure these conditions, including real wages, marital trends, proportion of children in two-parent households, minimum wage, wealth distribution, college tuition, average height, oversupply of lawyers, political polarization, income tax on the wealthy, visits to national monuments, trust in government, and other factors. Turchin points out that societies generally experience extended periods of integration and prosperity followed by periods of inequity, increasing misery and political instability that lead to disintegration, and that we're in the midst of the latter. Most of the variables that he measures began trending negatively between 1965 and 1980 and are now reaching near-crisis levels. By his analysis, "the US right now has much in common with the Antebellum 1850s [before the Civil War] and, more surprisingly, with…France on the eve of the French Revolution." He projects increased turmoil through 2020 and warns that "we are rapidly approaching a historical cusp at which American society will be particularly vulnerable to violent upheaval."

If there is a revolution, it is likely to be born of race and identity with automation-driven economics as the underlying force. A highly disproportionate number of the people at the top will be educated whites, Jews, and Asians. America is projected to become majority minority by 2045. African Americans and Latinos will almost certainly make up a disproportionate number of the less privileged in the wake of automation, as they currently enjoy lower levels of wealth and education. Racial inequality will become all the more jarring as the new majority remains on the outside. Gender inequality, too, will become more stark, with women comprising the clear majority of college graduates yet still underrepresented in many environments. Less privileged whites may be more likely to blame people of color, immigrants, or shifting cultural norms for their diminishing stature and shattered communities than they will automation and the capitalist system. Culture wars will be proxy wars for the economic backdrop.

This is already happening. Alec Ross, an author and Baltimore resident, described the Freddie Gray riots in 2015 as partially a product of economic despair. The protests injured 20 police officers, resulted in 250 arrests, damaged 300 businesses, caused 150 vehicle fires and 60 structure fires, and led to the looting of 27 drugstores. "While the triggering event [of the riots] was the death of a 25-year-old man in police custody, the protesters themselves consistently rooted their cause and rallying cry...in more than police brutality. It was about the hopelessness that came from growing up poor and black in a community that had been laid to waste with the loss of Baltimore's industrial and manufacturing base and then gone ignored. Black working-class families had effectively been globalized and automated out of jobs." The Charlottesville violence in 2017 over the removal of Confederate symbols can also be seen as engendered in part by economic dislocation. The driver of the car that plowed into the crowd, killing a young woman, was from an economically depressed part of Ohio and had washed out of the military. James Hodgkinson, the liberal activist who shot four people and critically wounded a congressman at a softball game in 2017, was a 66-year-old unemployed house inspector from Illinois whose marriage and finances were failing.

The group I worry about most is poor whites. Even now, people of color report higher levels of optimism than poor whites, despite worse economic circumstances. It's difficult to go from feeling like the pillar of one's society to feeling like an afterthought or failure. There is a strong heritage of military service in many white communities that will be subverted into antigovernment militias, white nationalist gangs, and bunkers in the woods. There will be more random mass shootings in the months ahead as middle-aged white men self-destruct and feel that life has no meaning. As the mindset of scarcity spreads and deepens, people's executive functioning will erode. It takes self-control to resist base impulses. Racism and misogyny will become more and more pervasive even as it is policed in certain sectors.

Contributing to the discord will be a climate that equates opposing ideas or speech to violence and hate. Righteousness can fuel abhorrent behavior, and many react with a shocking level of vitriol and contempt for conflicting viewpoints and the people who hold them. Hatred is easy, as is condemnation. Addressing the conditions that breed hatred is very hard. As more communities experience the same phenomena the catalysts will be varied and the reactions intense. Attacking other people will be a lot easier than attacking the system.

Could extreme behavior in some places even precede a political breakup of the country? One can imagine California, the most racially diverse, progressive, and wealthy state, holding a referendum to secede in response to events elsewhere in the country that are perceived as atavistic and regressive. There is already a nascent movement among technologists, libertarians, and others in California to secede on economic grounds, including the recent "Yes California" movement pushing "Calexit" and the California National Party—about one-third of Californians supported secession in a recent poll, up considerably from earlier levels. California would be the sixth-largest economy in the world as a separate country. If there were a successful vote, two-thirds of Congress and three-quarters of states would be required to approve it under the Constitution, which today seems impossible. However, California's departure would permanently tilt the country's political balance, which could be appealing to the party in power. Such a vote could also prompt a reprisal or punishment. Texas likewise has a long history of secessionist movements.

Earlier I wrote about truck drivers, who will soon start to lose their jobs or have their wages reduced as automated trucks enter the market. Let's imagine that one of them, Mike, owns a small trucking company with 10 trucks and 30 drivers. He sees his life savings about to go down the tubes because he owes the banks hundreds of thousands of dollars in loans he took out to buy his vehicles. Mike says to his guys, "Fuck this. We can't be replaced by robot trucks. Let's go to Springfield and demand our jobs back." He leads a protest in Illinois and hundreds of truckers join in, some of them bringing their vehicles and blocking roads. The police respond but they are reluctant to use force. The crowds multiply as more drivers and rioters arrive.

Inspired by what they see on social media, truckers begin to protest in other state capitals in the tens of thousands. The National Guard is activated and the president calls for calm, but disorder grows. Various antigovernment militias and white nationalist groups say, "This is our chance," and arrive in each state to support the truckers. Some of them bring various weapons, and violence breaks out. The protests and violence spread to the capitals of Alabama, Arkansas, Idaho, Indiana, Kentucky, Mississippi, Michigan, Ohio, and Nebraska. Locals take advantage of police preoccupation in these areas and begin looting drugstores nearby.

The president calls for a return to order and says that he will meet with the truckers. However, the protests morph into many distinct conflicts with unclear demands and fragmented leadership. Mike is held up as a symbol of the working man but has no control. The riots rage for several weeks. In the aftermath, there are dozens dead, hundreds injured and arrested, and billions of dollars' worth of property damage and economic harm. Images of the violence spread on the Internet and are seen by millions in real time.

After the riots, things continue to deteriorate. Hundreds of thousands stop paying taxes because they refuse to support a government that "killed the working man." A man in a bunker surrounded by dozens of guns releases a video saying, "Come and get your taxes, IRS man!" that goes viral. Anti-Semitic violence breaks out targeting those who "own the robots." A white nationalist party arises that openly advocates "returning America to its roots" and "traditional gender roles" and wins several state races in the South. Graffiti and literature for the new party appear on college campuses, which leads to protests and sit-ins. A shooter arrives in the lobby of a technology company in San Francisco and wounds several people. Technology companies hire security forces, but 30 percent of employees request to work remotely due to a sense of fear. Several tech companies move to Vancouver, citing a desire for employee safety. The California secession movement surges as state officials move to protect the border and implement checkpoints.

Maybe the scenario I sketched above seems unlikely. To me, it seems depressingly plausible. But this vision assumes that we keep the system as it is right now, where we prioritize capital efficiency above all and see people primarily as economic inputs. The market will continue to drive us in specific directions that will lead to extremes even as opportunities diminish at every turn.

Forestalling automation and retaining jobs might help. Some would argue we should require that a human is in every truck, only let doctors look at radiology films, and maintain employment levels in fast food restaurants and call centers. However, it would be nearly impossible to curb automation for any prolonged period of time effectively across all industries. The result would be that certain workers and industries would be protected while others in an industry that is less core—like retail—would be quickly displaced.

This reminds me of a story the economist Milton Friedman told about visiting a Chinese worksite. He notices that there are no big tractors or pieces of equipment, only men with shovels. He asks his guide, "Where are all of the machines to dig the holes and move the earth?"

His guide responds, "You don't understand. This is a program designed to create jobs."

Milton thinks for a second, then asks: "So why give them shovels?"

Time only flows in one direction, and progress is a good thing as long as its benefits are shared.

Doing nothing leads to almost certain ruin. Trying to forestall progress is likely a doomed strategy over time.

What's left?

When you're left with no other options, the unthinkable becomes necessary. We must change and reformat the economy and society to progress through a massive historical shift. Much of this book has likely come across as quite negative. This transition will indeed be very difficult. But the opportunities ahead are vast.

Robert Kennedy famously said that GDP "does not allow for the health of our children, the quality of their education, or the joy of their play... it measures everything, in short, except that which makes life worthwhile." We have to start thinking more about what makes life worthwhile.

PART
THREE:

SOLUTIONS
AND HUMAN
CAPITALISM

SIXTEEN

THE FREEDOM DIVIDEND

A t this point, you may be hanging your head, thinking, "Wow, this guy's view of the future is bleak." One friend who read early pages said to me, "Reading this feels like I'm getting punched in the face repeatedly." Another said, "You should change the title to *We're Fucked*."

There are potential solutions to these problems. Things will certainly be very difficult in the years ahead as jobs disappear. But there are things we can do that will make things dramatically better. They will require imagination, will, confidence, empathy, and a can-do spirit.

Peter Frase, author of *Four Futures*, points out that work encompasses three things: the means by which the economy produces goods and services, the means by which people earn income, and an activity that lends meaning or purpose to many people's lives. We should tackle these one at a time, with the easiest one first. In a future without jobs, people will need to be able to provide for themselves and their basic needs. Eventually, the government will need to intervene in order to prevent widespread squalor, despair, and violence. The sooner the government acts, the more high-functioning our society will be.

The first major change would be to implement a universal basic income (UBI), which I would call the "Freedom Dividend." The United States should provide an annual income of $12,000 for each American aged 18–64, with the amount indexed to increase with inflation. It would require a constitutional supermajority to modify or amend. The Freedom Dividend would replace the vast majority of existing welfare programs. This plan was proposed by Andy Stern, the former head of the largest labor union in the country, in his book *Raising the Floor.* The poverty line is currently $11,770. We would essentially be bringing all Americans to the poverty line and alleviate gross poverty.

A universal basic income is a version of Social Security where all citizens receive a set amount of money per month independent of their work status or income. Everyone from a hedge fund billionaire in New York to an impoverished single mom in West Virginia would receive a monthly check of $1,000. If someone is working as a waitress or construction worker making $18,000, he or she would essentially be making $30,000. UBI eliminates the disincentive to work that most people find troubling about traditional welfare programs—if you work you could actually start saving and get ahead. With the growing threat of automation, the concept has gained renewed attention, with trials being run in Oakland, Canada, and Finland as well as in India and other parts of the developing world.

Today, people tend to associate universal basic income with technology utopians. But a form of UBI almost became law in the United States in 1970 and 1971, passing the House of Representatives twice before stalling in the Senate. Versions of the idea have been championed by robust thinkers of every political persuasion for decades, including some of the most admired figures in American life. Here's a sampling:

Thomas Paine, 1796: Out of a collected fund from landowners, "there shall be paid to every person, when arrived at the age of twenty-one years, the sum of fifteen pounds sterling, as a compensation in part, for the loss of his or her natural inheritance,... to every person, rich or poor."

Martin Luther King Jr., 1967: "I am now convinced that the simplest approach will prove to be the most effective—the solution to poverty is to abolish it directly by a now widely discussed measure: the guaranteed income."

Richard Nixon, August 1969: "What I am proposing is that the Federal Government build a foundation under the income of every American family...that cannot care for itself—and wherever in America that family may live."

Milton Friedman, 1980: "We should replace the ragbag of specific welfare programs with a single comprehensive program of income supplements in cash—a negative income tax...which would do more efficiently and humanely what our present welfare system does so inefficiently and inhumanely."

Bernie Sanders, May 2014: "In my view, every American is entitled to at least a minimum standard of living...There are different ways to get to that goal, but that's the goal that we should strive to reach."

Stephen Hawking, July 2015: "Everyone can enjoy a life of luxurious leisure if the machine-produced wealth is shared, or most people can end up miserably poor if the machine-owners successfully lobby against wealth redistribution. So far, the trend seems to be toward the second option, with technology driving ever-increasing inequality."

Barack Obama, June 2016: "The way I describe it is that, because of automation, because of globalization, we're going to have to examine the social compact, the same way we did early in the 19th century and then again during and after the Great Depression. The notion of a 40-hour workweek, a minimum wage, child labor laws, etc.—those will have to be updated for these new realities."

Barack Obama, October 2016: "What is indisputable...is that as AI gets further incorporated, and the society potentially gets wealthier, the link between production and distribution, how much you work and how much you make, gets further and further attenuated...we'll be debating unconditional free money over the next 10 or 20 years."

Warren Buffett, January 2017: "[Y]ou have to figure out how to distribute it...people who fall by the wayside through no fault of their own as the goose lays more golden eggs should still get a chance to participate in that prosperity, and that's where government comes in."

Bill Gates, January 2017: "A problem of excess [automation] forces us to look at the individuals affected and take those extra resources and make sure they're directed to them in terms of re-education and income policies..." (Gates later suggested taxing robots.)

Elon Musk, February, 2017: "I think we'll end up doing universal basic income...It's going to be necessary...There will be fewer and fewer jobs that a robot cannot do better. I want to be clear. These are not things I wish will happen; these are things I think probably will happen."

Mark Zuckerberg, May 2017: "We should explore...universal basic income so that everyone has a cushion to try new ideas."

My mom, September 2017: "If you think it's a good idea, Andy, I'm sure it's a good idea."

You may be thinking, *This will never happen. And if it did, wouldn't it cause runaway inflation? Enable generations of wastrels?*

Twelve thousand dollars a year is not enough to do more than scrape by. Very few people will quit their jobs because of a guaranteed income at this level unless they were in a marginal or exploitative situation. The available data bears this out.

On the other hand, the benefits would be absolutely enormous:

- It would be a massive stimulus to lower-cost areas.
- It would empower people to avoid making terrible decisions based on financial scarcity and month-to-month needs.
- It would be a phenomenal boon to creativity and entrepreneurship.
- It would enable people to more effectively transition from shrinking industries and environments to new ones.
- It would reduce stress, improve health, decrease crime, and strengthen relationships.
- It would support parents and caretakers for the work that they do, particularly mothers.
- It would give all citizens an honest stake in society and a sense of the future.
- It would restore a sense of optimism and faith in communities around the country.
- It would stimulate and maintain the consumer economy through the automation wave.
- It would maintain order and preserve our way of life through the greatest economic and social transition in history.
- It would make our society more equitable, fair, and just.

An analysis by the Roosevelt Institute of this $12,000 per year per adult proposal found that adopting it would permanently grow the economy by 12.56 to 13.10 percent—or about $2.5 trillion by 2025—and it would increase the labor force by 4.5 to 4.7 million people. Putting money into people's hands and keeping it there would be a perpetual boost and support to job growth and the economy. The cost would be about an additional $1.3 trillion per year on top of existing welfare programs, most of which would be folded into the plan, as well as increased taxable revenue and cost savings. Conservatives would rejoice that the patchwork of 126 plans with perverse incentives and cumbersome bureaucracies would mostly disappear.

The cost of $1.3 trillion seems like an awful lot. For reference, the federal budget is about $4 trillion and the entire U.S. economy about $19 trillion. But there are myriad ways to pay for it. The most sensible way to pay for it in my view would be with a value-added tax (VAT)—a consumption tax—that would generate income from the people and businesses that benefit from society the most.

Here's the challenge: We need to extract more of the value from automation in order to pay for public goods and support displaced workers. But it turns out that "automation" and "robots" are very tricky things to identify or tax. If a CVS replaces a cashier with self-checkout and an iPad, is that considered automation? Or if a bank replaces 200 call center workers with a software program, what do they pay? Assuming appropriate staffing levels is impossible. Plus, you actually don't want to tax automation too heavily, because you don't want to discourage it too much—you need the value it's creating to pay for things.

Another thing to keep in mind—technology companies are excellent at avoiding taxes. Apple, for example, has $230 billion in overseas earnings it's holding abroad to avoid paying taxes. Microsoft has $124 billion and Google has $60 billion. Our current system of taxation will have a hard time harvesting the gains of automation from both the giant tech companies that will be among the biggest winners as well as from the small tech companies, which often aren't hugely profitable. Even taxing human income will become increasingly problematic as more and more work gets done by machines and software—hence Gates's suggestion that we should start taxing robots.

The best way to ensure public gains from the automation wave would be a VAT so that people and companies just pay the tax when they buy things or employ services. For businesses, it gets baked into the cost of production at every level. It makes it much harder for large companies, which are experts at reducing their taxes, to benefit from the American infrastructure and citizenry without paying into it. The biggest companies, like Amazon, would pay the most into the system because a VAT gets paid based on volume, not profits. It also would make it so that we'd all root for progress—the mechanic in Appalachia would feel like he's getting a stake every time someone gets rich.

Out of 193 countries, 160 already have a VAT or goods and services tax, including all developed countries except the United States. The average VAT in Europe is 20 percent. It is well developed and its efficacy has been established. If we adopted a VAT at half the average European level, we could pay for a universal basic income for all American adults.

A VAT would result in slightly higher prices. But technological advancement would continue to drive down the cost of most things. And with the backdrop of a universal basic income of $12,000, the only way a VAT of 10 percent makes you worse off is if you consume more than $120,000 in goods and services per year, which means you're doing fine and are likely at the top of the income distribution. Businesses will benefit immensely from the fact that their customers will have more money to spend each month—most Americans will spend the vast majority of their money locally.

The hedge fund billionaire who spends $10 million a year on private jets and fancy cars will pay $1 million into the system and receive $12,000. The single mom will pay about $2,500 and receive $12,000, and will also have the peace of mind that her child will start receiving $1,000 a month when he or she graduates from high school.

For people who consider this farcical, consider the bailouts that took place during the financial crisis. You may not recall that the U.S. government printed over $4 trillion in new money for its quantitative easing program following the 2008 financial collapse. This money went to the balance sheets of the banks and depressed interest rates. It punished savers and retirees. There was little to no inflation.

We did this nominally so that the banks would lend money to businesses, who would then create jobs and shore up the economy. In practice, most of the money went to the balance sheets of the banks and to inflate asset bubbles all over the country, primarily in assets like real estate in Manhattan and Silicon Valley and the stock prices of private companies like Uber and Airbnb. Many human beings did get rich from the money printing bonanza, but they were people among the best situated, not the least. We did this because we believed in institutions far more than we believe in our people.

With the Freedom Dividend, money would be put in the hands of our citizens in a time of unprecedented economic dislocation. It would grow the consumer economy. It's a stimulus of people. The vast majority of the money would go directly into the economy each month, into paying bills, feeding children, visiting loved ones, youth sports, eating at the local restaurant, piano lessons, extra tutoring help, car repairs, small businesses, housing improvements, prenatal vitamins, elder care, and so on. Most Americans are so cash-strapped that most of the money would be spent locally and quickly.

The government needs to adopt as its primary mission managing the economic transition that automation will bring. We are way behind the curve and need to catch up.

I'm relatively hopeful that the United States will wind up passing a UBI policy like the Freedom Dividend in the coming years. It's simple, it's fair, it's equitable, it's easy to understand, it benefits at least 80 percent of the population, and it will be necessary to maintain the fabric of society during the automation wave. It will become increasingly popular and commonsense. It would simply take an act of Congress, and the checks/transfers will start going out. Labor leader Andy Stern comments: "The government is not great at many things. But it is excellent at sending large numbers of checks to large numbers of people." Even in its current debilitated state, the government could easily start collecting a VAT and sending out the Freedom Dividend to end poverty as we know it and prepare society for the future.

To paraphrase Winston Churchill, "Americans will always do the right thing. After they've tried everything else." The question in my mind is what happens between now and then, and how bad things will get.

Believe it or not, the Freedom Dividend is the easy part of the transition. Money is easy. People are hard. For all of the immense good a UBI will do, it is just the first step. The ongoing challenge will be to preserve a mindset of growth, responsibility, community, humanity, family, and optimism in an era when so many bastions of the past are going to topple into obsolescence and so many ways of life will be changed irrevocably.

I never played Magic: The Gathering, but its creator, Richard Garfield, wrote about UBI in a way that I really liked: "UBI...is not shaming—everyone participates. It does not try to control the economy from the top—people can spend their money on what they want and therefore steer the economy as it has always been best steered, by the consumer. It could free up the job market in ways that are hard to appreciate...I am entranced by UBI, not just as a needed fix but as an institute that unleashes people's potential...I find myself convinced that UBI is natural, and would lead to a more productive and happier world—and it would allow us to fully harness people's creativity and the technology they create."

We're trying relative deprivation and it's not working. Half-measures are wasting time. Scarcity will not save us. Abundance will.

Before I get carried away with my argument for UBI, let's look back at the history of the concept—and how versions of it are already a reality.

SEVENTEEN

UNIVERSAL BASIC INCOME IN THE REAL WORLD

I
t's hard to fathom now, but the idea of a guaranteed annual income was mainstream political wisdom in the United States in the late 1960s and early 1970s. Medicare and Medicaid had just been passed in 1965, and the country had an appetite for solutions for social problems. In May 1968, over 1,000 university economists signed a letter supporting a guaranteed annual income. In 1969, President Nixon proposed the Family Assistance Plan, which would provide cash benefits of about $10,000 per family and serve as a guaranteed annual income with some eligibility requirements; this bill was supported by 79 percent of respondents polled at the time. The Family Assistance Plan passed the House of Representatives by a wide margin—243 to 155—but then stalled in the Senate due to, of all things, Democrats who wanted an even more robust plan. A Democratic congressman, William Ryan from New York, instead proposed an income floor equivalent to $33,000 today, and the original bill would be argued and reproposed for years thereafter.

The U.S. government funded a number of studies between 1968 and 1975 to gain insight into how guaranteed income would impact

individual families. The primary agenda was to see whether people would keep working if they were getting money from the government with no strings attached. The New Jersey Graduated Work
Incentive Experiment gave cash payments to more than 1,300 families between 1968 and 1971 to get above the poverty line. Researchers found minimal impact on work—men worked one hour less per
week, while women reduced their work weeks by five hours. Mothers spent more time with their children, whose performance at
school improved. High school graduation rates rose substantially
over the period, by as much as 30 percent.

Similar studies were rolled out in North Carolina, Iowa, Indiana, Colorado, and Washington. Most of these studies showed
results similar to the initial New Jersey population. However, the
most rigorous and generous study in Denver and Seattle found work
hour decreases of about 9 percent for men, 20 percent for wives,
and 14 percent for single mothers. The Denver study also showed
an increase in marriage dissolution, which surprised a lot of people and helped arm opponents of the legislation, who defeated it for
good in 1978. In 1988, scholars at the University of Wisconsin went
through the data and found that the effect on marriage was dramatically overstated based on an erroneous model. Other scholars later
questioned the work decrease as based on self-reported hours. But
by that time, the debate had passed.

The U.S. studies involved individual families and never tried to
measure communal impact. Canada tried it all in one small town.
In February 1974, Canada spent the equivalent of $56 million to get
everyone in the town of Dauphin, a 13,000-person town northwest
of Winnipeg, above the poverty line. One thousand families got a
check each month of different amounts with no restrictions. They
called it "Mincome," short for minimum income. It lasted for four

years, before a conservative government won control of the government and discontinued payments.

Many years later, in 2005, Evelyn Forget, an economist at the University of Manitoba, tracked down and analyzed the results. "Politically, there was a concern that if you began a guaranteed annual income, people would stop working and start having large families," recalls Forget. Instead, she found minimal effect on work. The only groups who worked substantially less were new mothers and teenagers, with the latter spending more time in school. Birth rates for women under 25 dropped. High school graduation rates went up. Perhaps most dramatically, Forget found that hospital visits went down 8.5 percent, with reductions in workplace injuries and emergency room visits. Domestic violence went down as did mental illness-related appointments and treatments. Basically, life got significantly better in a town without poverty.

It may be hard to believe, but one state in the United States has had something resembling a UBI for decades. In Alaska in 1976, the state started receiving billions in oil revenue from state-owned land. Governor Jay Hammond, a Republican, had an innovative plan—he pushed to place the revenue in a fund that would then pay out part of its earnings to state residents each year. He insisted that this fund had "a conservative political purpose" by putting a brake on government spending and distributing more of the money directly to people.

The Alaska Permanent Fund accrued earnings and started paying dividends in 1982. Each Alaskan now receives a petroleum dividend of between $1,000 and $2,000 per person per year; a family of four received more than $8,000 in 2015. The dividend reduces poverty by one-quarter and is one reason that Alaska has the second lowest income inequality in the country. Studies have shown that the dividend has increased average infant birthweight and helped keep rural Alaskans solvent. It has also created at least 7,000 jobs due to the increased economic activity each year. The program, now in its 36th year despite numerous changes in government, is overwhelmingly popular. Sixty-four percent of respondents even said that they would accept higher taxes if necessary to fund the dividend.

In 1995, a group of researchers began tracking the personalities of 1,420 low-income children in North Carolina. Then, something unexpected happened—25 percent of their families started receiving $4,000 per person. They were Cherokee Indians, and a casino had just been built nearby, with earnings flowing to tribal members. This development turned into a research treasure trove. "It would be almost impossible to replicate this kind of longitudinal study," said Randall Akee, an economics professor at UCLA. Akee found that the impact of the extra cash actually impacted the children's personalities over the years. Behavioral and emotional disorders went down. Two personality traits became more pronounced— conscientiousness and agreeableness. Both correlate strongly with holding a job and maintaining a steady relationship. These changes were most significant among children who started out the most deficient.

Akee surmised that the impact was due in part to less stressful environments. Relationships between spouses improved. Alcohol consumption went down. "We know that the thing poor couples fight about the most is money," said Akee. Removing that source of conflict resulted in "a more harmonious home environment."

"There is a lot of literature that shows in order to change outcomes among children you are best off treating the parents first," said Emilia Simeonova, an economics professor from Johns Hopkins who studied the same families. "[The money produced] clear changes in the parents." She concluded, "Now we have a sense of what even just a little money can do to change these things, to change their lives."

In 2008, Michael Faye and Paul Niehaus were graduate students at Harvard studying international development and doing fieldwork overseas. They visited Kenya, and everywhere they looked they saw misspent aid dollars in the forms of abandoned water pumps, unused clothing, and the like. They became convinced that more than food, bed nets, schoolbooks, sports equipment, cows, water jugs, or anything else, the people wanted cash. That summer, Michael and Paul gave a few thousand dollars of their own money to poor villagers and started to measure results. They found that among cash recipients, domestic violence rates dropped, mental health improved, and people started eating better.

They stuck with the idea and expanded it. In 2012, a friend introduced them to Google.org, which contributed $2.4 million to further their efforts. The more the pair measured, the more dramatically positive the results were. People started businesses. Children weighed more. Girls went to school more often. Women had more independence. It turns out that giving cash is very effective. Unlike most organizations, they documented all of their results and brought them back to show the world.

Since then, GiveDirectly has raised more than $120 million, in part to enable new ways to distribute money in developing countries. In 2016, they announced a $30 million 12-year basic income trial in a region in western Kenya. "GiveDirectly...has sent shockwaves through the charity sector," posited one article in the Guardian. "[Organizations] that ask for money on behalf of the poor should be able to prove they can do more good with it than the poor themselves... [for most NGOs] this is a compelling challenge." Basically, the global poor would be better served if most aid organizations got out of the way and handed them the money.

Today, economic inequality, frayed job markets, and the early signs of automation have produced a massive surge of enthusiasm for UBI worldwide. Finland started a two-year trial in 2017 in which 2,000 unemployed people between 25 and 28 receive a basic income of about $660 a month with no strings attached. India is actively considering implementing a modest basic income nationally in the next year after studies showed it would be more efficient than their existing programs. Canada is giving 4,000 participants in Ontario grants of up to $12,570 for individuals and $18,900 for couples from 2017 through 2020 and measuring results. The Netherlands and Scotland are each running a small trial.

Iran implemented a full-blown equivalent of UBI in 2011 of approximately $16,000 per year in response to heavy cuts to oil and gas subsidies. Economists measured labor rates and found no reduction in hours worked—if anything they found people in the service industry expanded their businesses. This is hugely indicative because of the enormous sample size—Iran has 80 million people, equivalent to the combined total of New York, California, and Florida—over an extended period of time.

Most recently, a small trial launched in the United States. Starting in early 2017 in Oakland, California, Sam Altman, the head of the technology firm Y Combinator, is giving 100 households in Oakland approximately $1,000 to $2,000 per month for about a year to measure the impacts on recipients. The goal is to roll out a larger five-year trial afterward. Sam and his friends are giving away $2 million and hiring researchers just to see what will happen. I love the fact that Sam is putting up the resources to study this problem. He's demonstrating the kind of leadership and vision that, in an ideal world, our government would be capable of.

Enthusiasm is building for a UBI based on both its intellectual and moral appeal and its real-world success thus far. The main counterarguments generally go something like this:

"We can't afford it."

Money has to come from somewhere. We're used to the government spending billions wastefully to no great effect. Trying to raise taxes is a tough assignment in any climate.

What's fascinating is that a UBI doesn't actually grow the government. It's almost cost-free to administer. It doesn't build a new bureaucracy. It is less an expenditure and more a transfer to citizens so they can use it to improve their lives, pay each other, patronize local businesses, and support the consumer economy. Instead of hiring a new army of government employees, every dollar will be put into the hands of an American citizen and then largely spent within the American economy.

By definition, none of the money would be wasted because it goes to citizens. It's analogous to a company giving dividends or moneys to its shareholders. No one regards that as a waste of money, because the shareholders theoretically are the owners of the company.

Are we not, as the citizens of the United States, the owners of this country?

As a country, we are easily wealthy enough to manage even a full UBI. Our economy has grown by more than $4 trillion in the past 10 years alone. The U.S. dollar remains the global reserve currency. We are the most technologically advanced society in human history, and increased automation will allow our economy to continue to grow well past its current level.

Not only that, but we will get a lot of the money back through new businesses and economic activity, better educational outcomes, improved health and preventative care, better mental health, reduced crime and incarceration, reduced services for homelessness, and many other social benefits.

You know what's really expensive? Dysfunction. Revolution.

Keeping people and families functional will largely pay for itself.

"It will destroy people's incentives to work."

All of the available data shows that work hours stay stable or at most decrease modestly with a basic income. To the extent that people spend less time working, they tend to be young mothers and teenagers, whom we might not mind working a little less if they're taking care of their kids or going to school.

There are two completely oppositional ideas that many people seem to hold simultaneously:

First, work is vital and the core of the human experience.

Second, no one will want to work if they don't have to.

These two ideas are at complete odds with each other. Either work is a core of the human experience and we'll do it even if we don't necessarily have to, or work is something we have no interest in doing and we do it only to survive.

Setting a Freedom Dividend of $12,000 a year would enable one to barely scrape by. Anyone who wants to accomplish anything, buy something nice, or build a better life for their children will still have to work.

Twelve thousand dollars a year is the equivalent of having $300,000 in savings and then living off the passive income at 4 percent a year. Have you ever heard of someone who gathered $300,000 and then just stopped working? I haven't. I have seen many people who saved some money and then wanted to save more.

Andy Stern jokes that most of the upper-middle-class children he knows have something called "parental basic income": their lives are partially subsidized by their parents. Cell phone bills, rent guarantees, family trips and vacations, and so on all come out of the Bank of Mom and Dad. This is the norm in most of the wealthy families I've seen. And most of their kids turn out fine in terms of work ethic.

Replacing work is going to be a generational challenge. It will require the great minds and hearts of this era. But getting money to live is an independent question. Getting money to live independent of work will enable us to figure out what work we actually want to do, even if that work is not necessarily in an office or store. This is a much deeper and more fundamental question than how one survives month to month.

"Wouldn't that cause rampant inflation?"

Inflation has been low for years, in part because technology and globalization have been reducing the costs of many things. Even the printing of $4 trillion in monetary easing after the financial crisis didn't cause meaningful inflation. If the universal basic income were paid for through a VAT as proposed above, we wouldn't be increasing the money supply, so inflation wouldn't be expected based on the amount of money floating around.

A universal basic income at the level of the Freedom Dividend would likely result in some inflation as vendors take advantage of the new buying power of the public to raise some prices, but costs would continue to decline for many things because technology would continue to lower the underlying cost of their production. If you reflect on your own costs, most things that are subject to economic competition, globalization, and technology have gotten either much cheaper or much better or both. I can't believe how cheap clothing has become—$8 T-shirts and $15 pants at H&M make me feel guilty for buying them. Cars cost the same in nominal terms as when I was growing up even though they feel like spaceships compared to my old cruddy Honda. Music, movies, and most forms of entertainment are cheaper than ever, particularly adjusted for inflation.

Of the major expenses that have shown inflation, the most conspicuous are health care costs and education costs, both of which have exploded in recent years. Health care and education are not truly subject to market forces and have thus far been resistant to both automation and increased efficiency. They are also some of the main reasons Americans have become stressed—our wages have been flat, but the cost of the staples we rely upon to provide a good life for our children have been spiraling out of control. Not only would a UBI not cause inflation, but putting purchasing power in the hands of Americans would help address the worst circumstances of where prices have gone up.

"People will spend the money on stupid things, like drugs and alcohol."

The data doesn't show this. In every basic income study, there has been no increase in drug and alcohol use. If anything, an improved sense of the future motivates people to figure out a plan for how to improve their lot. For example, many people in Alaska save a significant chunk of their oil dividend each year.

There are true addicts, and some people are self-destructive. But it's not like a lack of money is presently keeping people from using opioids and alcohol—they find a way to get both money and drugs right now, sometimes illicitly. A UBI would curb antisocial behaviors and give at least some an increased ability to seek treatment.

Here's the thing—poor people tend to be much more careful

with their money than rich people. I've never been truly poor. But I remember being young and feeling broke, bussing tables at a Chinese restaurant for $5.20 an hour plus tips as a teenager. I remember how much $50 in cash meant to me then, how careful I'd be with the money.

The idea that poor people will be irresponsible with their money and squander it seems to be a product of deep-seated biases rather than emblematic of the truth. There's a tendency for rich people to dismiss poor people as weak-willed children with no cost discipline. The evidence runs in the other direction. As the Dutch philosopher Rutger Bregman and others put it, "Poverty is not a lack of character. It's a lack of cash."

Scarcity research indicates that the best way to improve decision making is to free up people's bandwidth. People won't ever make perfect choices. But knowing that their basic needs are accounted for will lead to better choices for millions of people each day.

EIGHTEEN

TIME AS THE NEW MONEY

To be able to fill leisure intelligently is the last product of civilization...

—BERTRAND RUSSELL

A man... with no means of filling up time, is as miserable out of work as a dog on the chain.

—GEORGE ORWELL

Even with the Freedom Dividend attending to people's ability to feed themselves, the thing that still freaks everyone out about replacing jobs is this: What will people do all day? Work has been proven to be a vital part of a healthy life and society. Long-term unemployment is one of the most destructive things that can happen to a person. Getting a bit of money doesn't necessarily change that.

Should the government guarantee work or create jobs? Many idealistic people I know advocate for universal service opportunities. The problem is that it's very expensive to organize, train, and employ people. Teach for America spends approximately $51,000 per corps member on noncompensation costs over two years: recruitment, selection, training, programming, support, and so on. The Peace Corps's annual budget of $410 million is $56,000 per volunteer. Venture for America, the organization I started, spends about $30,000 per young entrepreneur on recruitment, training, and the like over two years. The U.S. military spends approximately $170,000 per soldier per year on salary, maintenance, housing, infrastructure, and the like.

Setting up a structure for people is wildly expensive. Guaranteeing work would cost tens of thousands of additional dollars for recruitment, training, and infrastructure before anyone even gets paid. You would also wind up creating very large organizations and bureaucracies. The Peace Corps has over 1,000 full-time employees supporting 7,200 volunteers, for example.

Many of the populations people are most eager to see employed and kept from idleness are among the least competent and able to be employed by the private sector. The natural tendency is to spend a lot of money on people doing things that aren't actually that valuable. Since we're talking about millions of people on the lower end of the education and skill range, this is likely where most efforts would lead if one tried to replace any significant proportion of private employment with government service jobs.

I believe in national service and the power of investing in people—the right people with the right mission can move mountains. But an economy where most people work for the government has been tried and failed in many environments—most notably Communist China before 1978 and the Soviet Union before it broke apart. Right now, the United States is relatively low among developed countries in terms of proportion of citizens who work for the government—around 15 percent as compared to Canada's 22.4 percent or the United Kingdom's 23.5 percent. Still, government-financed positions need to be created very carefully and judiciously and preferably focused on high-impact roles. They certainly will not be the cure for a nation without enough jobs to go around.

During the Great Depression in the 1930s, the U.S. government hired 40,000 recreation officers and artists at a cost of $3.3 billion—about $47 billion today—to make things more enjoyable and keep people engaged. That would be the equivalent of hiring about 100,000 people to go to towns around the country today based on how much our population has grown since then. This strikes me as something of an upper limit of what the government could do specifically for the purpose of citizen engagement. Areas of instruction during the Depression included single-sex sports and games, arts and crafts, music, dramatics, the reading of books, discussion groups, hiking parties, woodwork, metalwork, furniture making, glee clubs and orchestras, and lectures on hygiene, diet, and even social etiquette.

Reading that list probably makes one yearn for a simpler time. A better approach today would be to try to supercharge the existing interests and opportunities of businesses, people, and local organizations. A UBI would go a long way in this direction. For example, let's imagine a local nonprofit providing after-school recreation for underprivileged kids. It has five employees making $30,000 a year right now. With a UBI, they might be able to hire seven employees at $21,000 a year instead, a 40 percent increase in staffing, because people with a level of financial security might take the job for less. The same would go for a school's ability to utilize volunteers to provide teacher support, a church's ability to enlist mentors, and so on. Dutch professor Robert J. van der Veen and economist Philippe van Parijs observed that a UBI will bring down the average wage rate for attractive, intrinsically rewarding work. The fun things that people want to do that are socially and personally rewarding will pay less, but many more people will want to do them anyway. Jobs and purpose will in part be provided by more people teaching children, coaching others, caring for loved ones, and the like.

There will also be a dramatic expansion of painting, making music, shooting videos, playing sports, writing, and all of the creative pursuits many Americans would love to try, but can't seem to find the time for today. Many people have some artistic passion that they would pursue if they didn't need to worry about feeding themselves next month. A UBI would be perhaps the greatest catalyst to human creativity we have ever seen.

Perhaps most crucially, endless new businesses would form. If you are in a town of 5,000 people in Missouri and everyone is struggling to get by, starting, say, a bakery may not be that attractive. But with a UBI, there will be an additional $60 million being spent in that town next year. You personally will have an income to fall back on if the bakery doesn't work out. Now, the bakery may strike you as a great idea. Getting your friends and family excited about it would be a lot easier, too. This would play out over and over again throughout the economy, resulting in millions of new jobs— 4.7 million according to the Roosevelt Institute's analysis. A UBI would address a significant proportion of the lack of work through increased humanity, caring, creativity, and enterprise.

That said, we are going to have to do much more.

Picture the average truck driver who gets sent home in 2026. Let's call him Ted. He's 49, has health problems, dropped out of college after a year, had a series of construction jobs, and then was a trucker for 12 years before automation eliminated his job. He lives in a modest mobile home in Oklahoma. He has a child but is no longer with the mother, who lives a couple of towns away, and sees his son once or twice per month. He has some hobbies and interests that involve the outdoors. He's used to being on the road four days a week and talking to his fellow truckers on the radio. He likes to drink. He was brought up Christian but hasn't been to church in years. There aren't many job opportunities for Ted nearby, and he doesn't want to move. Thanks to his savings, the Freedom Dividend, and the settlement he received from the Trucker Transition Act of 2022, he can get by financially if he's frugal. Left to his own devices, Ted will likely spend a lot of time watching TV, drinking, and having his health deteriorate. The goal is for Ted to acquire a set of interests and relationships that replace the structure that work used to provide.

Now, let's imagine Ted is in his home in Oklahoma, settling into his recliner watching videos on his TV—he doesn't like the new VR goggles some of the kids use. He gets a message on his phone. It says, "One of your neighbors, Annie, could use some help changing her propane tank. Would you like to help her?" It includes a profile picture of Annie, who is a 60-year-old woman who lives nearby. Ted shrugs and responds "Yes" and puts in a time for later that day. At one p.m., Ted drives over to Annie's house and swaps out her depleted propane tank for a new one from Lowe's. His back hurts a little as he moves the tank, but it makes him feel useful. Annie profusely thanks him and they make some small talk. Annie worked as a secretary at a nearby hospital—her wrists are fragile. It turns out her children went to the same high school as Ted.

Ted returns to his house. Later, he gets a message saying, "Thanks for helping Annie! You have earned 100 Social Credits. You now have 1,600 Social Credits banked. You have earned 14,800 Social Credits over your lifetime." He also gets a message from Annie saying, "Thank you for the help. You're a lifesaver." He replies, "No problem. Happy to help." He takes on an assignment like this once or twice a day—generally moving something around or picking someone up. He's hoping to meet someone with a dog that he can borrow for the next time his son visits. His boy likes dogs. He could post a request on the Tulsa Digital Social Credit Exchange but would prefer not to—he doesn't really like asking for help. He prefers to help others and earn credits. He has his eye on a couple of deals for Thunder tickets or to buy a tent at Cabela's. He used a bunch of Social Credits to pay for a fishing trip earlier in the year. His local poker game just started using Social Credits instead of dollars, too—a couple of the guys had just started volunteering at the local youth center so they were swimming in credits.

Maybe you smirked in disbelief at my concept of Social Credits, but this scenario is based on a system currently in use in about 200 communities around the United States called time banking. Time banking is a system through which people trade time and build credits within communities by performing various helpful tasks— transporting an item, walking a dog, cleaning up a yard, cooking a meal, providing a ride to the doctor, and so on. The idea was championed in the mid-1990s in the United States by Edgar Cahn, a law professor and antipoverty activist as a way to strengthen communities.

For example, in Brattleboro, Vermont, today, 315 members of the local time bank have exchanged 64,000 hours of mutual work over the past eight years. The Brattleboro time bank was started by two graduate students with 30 members in 2009 and has grown each year. Amanda Witman, a 40-year-old single mother, wrote about her experience: "Three years ago, I was in a tough spot. My husband and I had separated, and I was in a large house that needed lots of repairs. I was home-schooling my kids and working part-time from home doing website customer service. I had a huge financial challenge. My friends knew I was overwhelmed, and more than one said I should join the Brattleboro Time Trade. At first I thought, Who has time to trade? Then I learned that you can run a deficit—get help immediately and pay back the time when you're able. So I posted requests on the website to fix up my house. I'd hoped one or two members would respond, but a bunch of people ended up offering assistance. Randy Bright fixed holes in the wall and replaced my water-pressure tank. Other people hauled a bunch of stuff to the dump, replaced ancient wiring and helped me plant a vegetable garden. Before joining the group, I never would have been comfortable requesting all that help. But you don't feel like you're pestering anyone, because people happily volunteer for the jobs and they always show up with a smile. And even though I'm so tight on time, I've always been able to find jobs that fit my schedule, like baby-sitting or making someone a meal. In fact, my whole family pitches in. I'll tell my kids—Everest, 15, Alden, 14, Ellery, 11, and Avery, 9—that we're stacking wood for our neighbor in order to get our light fixture fixed. It makes them feel useful. In fact, we've come to realize the value of some of our hobbies, like making music. Once, we earned four time-trade hours by playing together as a family at a local garden party: two fiddles, a guitar and a pennywhistle!"

Said Randy Bright, the 49-year-old handyman on the other end of the exchange, "When I joined, it was clear that handy people were in high demand. And, since I am divorced, I thought, Great, I'll meet single women! That hasn't panned out yet, but I have expanded my circle of friends. I've used some of my time-trade hours for home-cooked meals. It has aided me financially, too: I've developed a referral network that has helped get my own energy-efficiency business off the ground. My private business keeps me busy, but I still do time trades, and I often donate the hours I earn. The trades give me something intangible that just makes me feel good. I especially like showing my daughter, Nora (who's 14 and often comes along to help out) that not every exchange is about money."

Edgar Cahn, the founder of Time Banking, was the former speechwriter for Robert F. Kennedy, who was looking for new ways to fight poverty at a time when "money for social programs [had] dried up." He wrote, "Americans face at least three interlocking sets of problems: growing inequality in access by those at the bottom to the most basic goods and services; increasing social problems stemming from the need to rebuild family, neighborhood and community; and a growing disillusion with public programs designed to address these problems." He proposed that time banking could "[rebuild] the infrastructure of trust and caring that can strengthen families and communities."

Despite the success of time banks in communities like Brattleboro, they have not caught hold that widely around the United States in part because they require a certain level of administration and resources to operate.

Now imagine a supercharged version of time banking backed by the U.S. government where in addition to providing social value, there's real monetary value underlying it. This new currency— Digital Social Credits (DSCs or Social Credits)—would reward people for doing things that serve the community. The government would seed each market with an initial investment, but administrators would be local. DSCs would be targeted toward regions and communities that demonstrate a need for increased cohesion. You would earn a number of Social Credits anytime you do something for a neighbor—babysit a child, staff a garage sale, fix an appliance, play music at a party, and so on. You would also get Social Credits anytime you volunteer at the local shelter, participate in a town fair, coach the Little League, take a new course, paint a mural, play in a local band, mentor a young person, and so on. Existing organizations could award and earn Social Credits based on how many people they assist.

The government could put up significant levels of DSCs as prizes and incentives for major initiatives. For example, "100 million DSCs to reduce obesity levels in Mississippi" or "1 billion DSCs to improve high school graduation rates in Illinois" and then let people take various actions to collect it. Companies could help meet goals and create and sponsor campaigns around various causes. Nonprofits and NGOs would generate DSCs based on how much good they do and then distribute it back to volunteers and employees. New organizations and initiatives could be crowdfunded by DSCs instead of money, as people "vote" by sending points in. Events and media that draw crowds would receive DSCs based on the number of people that attend or upvote it; the currency would become a new way to support journalism, creativity, and local events.

Some might ask, "Why create a new digital currency instead of just using dollars?" First, people will respond to points in a different way than they would if they were paid very low monetary amounts. If you tell me I'm getting $2 to do something, I may ignore it. But if it's 200 points, I'll find it strangely compelling. People right now spend countless hours becoming Yelp Elite, King Wazers, Mayors on Foursquare, Google Local Guides, and other online equivalents based upon points and social rewards.

Second, everyone will feel much more open and comfortable sharing balances if it's a new social currency. You want people to advertise and reinforce their behavior. Behavior is much more likely to be reinforced if it's social and recognized. That's one reason why people are more likely to lose weight or achieve fitness goals when they are part of a group effort.

Third, by creating a new currency, the government could essentially induce billions of dollars of positive social activity without having to spend nearly that amount.

As individuals rack up DSCs, they would have both a permanent balance they've earned over their lifetime and a current balance. They could cash in the points for experiences, purchases with participating vendors, or support for causes, and transfer points to others for special occasions. As their permanent balance gets higher, they might qualify for various perks like throwing a pitch at a local ballgame, an audience with their local congressperson, or meeting their state's most civic-minded athlete or celebrity. Maybe the community's leading DSC earner would even get a special trip to the White House. People and companies could use cash to buy DSCs—this would help fund the system—but these DSCs would appear as a different color and be clearly purchased, not earned.

We could create an entire new parallel economy around social good.

The most socially detached would be the most likely to ignore all of this. But many people love rewards and feeling valued. I get obsessed with completing the 10-punch card for a free sandwich at my local deli. We could spur unprecedented levels of social activity without spending that much. Heck, DSCs could become cooler than dollars, because you could advertise how much you have and it's socially acceptable. If you wanted to spur adoption, you could target various rewards and campaigns toward particular demographics and areas; things done for people with lower levels of DSCs could count for extra.

The DSC system would be an example of harnessing market dynamics to spur social good. The federal government would help set up and fund the platform but it would be up to local governments, nonprofits, individuals, and companies to figure out the best ways to achieve various goals. The overall goal would be to improve social cohesion and maintain high levels of engagement for people in a post-work economy.

The Freedom Dividend would elevate society beyond a need for subsistence and scarcity. The Digital Social Credit would tie together communities and give people a way to both generate value and feel valued regardless of how the market regards their time.

NINETEEN

HUMAN CAPITALISM

Imagine an AI life coach with the voice of Oprah or Tom Hanks trying to help parents stay together or raise kids. Or a new Legion of Builders and Demolishers that installs millions of solar panels across the country, upgrades our infrastructure, and removes derelict buildings while also employing tens of thousands of workers. Or a digital personalized education subscription that is constantly giving you new material and grouping you with a few other people who are studying the same thing. Or a wearable device that monitors your vital signs and sends data to your doctor while recommending occasional behavior changes. Or voting securely in your local elections via your smartphone without any worry of fraud.

Each of these scenarios is possible right now with current technology. But the resources and market incentives for them do not exist. There is limited or no market reward at present for keeping families together, upgrading infrastructure, lifelong education, preventative care, or improving democracy. While our smartphones get smarter each season, propelled by tens of billions of dollars, our voting machines, bridges, and schools languish in the 1960s.

This is what we must change.

At present, the market systematically tends to undervalue many things, activities, and people, many of which are core to the human experience. Consider:

- Parenting or caring for loved ones
- Teaching or nurturing children
- Arts and creativity
- Serving the poor
- Working in struggling regions or environments
- The environment
- Reading
- Preventative care
- Character
- Infrastructure and public transportation
- Journalism
- Women
- People of color/underrepresented minorities

And now, increasingly,

- Unskilled labor and normal people
- Meaningful community connections
- Small independent businesses
- Effective government

There were periods when the market supported some of these things more than it does today. Today, it needs to be steered to do so. The United States has reached a point where its current form of capitalism is faltering in producing an increasing standard of living for the majority of its citizens. It's time for an upgrade.

THE NEXT STAGE OF CAPITALISM

Adam Smith, the Scottish economist who wrote *The Wealth of Nations* in 1776, is often regarded as the father of modern capitalism. His ideas of an invisible hand that guides the market, division of labor, and that self-interest and competition lead to wealth creation have been so deeply internalized that today we take most of them for granted. Our general thinking today is to contrast capitalism with socialism, which arose in the 1800s and advocated social ownership or democratic control of industries. Karl Marx published *Das Kapital* in 1867 and argued that capitalism contained internal tensions that would oppress the working class, who would eventually rise up and take control. Our perception is that capitalism— embodied by the West and the United States—won the war of ideas by generating immense growth and wealth and elevating the standard of living of billions of people. Socialism—represented by the Soviet Union, which collapsed in 1991, and China, which moderated its approach in the 1980s—didn't work in practice and was thoroughly discredited.

This simplistic assessment misses a couple important points. First, there is no such thing as a pure capitalist system. There have been many different forms of Western capitalist economies going back centuries, ever since money was invented around 7,000 years ago. The market feudalism of the Middle Ages evolved into the expansionist mercantilism of European trading companies, which evolved into the industrial capitalism of 20th-century America, and into the welfare capitalism of the 1960s when the United States and many other advanced countries established safety net programs like Medicaid. Our current form of institutional capitalism and corporatism is just the latest of many different versions.

Similarly, many forms of capitalism are in service around the world right now. Singapore is the fourth-richest country in the world in terms of per capita GDP. It has had an unemployment rate of 2.2 percent or lower since 2009 and is regarded as one of the most free, open, pro-business economies in the world. Yet the government in Singapore regularly shapes investment policy, and government-linked firms dominate telecommunications, finance, and media in ways that would be unthinkable in the United States. Singapore's system of capitalism is very different than Norway's and Japan's and Canada's and ours. Many countries' form of capitalism is steered not by an unseen hand, but by clear government policy.

Now imagine a new type of capitalist economy that is geared toward maximizing human well-being and fulfillment. These goals and GDP would sometimes go hand-in-hand. But there would be times when they wouldn't be aligned. For example, an airline removing passengers who had already boarded a plane to maximize its profitability would be good for capital but bad for people. So would a drug company charging extortionate rates for a life-saving drug. Most Americans, I think, would agree that the airline should simply accept the lost revenue and the drug company should accept a moderate profit margin. What if this idea was repeated over and over again throughout the economy?

Call it Human-Centered Capitalism, or Human Capitalism for short.

Human Capitalism would have a few core tenets:

1. Humanity is more important than money.
2. The unit of an economy is each person, not each dollar.
3. Markets exist to serve our common goals and values.

There's a saying in business that "what gets measured gets managed for." We need to start measuring different things.

The concept of GDP and economic progress didn't even exist until the Great Depression. It was invented so that the government could figure out how bad the economy was getting and how to make it better. The economist Simon Kuznets, upon introducing the concept of GDP to Congress in 1934, remarked that "economic welfare cannot be adequately measured unless the personal distribution of income is known. And no income measurement undertakes to estimate the reverse side of income, that is, the intensity and unpleasantness of effort going into the earning of income. The welfare of a nation can, therefore, scarcely be inferred from a measurement of national income as defined above." It's almost like he saw income inequality and bad jobs coming.

Our economic system must shift to focus on bettering the lot of the average person. Capitalism has to be made to serve human ends and goals, rather than have our humanity subverted to serve the marketplace. We shape the system. We own it, not the other way around.

In addition to GDP and job statistics, the government should adopt measurements such as:

- Median income and standard of living
- Levels of engagement with work and labor participation rate
- Health-adjusted life expectancy
- Childhood success rates
- Infant mortality
- Surveys of national well-being
- Average physical fitness and mental health
- Quality of infrastructure
- Proportion of elderly in quality care
- Human capital development and access to education
- Marriage rates and success

- Deaths of despair/despair index/substance abuse
- National optimism/mindset of abundance
- Community integrity and social capital
- Environmental quality
- Global temperature variance and sea levels
- Reacclimation of incarcerated individuals and rates of criminality
- Artistic and cultural vibrancy
- Design and aesthetics
- Information integrity/journalism
- Dynamism and mobility
- Social and economic equity
- Public safety
- Civic engagement
- Cybersecurity
- Economic competitiveness and growth
- Responsiveness and evolution of government
- Efficient use of resources

It would be straightforward to establish measurements for each of these and have them updated periodically, similar to what Steve Ballmer set up at USAFacts.org—a treasure trove of social metrics that pulls from many public and private sources. Everyone could then see how we're doing and be galvanized around improvement.

This could be tied in to the Digital Social Credit system, where people who help move society in a particular direction are rewarded. For example, a journalist who uncovered a particular source of waste, an artist who beautified a city, or a hacker who strengthened our power grid could be rewarded with Social Credits. So could someone who helped another person recover from addiction or helped acclimate an ex-convict into the workforce. Even someone who maintained a high level of physical fitness and helped others do so could be rewarded and recognized.

The power of this new marketplace and currency cannot be overstated. Most of the technologists and young people I know would be beyond pumped to work on these problems. They've been chomping at the bit to do so. We can harness the country's ingenuity and energy to improve millions of lives if we just create a way to monetize and measure these goals.

I'm no fan of big government. The larger an organization is, the more cumbersome and ridiculous it often gets. I have sat in Washington, DC, conference rooms and filled out forms and realize the limitations on what even well-intended public officials can do. I am, by nature, an entrepreneur who likes to operate close to the ground on the human level.

I've also spent time with people at the highest levels of government, and it's striking how stuck most of them feel. One congressman said to me, "I'm just trying to get one big thing done here so I can go home." He'd been in Congress for seven years at that point. Another joked that being in DC was like being in Rome, with the marble there to remind you that nothing will change. Government isn't magic. Quite the opposite. The system has become bigger than the people.

That said, I've concluded that there is no other way to make these changes and manage through the loss of jobs than to have the federal government reformat and reorganize the economy, particularly using technology to serve human needs.

I've been around some of the richest individuals, philanthropies, and companies in the world. Even the richest and most ambitious of them either operates at the wrong scale or has multiple stakeholders that make big, long-term commitments difficult to sustain. Most all of them are kind of waiting for government to reinvent itself and get its act together. Even billionaires operate on a scale of $100,000 to $10 million most of the time. We're staring at trillion-dollar problems, and we need commensurate solutions.

Grassroots efforts are admirable and inspiring. But the market to support most of them does not exist, and things are getting worse around them. No level of activism can compensate for the displacement of workers.

What is required is a new, invigorated government willing to build for the long term. We are in a slow-moving crisis that is about to speed up. It requires drastic intervention. Human Capitalism will reshape the way that we measure value and progress, and help us redefine why we do what we do.

TWENTY

THE STRONG STATE AND THE NEW CITIZENSHIP

LEADERS BEYOND MONEY

I was on the warm-up panel once for an event headlined by a duo of ex-presidents, Bill Clinton and George W. Bush. They were speaking to a room of wealthy clients of a financial institution. The event was very benign—the two didn't exactly share state secrets. They told funny stories about their time in office and their take on current events. The two had clearly become very friendly. They each had a Secret Service detail who made the whole thing much more cinematic with their crewcuts and headsets. Afterward, the assembled clients got in line for a photo-op with the two smiling ex-presidents.

There was a time not so long ago when this would have been unthinkable.

When Harry Truman left the office of the presidency in 1953, he was so poor that he moved into his mother-in-law's house in Missouri. All he had to live on was his pension as a former army officer of $112 a month. He refused to trade on his celebrity, turning down lucrative consulting and business arrangements. "I could never lend myself to any transaction, however respectable, that would commercialize on the prestige and dignity of the office of the presidency," he wrote. His only commercial gain from office was when he sold his memoirs to *Life* magazine.

For a long time, former presidents tended to recede from public and commercial life. This practice started changing with Gerald Ford joining the boards of American Express and 20th Century Fox after leaving office in 1977, and it has mushroomed ever since. Bill Clinton has amassed $105 million in speaking fees since leaving office. George W. Bush has collected a relatively modest $15 million. The going rate for one of the former presidents is $150,000 to $200,000 for a speaking engagement plus various expenses.

The irony is that back in 1958, President Eisenhower and Congress felt so bad for Harry Truman that they passed the Former Presidents Act, which authorized a lifetime pension that today pays former presidents $250,000 a year and gives them a budget for staff, health insurance, and the like. The money-making activities of former presidents surged after we started taking care of them.

Is it possible that even a president might go easy on various parties because he or she might be getting paid $200,000 or even $400,000 to speak to them a few years later? One of the reasons why we've lost our way as a society is that the market has overrun our leaders.

And it's not just presidents. Elites in general have gotten too cozy. We all went to the same colleges, have children in the same prep schools, live in the same neighborhoods, attend the same conferences and social functions, and often get paid by the same companies. There's a very powerful set of incentives to get along.

In order for humanity to trump capital, the state must represent the public interest above all. The goal should be to create a leadership class that can welcome the hatred of others with no fear of getting frozen out of opportunities afterward.

We should start at the top. We should give presidents a raise from their current $400,000 to $4 million tax-free per year plus 10 million Social Credits. But there would be one condition—they would not be able to accept speaking fees or any board positions for any personal gain after leaving office. This would keep them free and clear of any need to make powerful people happy. We should do the same for members of the Cabinet and the heads of all regulatory agencies.

It's tough working in DC. Most of the public servants I know are motivated by the right things. You go in hoping to make a difference. But you quickly get jaded by the system. You become quite influential in your own way, yet you interact with people who are making much more money than you at every turn. Many of them are classmates of yours. Your time in government runs out. Then what? Most government employees make about $100,000. Private industry may offer you 4 to 10 times as much. Industry implicitly becomes one of your most appealing options.

I have friends who have experienced versions of this. Government service can easily make you feel like a chump four years later. It's highly irrational for any regulator to come after industry too hard, because industry is waiting with the big paycheck afterward. At least one friend of mine swore up and down to me that he'd never become a lobbyist, only to become a lobbyist several years later. I don't blame him one bit—he'd spent years building up relationships and currency that people wanted to pay him for. And his options outside of DC were uncertain.

Sheila Bair, a former head of the Federal Deposit Insurance Corporation, lived through this conflict herself. She now advocates a lifetime ban on regulators working for the institutions they regulated in return for an increased government salary to $400,000.

"It would change the regulatory mindset," said Bair, and it would remove the "upside down" incentives for regulators to keep companies happy to command high salaries afterward.

For Human Capitalism to take hold, we need leaders who can truly ignore the market. That's the first step.

REAL ACCOUNTABILITY

The second step is to introduce a level of personal accountability for those who adopt practices that advantage capital over human interests. Recall the case of Purdue Pharma, the private company that was fined $635 million in 2007 by the Department of Justice for falsely promoting OxyContin as nonaddictive and tamper-proof. $635 million seems like a lot of money. But the company made $35 billion in revenue since releasing OxyContin in 1995, primarily from its signature product. The family that owns Purdue Pharma, the Sackler family, is now the 16th richest family in the country with a fortune of $14 billion—they have a museum at Harvard and a building at Yale named after them.

If you're going to make $35 billion, paying $635 million—only about 2 percent—seems like a fine price to pay for success. Meanwhile, the rest of us will be dealing with hundreds of thousands of opioid addicts for years to come. They have given us a modern-day plague with no end in sight. Thousands of families, lives, and communities have been ruined and affected, arguably to enrich one family.

A similar dynamic played out during and after the financial crisis—most of the major banks issued and profited from mortgage-backed securities in the tens of billions over multiple years. Then the market discovered these securities were worthless, the financial crisis ensued, the economy went into a tailspin, and all of the major banks needed taxpayer-funded bailouts. The big banks eventually

settled with the Department of Justice for billions of dollars—
JPMorgan Chase agreed to pay $13 billion in 2013, and Bank of
America agreed to pay $16.65 billion in 2014—but most everybody
kept their jobs and senior executives escaped culpability, despite the
havoc wreaked on the economy. Even the CEOs of the failed firms
Lehman Brothers, Merrill Lynch, and Bear Stearns each walked
away with hundreds of millions of dollars.

In the current system it pays financially for companies to be
aggressive and abuse the public trust, make as much money as possible, and then pay some modest fines. Often, no criminal laws are
broken, or if they are, violations are impossible to either prosecute
or prove. It's little wonder that our current version of institutional
capitalism sits so poorly with young people who grew up during the
recession. They were on the receiving end of a morality play that
ended with the bad guys walking away with bags of cash and a lousy
job market.

What could we do that would seriously mitigate this behavior and elevate the state and the public good above the interests of
multibillion-dollar corporations?

Here's an idea for a dramatic rule—for every $100 million a
company is fined by the Department of Justice or bailed out by the
federal government, both its CEO and its largest individual shareholder will spend one month in jail. Call the new law the Public Pro-
tection against Market Abuse Act. If it's a foreign company, this
would apply to the head of the U.S. operation and the largest American shareholder. There would be a legal tribunal and due process in
each case. The president would have the ability to pardon, suspend,
shorten, or otherwise modify the period or sentence. The president
would also have the ability to claw back the assets of any such individual to repay the public.

Admittedly, this drastic approach would stretch the bounds of the powers of the state. But there's a clear need for penalties with some teeth for executives and individuals who are being enriched by egregious behavior at public expense. If this rule had been in place during the financial crisis, we would have had the heads of the major banks all lined up for prison sentences. The Sacklers would have spent time behind bars. It would certainly set up a hierarchy where CEOs are not above the public good.

TECHNOLOGY ON OUR MINDS

Effectively regulating technological innovations like self-driving cars and artificial intelligence will require a much more activated and invigorated state. Elon Musk in 2017 called for proactive regulation of AI, calling it "a fundamental risk to the existence of civilization." Techies don't often call for regulation of their own industries, so you know it must be serious.

Another major technology issue that will require government intervention is the effect of smartphones on human minds, particularly those of young children. Recent research indicates that the increase in smartphone use by teenagers coincides with an unprecedented surge in depression, anxiety, reduced sociability, and even higher suicide rates. Tristan Harris, a former design ethicist at Google, has written compellingly about how apps are designed to function like slot machines, vying for our attention and giving us variable unpredictable rewards to keep us engaged. As individuals trying to moderate our own behavior and that of our children, we're outgunned by billion-dollar companies. Tristan wrote, "Imagine hundreds of engineers whose job every day is to invent new ways to keep you hooked." Another technologist lamented that "the best minds of my generation are thinking about how to make people click ads." And they're succeeding.

In a better world, one can imagine smartphones with settings like "maximum stimulation," "moderate engagement," and "serenity" and apps modifying their notifications and home screens accordingly. A government regulator—call it the Department of the Attention Economy—could dig into the guts of social media, gaming, and chat apps and allow for both user and parental visibility and control. Maybe there could even be notifications that flag excessive screen time; for example, "You are now entering hour 4 of continuous smartphone use. You may want to go outside or look at another human being now."

I have two little boys and am not eager to see them become antisocial homebody zombies trying to set new high gaming scores. Yet, in observing parents interact with their children, I can see how easily it happens. Parents know there are endless hours to fill. Change won't happen without some regulation, because the gaming and social media companies, many of them publicly traded, have strong financial incentives to maximize engagement.

THE NEW CITIZENSHIP

A renewal of citizenship and humanity will require a different experience at the user level of citizenship. What do I meant by that? The state has a few big responsibilities. Keeping people healthy and educating them are two of the main ones, which we'll turn to shortly.

Another aspect of citizenship is a sense of belonging and commonality. Most Americans have less and less exposure to those in other walks of life as we increasingly diverge into rural and urban enclaves. This leads to increasingly fraught politics as gaps become harder to bridge. Many of my friends advocate service year opportunities to foster more of a sense of unity. One idea is instituting an American Exchange Program or Citizenship Trip, during which all graduating high school seniors go on a month-long trip to several different parts of the country, hosted by host families and paid for by the government. They would volunteer for a local organization and participate in programming with 24 other high school graduates from diverse regions and backgrounds. The 25 young people would get to know each other in structured yet personal ways. It could be run by the top-rated schoolteachers and professors in the region each August and take place at high schools or community colleges. There would be some required programming on the basics of citizenship and civic investment.

Afterward, everyone would have at least a few friends from vastly different backgrounds. Young people have the potential to develop significant relationships in short periods of time in the right context. It would permanently alter our politics by making it impossible to cast other Americans as anything other than fellow citizens who want better lives for themselves and their loved ones.

People can tell when you actually invest in them—it's one reason all of the high-end companies conduct elaborate trainings. Done well, the American Exchange Program would give people more of a reason to explore other parts of the country and maybe even move someplace different if an opportunity calls for it. It would open minds and hearts.

In order for our society to prosper through the automation wave, the state must become a newly invigorated force. Citizenship must grow to mean something again. And we have to make clear that we value people intrinsically, independent of any qualities or qualifications.

TWENTY-ONE

HEALTH CARE IN A WORLD WITHOUT JOBS

As jobs disappear and temporary employment becomes more prevalent, reforming our health care system will be more and more crucial. Right now, many of us rely upon our employers to pay for and provide health insurance, in whole or in part. This will be increasingly difficult to sustain as jobs with benefits become harder and harder to come by. On the consumer side, spiraling health care costs have already become a crushing burden for Americans. Health care bills were the number one cause of personal bankruptcy in 2013, and a study that year found that 56 million Americans—over 20 percent of the adult population—struggled with health care expenses they couldn't afford to pay. We've all seen and heard the horror stories of people coming back from the hospital with a bill for tens of thousands of dollars. For many Americans it's a double whammy if you get sick—you not only have to deal with the illness or injury, but you have to figure out how to pay for treatment.

I worked at a health care software startup based in New York from 2002 to 2005. I was 27 years old at the time. Our CEO was a talented former physician named Manu Capoor. We were one of the early electronic medical records companies that specialized in taking paper info and digitizing it. Our niche was presurgical info, so our clients were large hospitals that hosted a lot of surgeries. I was the head of client engagement—I led small teams that rolled out our software to clerks, doctors' offices, secretaries, nurses, office managers, residents, anesthesiologists, and the occasional surgeon. It took a while to train the dozens or hundreds of people who could be touching a particular patient file—we were modifying behavior from paper to digital. I would spend weeks and months in urban hospitals in the Bronx, Morningside Heights, or West Palm Beach distributing usernames and passwords, training people, troubleshooting, and answering the occasional angry phone call. I hung out outside operating rooms at seven a.m. because surgeons like to start early, and I ate at the IHOP across the street from the UMDNJ hospital in Newark so many times that I still can't set foot in one today.

Although we passionately believed in the benefits of our product, we found that it was difficult to make what seemed like a pretty simple and straightforward process change. There were many reasons for this, not the least of which was that the hospitals had a limited ability to police doctor's office behavior. The surgeons were in charge; their procedures were the big money generators. Each surgeon's office was its own business with different systems and practices. Some doctors liked to invest in technology and people, while others were clearly happy spending very little in order to maximize profitability. They just wanted to come in 3.5 days a week and get to their golf courses or boats as fast as possible. It was like a fast-moving assembly line filled with people scrambling to get through each day and little accountability or incentive to improve.

We used to joke around as the months wore on that "health care is where good ideas go to die." We never did accomplish our heady goals, as adoption was painstaking and difficult. I left after four years, having helped build a client base of about a dozen hospitals. I learned firsthand how even something that made sense and should make things more efficient would be slow going in the health care industry. There's no real reason for them to change.

I know my experiences in the early 2000s have played over and over again for others who have tried to improve the health care system with technology. In general, the use of technology has not transformed health care the way that optimists would hope. Health care costs have continued to climb to a record 17.8 percent of the economy in 2016, up from 11.4 percent in 1989 and less than 6 percent in 1960. We spend about twice what other industrialized countries do on health care per capita with lesser results. According to a 2014 Commonwealth Fund report, we are last among major industrialized nations in efficiency, equity, and health outcomes attributable to medical care despite spending much more than anyone else. Another study had the United States last among developed countries in basic measurements such as rate of women dying due to pregnancy or childbirth and rate of survival to age five. To the extent that new technology is used, it tends to be expensive new devices and implants that drive costs ever higher. The basic practice of medicine, as well as the training, is the same as it's been for decades.

Our job-based health insurance system does the very thing we most want to avoid—it discourages businesses from hiring. I've now run a couple of companies, and if I hire a full-time entry-level worker in New York at $42,000, I have to factor in an additional $6,000 for health care insurance costs. For employers, company-subsidized health insurance costs are a major impediment to hiring and growth. The costs get a lot higher for senior people with families—my last company was spending more than $2,500 a month on certain people's insurance plans. If these costs weren't on our books we definitely would have hired more people.

Health insurance also pushes companies to make as many

employees as possible into part-time gig workers or contractors. The organizations I ran were generous—my education company made instructors who worked more than 20 hours a week full-time employees and provided benefits accordingly. This was highly unusual in our industry and very expensive—we could do it because we were growing and profitable, and it was always important to me to take care of people. For many companies, insurance costs are increasingly out of control, and they can make or break a business. It's very difficult to pass increased costs on to employees or take back benefits after they've been provided, so you're setting yourself up for increased costs in good times and bad.

On the worker side, I know tons of people who hang on to jobs that they do not want to be in just for the health insurance. Economists refer to this as "job lock"; it makes the labor market much less dynamic, which is bad in particular for young workers. Replacing health insurance is a major source of discouragement for people striking off on their own and starting a new business, especially if they have families. In a world where we're trying to get more people to both create jobs and start companies, our employer-based health insurance system serves as a shackle holding us in place and a reason not to hire.

As jobs disappear, having one's health care linked to employment will become increasingly untenable. The need for a different approach is growing.

Health care is not truly subject to market dynamics for a host of reasons. In a normal marketplace, companies compete for your business by presenting different value propositions, and you make an informed choice. With health care, you typically have only a few options. You have no idea what the real differences are between different providers and doctors. Costs are high and extremely unpredictable, making it hard to budget for them. The complexity leaves many Americans overwhelmed and highly suggestible to experts or institutions. When you actually do get sick or injured, you become cost-insensitive, just trying to get well. Hospitals often employ opaque pricing, resulting in patient uncertainty over what their insurance will actually cover. Moreover, when you're ill, it's possible your faculties can be impaired because of illness, emotional distress, or even unconsciousness.

As Steven Brill wrote in his seminal *Time* magazine article on health care costs, "Unless you are protected by Medicare, the health care market is not a market at all. It's a crapshoot." The lack of real market discipline or cost control incentives has driven costs ever higher. Technology that should decrease costs has been kept at the door, because for most actors in the system, the goal is to increase revenue and profitability. The more services, tests, appointments, procedures, and expensive gadgets you use, the better. The system rewards activity and output over health improvements and outcomes.

Changing these incentives is key. The most direct way to do so would be to move toward a single-payer health care system, in which the government both guarantees health care for all and negotiates fixed prices. Medicare—the government-provided health care program for Americans 65 and over—essentially serves this role for senior citizens and has successfully driven down costs and provided quality care for tens of millions. Most everyone loves Medicare—it's politically bulletproof. Sam Altman, the head of Y Combinator, suggests rolling out Medicare across the population by gradually lowering the eligibility age over time. A gradual phase-in would give the industry time to plan and adjust. This is an excellent way forward, and a "Medicare-for-all" movement is currently gathering steam.

There would inevitably remain a handful of private options for the super-affluent, but most everyone would use the generalized care.

One harsh reality is that any rationalization of health care costs will hit tons of resistance because it's going to reduce a lot of people's incomes. Dean Baker, co-director of the Center for Economic and Policy Research, has written about the high cost of health care, including doctor salaries. "We do waste money on insurance, but we also pay basically twice as much for everything," he writes. "We pay twice as much to doctors. Would single-payer get our doctors to accept half as much in wages?" Moving toward a single-payer system, Baker says, would mean "fights with all of these powerful interest groups."

At least some doctors have been voicing their discontent with the current arrangement that puts money and efficiency over time spent with patients. Dr. Sandeep Jauhar, a cardiologist and author, writes that doctors today see themselves not as "pillars of any community" but as "technicians on an assembly line" or "pawn[s] in a money-making game for hospital administrators." Jauhar notes that only 6 percent of doctors "described their morale as positive" in a 2008 survey, and most are pessimistic about the future of the medical profession.

A 2016 survey of American doctors by the Physicians Foundation found that 63 percent have negative feelings about the future of the medical profession, 49 percent said they often or always experience feelings of burnout, and 49 percent would not recommend a career in medicine to their children. The same survey found that excessive paperwork and regulation was a consistent burden, with only 14 percent of doctors believing they had enough time to provide patients the highest quality of care. Almost half were planning on retiring, taking a nonclinical position, going part-time, or reducing their patient hours due to various frustrations. The low amount of time spent per patient makes doctors unhappy, cuts patients short, and drives up costs. Jauhar notes that many doctors work at "hyperspeed" and call in specialists just to "cover their ass" in case they missed something, resulting in ever more tests and costs.

When I went to Brown in the mid-1990s, about half of the people around me were pre-med. I remember how hard they all studied for organic chemistry, which was the weed-out class that separated the people who were going to go on to med school successfully from those who were going to have to rethink their ambitions. Many people who wanted very badly to be doctors didn't make it. One friend in particular I remember being crushed by the realization that she wasn't going to fulfill her childhood ambition. None of my friends who are doctors today actually use organic chemistry for anything. It was just intended to make things really difficult.

Becoming a doctor is a climb through a very competitive and hierarchical system. You study to get a high GPA in your pre-med coursework, take the MCAT, spend a summer caddying for a doctor or researcher, compete in med school to graduate with honors, apply to match with a desirable residency, then pursue the right internship and fellowship. At every level, the people become smarter and smarter. Some specializations take as many as six years after medical school, or 10 full years after college. Different specialties take on different personalities—the anesthesiologists are mellow, the orthopedic surgeons are jocks, the pediatricians love children, and so on. The amount of money you make largely corresponds to how many years you spend in specialized training. Family medicine doctors make about $200,000 a year on average, while orthopedic surgeons make more than $500,000 per year. The average educational debt load for a medical school graduate is $180,000, with 12 percent of doctors owing a whopping $300,000 for their training.

In part as a result of this system, there's a national shortage of both primary care doctors and doctors who practice in rural areas. About 65 million Americans live in what one expert called basically "a primary care desert." The Association of American Medical Colleges estimated that the number of additional doctors necessary to provide appropriate care to underserved areas was 96,200 in 2014, with a gap of about 25,000 in primary care alone. Many states are offering grants and incentives to address doctor shortages, as 12 states have fewer than half the number of primary care doctors necessary to provide adequate coverage. After all of the competition, schooling, and debt, many doctors don't want to sign up for less pay and prestige to work in underserved areas.

The process is also not selecting people for empathy. Most medical schools apply a mechanical screen to determine who to interview based solely on college GPA, course of study, and MCAT score. Though some schools say they are trying to identify applicants who display various personal traits, we're still talking about 21,030 people per year who studied science and did well on the MCAT attending med school, which is a very restricted group of people.

Martin Ford, the author of *Rise of the Robots*, suggests that we create a new class of health care provider armed with AI—college graduates or master's students unburdened by additional years of costly specialization, who would nonetheless be equipped to head out to rural areas. They could help people monitor chronic conditions like obesity and diabetes and refer particularly hairy problems to more experienced doctors. Call them primary care specialists. AI will soon be at a point where technology, in conjunction with a non-doctor, could offer the same quality of care as a doctor in the vast majority of cases. In one study, IBM's Watson made the same recommendation as human doctors did in 99 percent of 1,000 medical cases and made suggestions human doctors missed in 30 percent of them. AI can reference more cases than the most experienced physician while keeping up to date with the latest journals and studies.

Predictably, doctors have lobbied against nurse practitioners and unsupervised residents seeing patients, and they would doubtless feel even more negatively about this new class of primary care specialist. But this change would make health care much more widely available, open up a new employment category for smart and empathetic college graduates who genuinely want to spend time with patients, and eventually lighten the time burden on individual physicians.

This brings us back to how to implement a new single-payer system. We need to do more than rationalize current costs—we need to transform the way that doctors get paid.

Adopting Medicare-for-all or a single-payer system will solve the biggest problems of rampant overbilling and ever-increasing costs. But Medicare still generally reimburses based on individual appointments, procedures, and tests, which maintain the incentives for doctors to do more to get paid more. There is a movement toward "value-based" or "quality-based reimbursement," which tries to measure patient outcomes, readmission rates, and the like and reward providers accordingly. One startup based in Maryland, Aledade, is having success by giving primary care doctors incentives to reduce costs. But these "pay for performance" plans are tough to measure, influence a very low proportion of the funds currently being received by providers, and have had mixed results.

The best approach is what they do at the Cleveland Clinic—doctors simply get paid flat salaries. When doctors aren't worried about billing, they can focus on patients. Dr. Delos Cosgrove, the CEO of the Cleveland Clinic, said, "I think you have to recognize that people do what you pay them to do. If you pay doctors to do more of something, then that's what they'll do. If you put the emphasis on looking after patients, they'll do that." The Cleveland Clinic is consistently ranked among the top hospitals in the country. And physician turnover is only 3.5 percent per year, much lower than normal.

The Cleveland Clinic has achieved financial success in part by universalizing a sense of cost control. They put price tags on things so everyone knows how much it costs to, say, open up a new set of sutures. They don't allow redundant tests. They include doctors in purchasing decisions. Everyone is interested in the company's financial sustainability because they feel a sense of ownership and mission. Plus, if the hospital does well, you're more likely to get a raise.

What's required is an honest conversation in which we say to people who are interested in becoming doctors, "If you become a doctor, you'll be respected, admired, and heal people each day. You will live a comfortable life. But medicine will not be a path to riches. On the bright side, we're not going to burn you out by forcing you to see a million patients a day and fill out paperwork all the time. We're going to supplement you with an army of empathetic people equipped with AI who will handle most routine cases. We'll only call you when the case genuinely requires distinct human judgment or empathy. We want you to become the best and most human version of yourself, not Dr. Speed Demon who can bang out a nine-minute appointment. Let's leave that to Watson."

I'm sure that many doctors would enjoy this shift in role and embrace becoming better, more empathetic clinicians. Changing their incentives would change everything.

A shift in incentives would also allow doctors to treat patients holistically. The Southcentral Foundation, a health care provider for Alaska Natives, treats health problems and behavioral problems as related issues. When you get a health checkup, you also get a psychological appointment. It turns out that problems like obesity and depression are linked, and the local citizens' top concerns—child sexual abuse, child neglect, domestic violence, and addictions—all involve psychology and behavior as much as medicine and drugs. Integration of physical and psychological services at Southcentral lowered hospital admissions and visits to the emergency room by more than a third between 2000 and 2015, and 97 percent of patients said they were satisfied with the care. Integrating medical and behavioral health care could save tens of billions of dollars each year from the nation's health care costs. Southcentral CEO Katherine Gottlieb, an Alaska Native, received a MacArthur "genius" grant for her work.

In time, freedom from being paid a fee for service would give physicians and organizations the opportunity to solve problems in new ways. At first, the goal would be to measure patient outcomes and decrease readmissions and errors. Eventually, one can imagine hospitals being measured against statistics on the health of the surrounding population. Primary care specialists could distribute biometric devices, monitor a patient's interactions with other doctors, and encourage preventative measures. AI coaches could be employed to remind people to stick to their treatment or regimen, or to assist with psychological disorders. Patients could volunteer to share their health data to usher in revolutionary new approaches. The goal would be to make each hospital a hub of health and vitality that solves or reduces problems beyond its walls. Technology that streamlines costs and improves patient care would become a clinician's best friend.

We have so many brilliant doctors—they should be innovators, detectives, guides, and sources of comfort, not glorified assembly line workers. And freeing health care from being locked to a job would be a massive boon to economic growth and dynamism.

TWENTY-TWO

BUILDING PEOPLE

EDUCATION IN THE AGE OF AUTOMATION

Reimagining college in the age of automation begs the fundamental question—what are people sent to college to learn? Originally, the idea of an education was to develop a sense of morality. As Mary Woolley, the president of Mount Holyoke, stated in 1901, "Character is the main object of education." The Harvard psychologist and philosopher William James wrote around the same time that character and moral significance are built through adopting a self-imposed, heroic ideal that is pursued through courage, endurance, integrity, and struggle. It's the development of these ideals that was once the purpose of a university education.

Of course, for many decades now, the point of college has been to set people up for jobs. But what happens when the jobs disappear? Similar to health care, the automation wave should lead us to invest more people in education and human capital development. It should also drive us to dramatically increase our emphasis on technical and vocational training and apprenticeships at the high school level to take advantage of the jobs that will continue to exist. The difficulty is that schools will need to reinvest and adapt even as the monetary returns on education diminish and jobs become harder to come by.

Some believe that we can inexpensively educate large numbers of people using the latest technology. A couple years ago I spoke at an awards dinner with Sal Khan, the founder of the Khan Academy. If you don't know Khan Academy, you should—they make education videos that are used by millions around the world on everything from basic arithmetic to great literature to quantum physics. Sal was a hedge fund analyst turned explainer of all things. Bill Gates's kids used to watch the videos to supplement their schooling, leading Bill to become one of the many million-dollar donors to Khan Academy. Their mission is to educate the world.

Sal gave an inspiring talk that night. The high point went something like this: "Back in the Middle Ages, if you asked the literate monks and scholars how many of the farmers and peasants walking around would be capable of learning to read, they'd scoff and say, 'Read? Most of these peasants could never learn to do something like that.' They might guess that 2 to 3 percent of the peasants would be capable of becoming literate. Today we know that the real number is closer to 99 percent. Virtually everyone is capable of learning to read. But if I ask you today how many people are smart enough to study quantum physics, you might say only 2 or 3 percent. This is as shortsighted as the monks were in the Middle Ages. We are just scratching the surface of how smart people can become if we give them the proper tools to learn. In the years ahead, we will find that people are capable of much more than we can imagine."

Sal's speech received a rousing ovation. It was an exhilarating vision. Technology and universally accessible, low-cost education materials would accelerate a new age of smarter human beings. Presumably, these new smarter human beings would innovate and create new jobs and businesses.

As we walked away, I found myself asking, "Is he right?"

At least here in the United States, it's very hard to say that he is. The Internet became widely available and adopted in 2002. A majority of American households have had broadband Internet at home for more than 10 years now, and 85 percent today have either a broadband home connection or a smartphone. We have years of information about how unlimited access to materials like Khan Academy has influenced learners around the country. Unfortunately, SAT scores have declined significantly in the last 10 years. High school graduation rates have edged upward. College readiness is generally down. We don't seem to be getting any more enlightened despite ubiquitous online lessons.

It's impossible not to love Khan Academy. I fully intend to strap my kids in as soon as they're ready for it, and I fantasize about coming home and having them say things like, "I learned thermodynamics today!" But if one gives a 12-year-old access to high-speed Internet, they are infinitely more likely to chat with their friends, play video games, or watch the latest Honest Trailers video than delve into a deep, thought-provoking discussion of *War and Peace*. Among the biggest gainers from Khan Academy are people abroad and learners like Bill Gates's kids, who already had some things going for them.

The clearest impact of technology on teen development to date has been starkly negative. According to psychologist Jean Twenge's 2017 book, *iGen*, smartphone use has caused a spike in depression and anxiety among people born from 1995 on, and a diminution in sociability and independence. An excerpt of her book in *The Atlantic* was aptly titled, "Have Smartphones Destroyed a Generation?" They are not using their smartphones to learn calculus, but they are trying to keep their Snapstreaks going.

In 2011, everyone began taking about massive open online

courses (MOOCs), and many believed they were going to revolutionize education. In 2013, Udacity rolled out the core coursework of Stanford and MIT in topics like artificial intelligence. Tens of thousands of students around the world enrolled. Pundits and experts predicted the disruption of college as an institution. Instead, these MOOCs kind of flopped. Only about 4 percent of students completed the average course, with many quitting after only one or two sessions. In one case, an online math course was found to be less effective than a remedial college class in person and scaled back. Though these online courses continue to improve, college applications remain higher than ever.

PEOPLE (STILL) LEARN FROM OTHER PEOPLE

Too often people mistake content for education and vice versa. We act as if we can take a textbook or lesson online and make it interactive, and then that will educate someone. But no one would consider putting a child in an empty classroom with a textbook "education." We would call that reading or maybe punishment. Max Ventilla, the founder and CEO of AltSchool, has said that "the worst use of software in [education] is in replacement of humans…that's craziness…It's about the relationship that kids have with their peers, with adults. That's what creates the motivation that creates the learning." AltSchool is a company founded in 2014 to personalize education for all children across the country. AltSchool has raised over $175 million from Mark Zuckerberg, Emerson Collective, and others. It has opened six schools that collectively serve hundreds of elementary school students in San Francisco and New York. It employs more than 50 engineers who are developing tools each day that teachers request. The school uses video cameras to monitor tiny student interactions for playback.

"We believe that the vast majority of the learning should happen non-digitally," Max explains. He is the former head of personalization at Google and parent to three young children, and he wants to build schools that prepare children for the future. "In any AltSchool classroom, most of what a kid is doing is not on a screen, but for every kid, we have a digital representation of the important things that relate to that child's learning, not just their academic learning but also their non-academic learning. [They learn] that their character skills matter, that their grit, their perseverance, that their experience with being successful after failing a bunch of times is as much a part of the education as...learning history facts and knowing how to multiply two numbers."

AltSchool represents a sophisticated blend of using software to do the things that technology is excellent at—recording and synthesizing large amounts of data over a growing number of people and making recommendations—while retaining the essence of how people learn: from other people. I had dinner with Max and his wife, Jenny, in San Francisco last year. I could see how AltSchool raised $175 million; Max is an exceptional guy and completely sincere in his mission of furthering how our children learn. He's in it for the long term. It probably helps that his mother and sister are teachers.

Perhaps the best thing about AltSchool is that it focuses on character skills. In an age with less and less employment, the abilities to self-manage and socialize will become the new keys to success in life. We should recognize that the majority of high school students will not go to college, and that their ability to function should be independent of further education. Grit, persistence, adaptability, financial literacy, interview skills, human relationships, conversation, communication, managing technology, navigating conflicts, preparing healthy food, physical fitness, resilience, self-regulation, time management, basic psychology and mental health practices, arts, and music—all of these would help students and also make school seem much more relevant. Our fixation on college readiness leads our high school curricula toward purely academic subjects and away from life skills. The purpose of education should be to enable a citizen to live a good, positive, socially productive life independent of work.

EDUCATION STARTS AT HOME

One enormous favor we could do for teachers would be to try to keep parents together. Children raised in two-parent households have better outcomes by most dimensions. Technology could potentially help here—one can imagine an AI life coach with the voice of Morgan Freeman trying to help people manage their differences. The government should provide or subsidize marriage counseling to essentially anyone who wants it. If you have kids and you want to stay together, we should help you do it. Even successful married couples shudder if you bring up the early years when their children were first born. Any marriage or relationship that remains whole is a win for the next generation.

We should also make sure that parents have ample time to spend time with their children. Our lack of family leave for new parents is barbaric, antifamily, sexist, regressive, economically irrational, and just plain stupid. Studies have shown that robust family leave policies improve children's health and heighten women's employment rates because they don't feel they need to leave work entirely in order to be successful. The United States is one of only four out of 196 countries in the world—and the only industrialized country— that does not have federally mandated time off from work for new mothers. The other three are Lesotho, Swaziland, and Papua New Guinea—not exactly a list of world beaters. We're in the bottom 2 percent of recognizing that new parents might need to spend time with their new baby—it's the most obvious example of our prioritizing capital in a misguided way over humanity. In contrast, Denmark gives parents 52 weeks of paid leave they can split between them, with a minimum of 18 weeks of full pay for the mother.

If current trends continue, there are going to be many more single moms in the years ahead; there are already 11.4 million single mothers raising 17.2 million children in the United States, 40 percent of whom live in poverty. Single mothers make up more than 82 percent of single parents, and 40 percent of them work in low-wage jobs, one of the highest proportions in the world. Ideally we would create communal living arrangements specifically for single moms to be able to pool resources, cooking time, and babysitting, and to be able to put their kids down without worry. The trend of cohousing is increasingly popular among millennials, and there are already 150 cohousing communities in the United States. Communal living arrangements have been shown to increase social cohesion, which is very helpful for children, parents, and older people alike.

We also should start school earlier. The benefits to children, particularly those most in need, are massive and clear. There is a movement toward pre-kindergarten offerings in New York, San Antonio, and other cities. The United Kingdom now offers universal pre-kindergarten options for all three- and four-year-olds, and China and India are undergoing massive expansions.

When children get to school, there are a few things that have been shown to be helpful and effective. Unfortunately, additions like laptops and software have thus far been shown to be largely unhelpful in making poor schools better. Technology is additive to existing environments; in a strong school with good teachers, it's helpful. In a low-performing school, it doesn't really solve anything. We know what works—better teachers, better cultures, teamwork, and individualized attention. We're just not very good at delivering these things. We fall in love with scale and solutions that promise more for less.

I ran an education company, Manhattan Prep, that started as a solo tutoring shop and eventually grew to serve tens of thousands of students per year. We used current technology, but we became the industry leader primarily by finding the best teachers, compensating them more, and then empowering them to teach their classes how they saw fit. People teach other people. If you want to teach thousands of students well, you teach one student well. Then you do it thousands of times.

COLLEGE ISN'T ALWAYS THE ANSWER

Starting at the grade school level, we overemphasize college readiness and stigmatize vocational training. Only 6 percent of American high school students were enrolled in a vocational course of study in 2013, compared to 42 percent in the United Kingdom, 59 percent in Germany, and 67 percent in the Netherlands. Many available categories of employment will fall into nonroutine middle-skill jobs of welding, glass installation, electricians, machinists, maintenance, line repair, technicians, and the like even as the economy changes. A Georgetown center estimated that there are 30 million good-paying jobs that don't require a college degree, many of which need some specialized training. A few summers ago my office's air conditioning system broke and we had to pay a couple thousand to get it repaired as fast as possible. There are going to be old air conditioning systems in the United States for decades to come.

College is being dramatically overprescribed and oversold as the answer to all of our job-related economic problems. The most recent graduation rate for first-time, full-time undergraduate students who began seeking a bachelor's degree was 59 percent after six years. That is, only 59 percent of students who started college in 2009 had completed a bachelor's degree by 2015, and this level has been more or less consistent the past number of years. For those who attended private, selective colleges, this number will seem jarringly low; the same number at selective schools is 88 percent. Among schools with open admissions policies the rate is only 32 percent, and among for-profit universities the six-year graduation rate is 23 percent. Similarly, the graduation rate from two-year associate's degree programs within three years is only 29.1 percent. College, more than high school, is America's true dropout factory.

The main reasons cited for dropping out are being unprepared for the rigors of academic work; inability to cope with the competing demands of study, family, and jobs; and cost. The worst part is that no school will refund you your tuition if you don't get your degree. Millions of high school graduates show up to college or community college, rack up significant debt, and then don't graduate. We are up to a record $1.4 trillion in educational debt that serves as an anchor on the futures of many of our young people.

Meanwhile, the New York Federal Reserve estimated the under-employment rate of college graduates to be as high as 44 percent for recent grads and 34 percent overall. One-third of college graduates are working in jobs that don't require a degree. We pretend that a college degree will prepare one for the future and ensure gainful opportunities when that's often not the case.

WHY IS COLLEGE SO EXPENSIVE?

This raises a central question: Why is college so expensive? There is no real measure of the effectiveness of college; it's not like they give you the SAT again and see how much better you got at it. And yet, college tuition has risen at several times the rate of inflation the past 20 years, more dramatically than all other costs, including health care. Thousands of parents right now are sitting there thinking, "Gosh, sending two kids to college might cost half a million dollars." The real income received by college graduates has declined even as the cost of a degree has gone through the roof.

Relative Changes in U.S. Consumer Price Index (1978-2017)

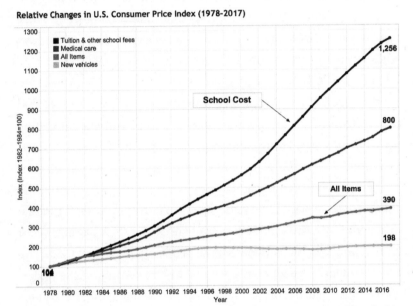

Source: U.S. Bureau of Labor Statistics, Consumer Price Index for All Urban Consumers, retrieved from FRED, Federal Reserve Bank of St. Louis.

Private university tuition is up to $50K per year at some schools, with public university fees rising to about $10K for in-state residents and $25K for out-of-state students, all before living expenses. Average college tuition has risen as much as 440 percent in the last 25 years. It's little wonder that students are being forced to load up on government-provided loans to go to college.

It's not that professors are getting paid more. It's not even all the new buildings and facilities. It's that universities have become more bureaucratic and added layers of administrators. According to the Department of Education and Bloomberg, administrative positions at colleges and universities grew by 60 percent between 1993 and 2009, 10 times the rate of tenured faculty positions during the same period. An analysis of a university system in California showed a 221 percent increase in administrators over a multiyear period even as the number of full-time faculty members only grew 5 percent. One report observed that "America's universities now have more full-time employees devoted to administration than to instruction, research and service combined."

I understand it. I've run a nonprofit. If you get more resources, you hire people to work for you. Everyone is well intentioned and pleasant. You do great work. An organization's imperative over time becomes its own growth and self-maintenance. But in this context, it's critical to bring education costs down for the sake of the public good in the age of automation.

At the high end, universities are spending a lot of money on making more money. In 2015, a law professor pointed out that Yale spent more the previous year on private equity managers managing its endowment—$480 million—than it spent on tuition assistance, fellowships, and prizes for students—$170 million. This led Malcolm Gladwell to joke that Yale was a $24 billion hedge fund with a university attached to it, and that it should dump its legacy business.

Yale and all other nonprofit universities are tax-exempt and receive millions in research money from the government, which means that American taxpayers are paying for and subsidizing the accrual of billions to both the universities and their endowments. A research group documented the cost of taxpayer subsidies for a community college student as between $2,000 and $4,000 per student per year, with that figure climbing to $10,000 per student per year at a typical state university. For Harvard the taxpayer subsidy jumped up to $48,000 per year, for Yale it was $69,000 per student per year, and for Princeton it was $105,000 per student per year. Being tax-exempt is more valuable the more money you're generating.

This is a perverse use of taxpayer resources—it's literally just helping rich schools get richer as opposed to spending money on education. One way to change this would be a law stipulating that any private university with an endowment over $5 billion will lose its tax-exempt status unless it spends its full endowment income from the previous year on direct educational expenses, student support, or domestic expansion. This would spur Harvard, Yale, Stanford, Princeton, MIT, Penn, Northwestern, and others to spend billions each year directly on their students and expansion within the United States. There could be a Harvard center in Ohio or Michigan as well as the new one they just opened in Shanghai. This would also induce investment from schools that approach the $5 billion threshold, such as Dartmouth and USC, who would want to stay below this level. Another possible approach would be to simply tax rich universities' endowments and use the proceeds to subsidize students at community colleges and public schools, which has been advocated by at least one progressive group. One could also mandate that they spend a certain percentage—say 6 to 8 percent—of their endowments each year.

The trickiest part is to introduce cost discipline and discourage administrative bloat at universities. Capping cost increases now won't be that helpful because the horse is already out of the barn. In 1975, colleges employed one professional staffer—admissions officers, information technology specialists, and the like—for every 50 students. By 2005, the proportion had risen more than 138 percent to one for every 21 students. Media coverage calling out administrative efficiency and bloat could be a useful galvanizer. But it will likely be necessary for the government to install benchmarks around the proper ratios of administrators to students and administrators to faculty and then give institutions time to move in that direction. The government subsidizes education through research money, the tax-exempt status of universities, and the provision of hundreds of billions of dollars of school loans—it needs to help rationalize all of this spending without blindly saying "more college will fix everything." It won't.

We also need to amend or ignore the *U.S. News and World Report* college rankings. At present, the rankings reward colleges for accepting more rich students by including measures like financial strength, student-to-teacher ratio, and alumni giving. Perhaps not surprisingly, Yale and Princeton admit more children from the top 1 percent than from the bottom 60 percent combined. Schools that admit more varied types of students or even operate more efficiently will be penalized in the rankings. Brit Kirwan, the former chancellor of the University of Maryland, said, "If some foreign power wanted to diminish higher education in America, they would have created the *U.S. News and World Report* rankings. You need both more college graduates in the economy and you need many more low-income students getting the benefit of higher education— and *U.S. News and World Report* has metrics that work directly in opposition to accomplishing those two things." It's insane that the rankings of a single publication shape the behavior and policies of dozens of billion-dollar organizations against the public interest.

NEW SCHOOLS

We have been grasping for more economical ways to educate people for years as the cost of college has escalated. There are high hopes for coding boot camps that can train people in coding and get them high-paying jobs in four months. Flatiron School and General Assembly took the world by storm with successful job placement rates as high as 95 percent. After some early success and an excess of investment, a number of the larger boot camps have recently closed, and the industry as a whole is consolidating. The 90 coding boot camps across the country produced about 23,000 graduates in total and have almost exclusively found success with immersive in-person programs. "Online boot camp is an oxymoron," said Ryan Craig, an investor at University Ventures. "No one has figured out how to do that yet."

Perhaps the most interesting application of technology in college education is the Minerva Project, a startup university now entering its fifth year. At Minerva, students take classes online, but they do so while living together in dorm-style housing. Minerva's online inter-face is unusual in that the student's face is shown the whole time, and they get called on to ensure accountability and engagement. This "facetime" is even the main performance metric—there aren't final exams. Professors review the classes to see if individual students are demonstrating the right "habits of mind." Minerva saves money by not investing in libraries, athletic facilities, sports teams, and the like. Students spend up to one year each in different dorms in San Francisco, Buenos Aires, Berlin, Seoul, and Istanbul. Minerva is selective—the acceptance rate for the latest class was only 1.9 percent. Students socialize and build connections because they live and travel together. Minerva delivers learning but it also delivers the credentialing, network, socialization, and identity that students crave. And it does this at $28K a year, a little more than half of what similarly selective universities charge. I met a group of Minerva students in San Francisco last year, and they struck me as unusually self-determined and thoughtful.

One thing I love about Minerva is that it's a new school. Ben Nelson, the founder and CEO, has made the point that if everyone wants to attend a great university, why don't we create more of them? It's truly odd that we've maintained a similar number of slots at selective schools even as admissions rates have plummeted to record lows. It may serve a school's interest to remain small and selective, but it's better for society if they were to try to expand. Dartmouth recently announced it may grow its entering class by as much as 25 percent, which is a step in the right direction.

REDISCOVERING IDEALS

The single best thing that universities could do would be to rediscover their original missions. What do you stand for? What should every graduate of your institution hold or believe? Teach and demonstrate some values. They're not your customers or your reviewers or even your community members; they're your students. They can tell if you're primarily sitting there selecting them, trying to connect them to jobs, building your endowment for the future, and encouraging them to donate.

Harvard was originally founded to prepare clergy for their work. Now its main purpose seems to be to make sure that at least one banker a year used to play the cello. I spoke at Princeton a while back, and the students literally laughed when someone mentioned their motto: "In the Nation's Service and the Service of Humanity." I'm sure if someone had said it was "For the Wealth of Princeton" or "In Service of the Markets" they would have laughed, too, for different reasons.

In his book *Self and Soul*, Mark Edmundson, a University of Virginia professor, writes that Western culture historically prized three major ideals:

- *The Warrior.* His or her highest quality is courage. Historical archetypes include Achilles, Hector, and Joan of Arc.
- *The Saint.* His or her highest quality is compassion. Historical archetypes include Jesus Christ and Mother Theresa.

- *The Thinker.* His or her highest quality is contemplation. Historical archetypes include Plato, Kant, Rousseau, and Ayn Rand.

Edmundson mourns that these ideals today have been largely abandoned. The new ideal is what he calls "the Worldly Self of middle-class values." To get along and get ahead. To succeed and self-replicate. The three great ideals live on in diluted form (e.g., spin classes and Spartan races for the Warrior, nonprofits and social entrepreneurship for the Saint, Ta-Nehisi Coates and the blogosphere for the Thinker). But anyone who pursues one of these ideals to their extremes in modern life would seem ridiculous, impractical, unworldly, and even unbalanced. I'm sure most college students would agree.

Personal qualities today are increasingly marginalized in favor of technocratic, market-driven skills. Instead, finance is the new courage, branding is the new compassion, and coding is the new contemplation. Schools today don't believe it's their place to teach toward the big questions. They can barely remember what ideals look like. If they can remember, there will be much more hope for us all.

CONCLUSION: MASTERS OR SERVANTS

realize the vision I paint of our present and future challenges in this book has been a lot to take. The challenges of this era are massive. Automation-led job destruction has had a running start weakening our society. We feel paralyzed because we fear that our institutions and leaders are no longer able to operate and the solutions require many to act against their own immediate interests. We strive to make more people and communities capital-efficient and market-friendly even as the water level rises. The logic of the market has overtaken most of our waking lives. Normal Americans will increasingly suffer as the market grinds on and eliminates opportunities and paths to a better life.

A majority of the technologists I speak to are already 100 percent certain that the automation wave is coming. They skip to the logical end. The time frame is unclear, but it really doesn't matter that much if it's 5, 10, or 15 years. They've already gotten there in their minds. Most are ready to head for the hills.

I am fighting for my soul because I'm right there with them. I see it, too. I see the path from here to there filled with broken people and communities, and a society torn apart by ever-rising deprivation and disability. People will blame each other because they are locked in a fight for scarcity. Experts will squabble while the average person suffers. Families will deteriorate into dysfunction. Children will come of age with no real hope of a better life and with institutions selling them false promises.

The age of automation will lead to many very bad things. But it will also potentially push us to delve more deeply into what makes us human.

I spent the past six years raising a small army of idealistic entrepreneurs who have fanned out to 18 cities around the country. Dozens of our alumni have started companies ranging from a crawfish restaurant to a company connecting brand sponsors to Little Leagues to a chickpea pasta company to a company that helps make construction projects more environmentally friendly. We have helped create more than 2,500 jobs. It's amazing. It's inspiring.

It won't be nearly enough. It will be like a wall of sand before an incoming tide.

I created a multimillion-dollar organization out of people and ideals. I have lived in Manhattan, Silicon Valley, and San Francisco while working in Providence, Detroit, New Orleans, Cincinnati, Las Vegas, Baltimore, Cleveland, Philadelphia, Pittsburgh, St. Louis, Miami, Columbus, San Antonio, Charlotte, Atlanta, Nashville, Birmingham, Denver, Kansas City, and Washington, DC.

I have been in the room with the people who are meant to steer our society. The machinery is weak. The institutionalization is high. The things you fear to be true are generally true.

I wrote this book because I want others to see what I see. We are capable of so much better.

There's a very popular notion out there that ideas change the world. That's wrong. People change the world. People making commitments and sacrifices and doing something about the forces that are tearing our society apart. Whom do we serve, Humanity or the Market?

Are we the opiated masses, the elites in our enclaves, careening toward a conjoined bleak destiny that we are powerless to stop?

Is there enough character and will and confidence and independence left to build the world and do what is required? Is there enough empathy? Capital doesn't care about us. We must evolve beyond relying upon it as the primary measurement of value. Human Capitalism will give us the chance to define what's important and pursue it.

I'm now a grown man with a family. I know the difference between talking about something and actually doing something about it. There is no hiding from what one knows. I even know the difference between writing a book about something and fighting for it. The choice is essentially to cut and run or to stand and fight. We must convert from a mindset of scarcity to a mindset of abundance. The revolution will happen either before or after the breakdown of society. We must choose before.

It will not be easy. We all have dysfunction within us. Darkness and pain. Contempt and resentment. Greed and fear. Pride and self-consciousness. Even reason will hold us back.

Through all of the doubt, the cynicism, the ridicule, the hatred and anger, we must fight for the world that is still possible. Imagine it in our minds and hearts and fight for it. With all of our hearts and spirits. As hands reach out clutching at our arms, take them and pull them along. Fight through the whipping branches of selfishness and despair and resignation. Fight for each other like our souls depend on it. Climb to the hilltop and tell others behind us what we see.

What do you see?

And build the society we want on the other side.

Evelyn, thank you for all that you do for me and our boys. They will grow up to be strong and whole.

The rest of you, get up. It's time to go. What makes you human? The better world is still possible. Come fight with me.

ACKNOWLEDGMENTS

Thank you to my editor, Paul Whitlatch, for being such an incredible reader and collaborator. And thank you to my agent, Byrd Leavell, for being a great friend and the best in the business. Belief in someone is a powerful thing.

Thank you to everyone who has helped build Venture for America over the years. I hope that you recognize the ideas in this book as springing from our mission. A dedicated group of the right people can indeed change the world. I've lived it and been the beneficiary of this truth, thanks to you.

As an entrepreneur, I'm a big fan of borrowing. I owe an intellectual debt to Martin Ford for breaking this ground and Andy Stern for orienting me toward solutions. David Freedman inspired the title of this book. Lauren Zalaznick, Cheryl Houser, Eric Bahn, Miles Lasater, Bernie Sucher, Kathryn Bendheim, Daniel Tarullo, Miika Grady, Scott Krase, Eric Cantor, Lawrence Yang, Owen Johnson, Chip Hazard, Chris Boggiano, Marian Salzman, Guillermo Silberman, and many others provided phenomenal insight into early drafts.

Albert Wenger, Josh Kopelman, Rutger Bregman, David Brooks, J. D. Vance, Jean Twenge, Lisa Wade, Victor Tan Chen, Yuval Harari, Steve Case, David Autor, Krystal Ball, Ryan Avent, Alec Ross, Mark Zuckerberg, Sam Altman, Chris Hughes, Derek Thompson, Steve

Glickman, John Lettieri, Rana Foroohar, Tim O'Reilly, Dylan Matthews, Annie Lowrey, Ross Baird, Nick Hanauer, David Rose, and Scott Santens shaped my thinking on many points, generally without knowing it.

Thank you to Zeke Vanderhoek for being such a great partner and friend. This, too, is your legacy.

Thank you to Muhan Zhang, Andrew Frawley, Katie Bloom, Matt Shinners, and Zach Graumann for being a part of the new story very early on. We will have a lot of company soon, I believe.

Thank you to my researcher, Ovidia Stanoi, for tracking down so many pieces of information, helping visualize data, and bearing with me.

Thank you, Evelyn, for being the best wife and partner anyone could hope for. You are to mothers what Universal Basic Income is to solutions. Christopher and Damian, I hope this helps make your country stronger in the ways that matter.

NOTES

INTRODUCTION: THE GREAT DISPLACEMENT

Seventy percent of Americans consider themselves part of the middle class: Emmie Martin, "70 Percent of Americans Consider Themselves Middle Class—but Only 50 Percent Are," CNBC.com, June 30, 2017.

...83 percent of jobs where people make less than $20 per hour will be subject to automation or replacement...: "Artificial Intelligence, Automation, and the Economy," Executive Office of the President, December 2016.

Driving a truck is the most common occupation in 29 states: Barbara Kollmeyer, "Somewhere along the Way the U.S. Became a Nation of Truck Drivers," *Marketwatch*, February 9, 2015.

Automation has already eliminated about 4 million manufacturing jobs in the United States since 2000: Federica Cocco, "Most US Manufacturing Jobs Lost to Technology, Not Trade," *Financial Times*, December 2, 2016.

The U.S. labor force participation rate is now at only 62.9 percent: Data and table retrieved from the Bureau of Labor Statistics at https://data.bls.gov.

...95 million working-age Americans are not in the workforce: Data and table retrieved from the Bureau of Labor Statistics at https://data.bls.gov.

...40 percent percent of American children are born outside of married households: National Center of Health Statistics, Centers for Disease Control and Prevention. Data retrieved from https://www.cdc.gov/nchs/fastats/unmarried-childbearing.htm.

…overdoses and suicides have overtaken auto accidents as leading causes of death: Drug Overdose Deaths in the United States, 1999–2015, Centers for Disease Control and Prevention. For suicides, see Alexander Abad-Santos, "3,026 More People Die from Suicide in America Each Year Than in Car Crashes," *The Atlantic*, May 2, 2013.

More than half of American households already rely on the government for direct income in some form: George Will, "Our Mushrooming Welfare State," *The National Review*, January 21, 2015.

…20 percent of working-age adults are now on disability, with increasing numbers citing mood disorders: Brendan Greeley, "Mapping the Growth of Disability Claims in America," *Bloomberg Businessweek*, December 16, 2016.

The budget for research and development in the Department of Labor is only $4 million: Email exchange with senior Obama official Thomas Kalil. Research and Development does not appear as a budget category on the Department of Labor website https://www.dol.gov/general/budget.

CHAPTER 1: MY JOURNEY

America is starting 100,000 fewer businesses per year than it was only 12 years ago: Ben Schiller, "Is This the Golden Age of Entrepreneurialism? The Statistics Say No," *Fast Company*, June 1, 2017.

…a CNN article that detailed how automation had eliminated millions of manufacturing jobs…: Patrick Gillespie, "Rise of the Machines: Fear Robots, Not China or Mexico," CNNMoney, January 30, 2017.

CHAPTER 2: HOW WE GOT HERE

Most community banks were gobbled up by one of the mega-banks in the 1990s…: Rana Foroohar, *Makers and Takers: The Rise of Finance and the Fall of American Business* (New York: Crown Business, 2016), p. 14.

Union membership fell by 50 percent: Quoctrung Bui, "50 Years of Shrinking Union Membership, in One Map," *Planet Money*, National Public Radio, February 23, 2015.

Real wages have been flat or even declining: Drew Desilver, "For Most Workers, Real Wages Have Barely Budged for Decades," Pew Research Center, October 9, 2014.

Ninety-four percent of the jobs created between 2005 and 2015 were temp or contractor jobs without benefits: Dan Kopf, "Almost All the US Jobs Created since 2005 Are Temporary," QZ.com, December 5, 2016.

The chances that an American born in 1990 will earn more than their parents are down to 50 percent . . . : Tim O'Reilly, *WTF: What's the Future and Why It's Up to Us* (New York: Harper Business, 2017), p. xxi.

The ratio of CEO to worker pay rose from 20 to 1 in 1965 to 271 to 1 in 2016: Lawrence Mishel and Jessica Schnieder, "CEO Pay Remains High Relative to the Pay of Typical Workers and High-Wage Earners," Economic Policy Institute, July 20, 2017.

The securities industry grew 500 percent as a share of GDP between 1980 and the 2000s . . . : Rana Foroohar, *Makers and Takers* (New York: Crown Business, 2016), p. 9.

U.S. companies outsourced and offshored 14 million jobs by 2013: Sarah P. Scott, "Activities of Multinational Enterprises in 2013," Bureau of Economic Analysis report, August 2015.

The share of GDP going to wages has fallen from almost 54 percent in 1970 to 44 percent in 2013 . . . : Tim O'Reilly, *WTF: What's the Future and Why It's Up to Us* (New York: Harper Business, 2017), p. 246.

The top 1 percent have accrued 52 percent of the real income growth in America since 2009: Rana Foroohar, *Makers and Takers* (New York: Crown Business, 2016), p. 9. Citing Emmanuel Saez, "Striking It Richer: The Evolution of Top Incomes in the United States," June 30, 2016.

The wealthy experience higher levels of depression and suspicion in unequal societies: Rutger Bregman, *Utopia for Realists: The Case for a Universal Basic Income, Open Borders, and a 15-Hour Workweek* (Boston: Little, Brown and Company, 2016), p. 67.

... *"People are falling behind because technology is advancing so fast...
and our organizations aren't keeping up"*: Alec Ross, *The Industries of
the Future* (New York: Simon and Schuster, 2015), p. 40.

CHAPTER 3: WHO IS NORMAL IN AMERICA

*The average American achieves something between one credit of college and
an associate's degree...*: Camille L. Ryan and Kurt Bauman, "Educational
Attainment in the United States: 2015," U.S. Census Bureau, Department
of Commerce, Economics and Statistics Administration, March 2016.

The median household income was $59,309 in 2016: See Bureau of the
Census for the Bureau of Labor Statistics, Current Population Survey, 2017
Annual Social and Economic Supplement, U.S. Census Bureau, 2017.

*The median personal income in the U.S. was $31,099 in 2016 and the mean
was $46,550*: Median personal income retrieved from the Federal Reserve
Bank of St. Louis website at https://fred.stlouisfed.org. Also see Bureau of
the Census for the Bureau of Labor Statistics, Current Population Survey,
2017 Annual Social and Economic Supplement, U.S. Census Bureau, 2017.

... *only 26 percent of people identified their neighborhood as urban...*: Jed
Kolko, "How Suburban Are Big American Cities?" Fivethirtyeight.com,
May 21, 2015.

*In 2016, the District of Columbia had the highest per capita income at
$50,567...*: Data retrieved from the U.S. Census Bureau at https://www
.census.gov/data/tables/time-series/demo/income-poverty/historical
-income-households.html.

... *59 percent of Americans don't have the savings to pay an unexpected
expense of $500*: Jill Confield, "Bankrate Survey: Just 4 in 10 Americans
Have Savings They'd Rely on in an Emergency," Bankrate, January 12,
2017.

... *63.7 percent of Americans own their home, down from a high of 69
percent in 2004*: U.S. Bureau of the Census, Homeownership Rate for the
United States, retrieved from FRED, Federal Reserve Bank of St. Louis,
November 6, 2017.

Women-led households have 12 percent less wealth than male-led households...: Data retrieved from the U.S. Census Bureau at https://www.census.gov/data/tables/time-series/demo/income-poverty/historical-income-households.html.

...the median level of stock market investment is close to zero: Danielle Kurtzleben, "While Trump Touts Stock Market, Many Americans Are Left Out of the Conversation." National Public Radio, March 1, 2017.

CHAPTER 4: WHAT WE DO FOR A LIVING

...between 64 and 69 percent of data collecting and processing tasks common in administrative settings are automatable: McKinsey Global Institute, *A Future That Works: Automation, Employment, and Productivity,* January 2017.

Rob estimates...: Rob LoCascio, "We Need a New Deal to Address the Economic Risks of Automation," *TechCrunch,* March 31, 2017.

...8,640 major retail locations are estimated to close in 2017: Tyler Durden, " 'The Retail Bubble Has Now Burst': A Record 8,640 Stores Are Closing In 2017," *Zero Hedge,* April 22, 2017.

Dozens and soon hundresds of malls are closing...: Sharon O'Malley, "Shopping Malls: Can They Survive in the 21st Century?" *Sage Business Research,* August 29, 2016.

...map of scheduled Macy's, Sears and Kmart closures as of 2017: Hayley Peterson, "A giant wave of store closures is wreaking havoc on shopping malls," *Business Insider,* January 9, 2017.

One declining Memphis-area mall reported 890 crime incidents...: Hayley Peterson, "Dying Shopping Malls Are Wreaking Havoc on Suburban America," *Business Insider,* March 5, 2017.

...the plight of towns in upstate New York...offering some unrealistic solutions: Louis Hyman, "The Myth of Main Street," *New York Times,* April 8, 2017.

On average, sellers' income from Etsy contributes only 13 percent to their household income...: "Crafting the Future of Work: The Big Impact of Microbusinesses." 2017 Seller census report. Etsy.com, 2017.

McDonald's just announced an "Experience of the Future" initiative: Tae Kim, "McDonald's Hits All-Time High as Wall Street Cheers Replacement of Cashiers with Kiosks," CNBC, June 20, 2017.

The former CEO of McDonald's suggested...: Tim Worstall, "McDonald's Ex-CEO Is Right When He Says A $15 Minimum Wage Would Lead to Automation," *Forbes*, May 26, 2016.

...food delivery robots...: Kat Lonsdorf, "Hungry? Call Your Neighborhood Delivery Robot," National Public Radio, March 23, 2017.

CHAPTER 5: FACTORY WORKERS AND TRUCK DRIVERS

More than 80 percent of the jobs lost...were due to automation: Federica Cocco, "Most US Manufacturing Jobs Lost to Technology, Not Trade," *Financial Times*, December 2, 2016.

Men make up 73 percent of manufacturing workers: Natalie Schilling, "The Coming Rise of Women in Manufacturing," *Forbes*, September 20, 2013.

About one in six working-age men in America is now out of the workforce: Derek Thompson, "The Missing Men," *The Atlantic*, June 27, 2016.

...41 percent of displaced manufacturing workers...were either still unemployed or dropped out of the labor market...: "Where Did All the Displaced Manufacturing Workers Go?" Manufacturers Alliance for Productivity and Innovation, May 21, 2013.

...44 percent of 200,000 displaced transportation equipment and primary metals manufacturing workers...: Alana Semuels, "America Is Still Making Things," *The Atlantic*, January 6, 2017.

Jobs in manufacturing for people with graduate degrees grew by 32 percent after 2000...: Alana Semuels, "America Is Still Making Things," *The Atlantic*, January 6, 2017.

"The recession led to this huge wiping out of one-industry towns...": Ben Schiller, "Is This the Golden Age of Entrepreneurialism? The Statistics Say No," *Fast Company*, June 1, 2017.

5.2 percent of working-age Americans received disability benefits in 2017, up from only 2.5 percent in 1980...: Social Security Agency, "Selected Data from Social Security's Disability Program," Graphs of disabled worker data (number 2), Social Security Agency, August 2017.

...about half of the 310,000 residents who left the workforce in Michigan between 2003 and 2013 went on disability: Chad Halcon, "Disability Rolls Surge in State: One in 10 Workers in Michigan Collecting Checks," *Crain's Detroit Business*, June 26, 2015.

The average age of truck drivers is 49...: Sean Kilcarr, "Demographics Are Changing Truck Driver Management," *FleetOwner*, September 20, 2017.

Morgan Stanley estimated the savings of automated freight delivery...: *Autonomous Cars: Self-Driving the New Auto Industry Paradigm*, Morgan Stanley Blue Paper, November 6, 2013.

Crashes involving large trucks killed 3,903 people...: Olivia Solon, "Self-Driving Trucks: What's the Future for America's 3.5 Million Truckers?" *The Guardian*, June 17, 2016.

...88 percent of drivers have at least one risk factor for chronic disease: W. Karl Sieber et al., "Obesity and Other Risk Factors: The National Survey of U.S. Long-Haul Truck Driver Health and Injury," *American Journal of Industrial Medicine*, January 4, 2014.

...ripple effects far and wide: Michael Grass, "What Will Happen to Truck Stop Towns When Driverless Truck Technology Expands?" *Free Republic*, May 18, 2015.

About 13% of truck drivers today are unionized: David McGrath, "Truckers Like My Friend Claude Are Extinct—and the Reason Is Sad," *Chicago SunTimes*, September 1, 2017.

About 10 percent of truck drivers...own their own trucks: Owner Operator Independent Drivers Association, https://www.ooida.com/MediaCenter/trucking-facts.asp.

...about 5 percent of Gulf War veterans...worked in transportation in 2012:
Linda Longton, "Fit for Duty: Vets Find New Life in Trucking," *Overdrive*,
August 9, 2012.

CHAPTER 6: WHITE-COLLAR JOBS WILL DISAPPEAR, TOO

*...Narrative Science produces thousands of earnings previews and stock
updates...*: Joe Fassler, "Can the Computers at Narrative Science Replace
Paid Writers?" *The Atlantic*, April 12, 2012.

...Moore's Law, which states that computing power grows exponentially...:
Annie Sneed, "Moore's Law Keeps Going, Defying Expectations," *Scientific
America*, May 19, 2015.

People didn't think that Moore's Law could hold for the past 50 years...:
Russ Juskalian, "Practical Quantum Computers: Advances at Google, Intel,
and Several Research Groups Indicate That Computers with Previously
Unimaginable Power Are Finally within Reach," *MIT Technical Review*,
2017.

*By 2020 about 1.7 megabytes of information will be created every second
for every human being on the planet*: Bernard Marr, "Big Data: 20 Mind-
Boggling Facts Everyone Must Read," *Forbes*, September 30, 2015.

*...financial services...are already being transformed to take advantage
of new technologies...*: Claer Barrett, "Wealth Management Industry in
Disruption" *Financial Times*, May 6, 2016.

Goldman Sachs went from 600 NYSE trader...: Nanette Byrnes, "As
Goldman Embraces Automation, Even the Masters of the Universe Are
Threatened," *MIT Technology Review*, February 7, 2017.

In 2016 the president of the financial services firm State Street predicted,...:
Deirdre Fernandes, "State Street Corp. Eyes 7,000 Layoffs by 2020," *Boston
Globe*, March 29, 2016.

*A new AI for investors platform called Kensho has been adopted by the
major investment banks...*: Nathaniel Popper, "The Robots Are Coming
for Wall Street," *New York Times*, February 28, 2016.

...Bloomberg reported that Wall Street reached "peak human" in 2016...: Hugh Son, "We've Hit Peak Human and an Algorithm Wants Your Job. Now What?" *Bloomberg Markets,* June 8, 2016.

The insurance industry, which employs 2.5 million Americans...: "Number of Employees in the Insurance Industry in the United States from 1960 to 2015 (in millions)." Statista, 2016.

McKinsey predicts a massive diminution in insurance staffing...: Sylvain Johansson and Ulrike Vogelgesang, "Automating the Insurance Industry," *McKinsey Quarterly,* January 2016.

There are 1.7 million bookkeeping accounting and auditing clerks...: Bureau of Labor Statistics, "Bookkeeping, Accounting, and Auditing Clerks," *U.S. Occupational Outlook Handbook,* 2016–2017 edition (Washington, DC: Bureau of Labor Statistics, U.S. Department of Labor, 2017).

...39 percent of jobs in the legal sector will be automated...: Deloitte Insight, "Developing Legal Talent: Stepping into the Future Law Firm," Deloitte, February 2016.

...Google's neural network...has produced art...: Jane Wakefield" Intelligent Machines: AI Art Is Taking on the Experts," BBC News, September 18, 2015.

CHAPTER 7: ON HUMANITY AND WORK

Yuval Harari in Homo Deus makes the point that our cab driver...: Yuval Harari, *Homo Deus: A Brief History of Tomorrow* (New York: HarperCollins, 2017), p. 315.

...Terry Gou...comparing humans to animals: Henry Blodget, "CEO of Apple Partner Foxconn: 'Managing One Million Animals Gives Me a Headache,'" *Business Insider,* January 19, 2012.

Only 13 percent of workers worldwide report being engaged with their jobs: Employee Engagement Insights and Advice for Global Business Leaders: State of the Global Workplace, Gallup Research, October 8, 2013.

"Purpose, meaning, identity, fulfillment, creativity, autonomy—all these things that positive psychology has shown us to be necessary for well-being are absent in the average job": Derek Thompson, "A World without Work," *The Atlantic*, July–August 2015.

4 in 10 Americans reported working more than 50 hours…: Bob Sullivan, "Memo to Work Martyrs: Long Hours Make You Less Productive, CNBC, January 26, 2015.

CHAPTER 8: THE USUAL OBJECTIONS

"You have to recognize realistically that AI is qualitatively different…": Andrew Ross Sorkin, "Partisan Divide over Economic Outlook Worries Ben Bernanke," *New York Times*, April 24, 2017.

Fifty-eight percent of cross-sector experts polled by Bloomberg in 2017…: Shift: The Commission on Work, Workers, and Technology, "Report of Findings," May 16, 2017.

…employers think you're a major risk if you haven't been unemployed for six months…: Nicholas Eberstadt, *Men without Work: America's Invisible Crisis* (West Conshohocken, PA: Templeton Press, 2016), p. 95.

The field has a high rate of turnover…: Alana Semuels, "Who Will Care for America's Seniors?" *The Atlantic*, April 27, 2015.

"Some would call it a dead-end job": Alana Semuels, "Who Will Care for America's Seniors?" *The Atlantic*, April 27, 2015.

…Mathematica Policy Research compared TAA recipients…: Ronald D'Amico and Peter Z. Schochet, "The Evaluation of the Trade Adjustment Assistance Program: A Synthesis of Major Findings," Mathematica Policy Research, December 2012.

A similar evaluation of Michigan's No Worker Left Behind program…: Victor Tan Chen, *Cut Loose: Jobless and Hopeless in an Unfair Economy* (Berkeley: University of California Press, 2015), pp. 63–71.

"I still haven't got a job in my skill": Victor Tan Chen, *Cut Loose: Jobless and Hopeless in an Unfair Economy* (Berkeley: University of California Press, 2015), pp. 63–71.

The unemployment rate also doesn't take into account people who are underemployed…: Nicholas Eberstadt, *Men without Work: America's Invisible Crisis* (West Conshohocken, PA: Templeton Press, 2016), p. 39.

…underemployment rate of recent college graduates…: "The Labor Market for Recent College Graduates," Federal Reserve Bank of New York, October 4, 2017.

The U6 unemployment rate was 8.3 percent in September 2017: "Unemployment Rate—U6 (2000–2017)," PortalSeven.com, September 2017.

CHAPTER 9: LIFE IN THE BUBBLE

The data presented in Tables 9.1. and 9.2. was retrieved from those universities' Career Services Offices or their reports on the students' destinations after graduation. The sources of information used are noted below:

Harvard Crimson Report: Harvard Crimson Report, "The Graduating Class of 2016 by the numbers," http://features.thecrimson.com/2016/senior-survey/post-harvard/, retrieved May 15, 2017.

Yale Office of Career Strategy, "First Destination Report: Class of 2016," http://ocs.yale.edu/sites/default/files/files/OCS, retrieved May 15, 2017.

Princeton Career Services, "Annual Report 2014–2015," https://careerservices.princeton.edu/sites/career/files/Career Services, retrieved May 15, 2017.

University of Pennsylvania Career Services, "Class of 2016 Career Plans Survey Report," http://www.vpul.upenn.edu/careerservices/files/CAS _CPSurvey2016.pdf, retrieved May 15, 2017.

Massachusetts Institute of Technology, "Students after Graduation," http://web.mit.edu/facts/alum.html, retrieved May 15, 2017.

Office of the Provost, MIT Institutional Research, "2016 MIT Senior Survey," http://web.mit.edu/ir/surveys/senior2016.html, retrieved May 15, 2017.

Stanford BEAM, "Class of 2015 Destinations Report," https://beam.stanford.edu/sites/default/files/stanford-_destinations_final_web_view.pdf, retrieved May 15, 2017.

Brown University Center for Careers, "CareerLAB by the Numbers, 2015–2016 Academic Year," https://www.brown.edu/campus-life/support/careerlab/sites/brown.edu.campus-life.support.careerlab/files/uploads/15166_CLAB_By the Numbers Flyer_FNL_0.pdf, retrieved May 15, 2017.

Dartmouth Office of Institutional Research, "2016 Senior Survey," https://www.dartmouth.edu/~oir/2016seniordartmouth.html, retrieved May 15, 2017.

Dartmouth Office of Institutional Research, "2016 Cap and Gown Survey—Final Results," https://www.dartmouth.edu/~oir/2016_cap_and_gown_survey_results_infographic_final.pdf, retrieved May 23, 2017.

Cornell Career Services, "Class of 2016 Postgraduate Report," http://www.career.cornell.edu/resources/surveys/upload/2016_PostGrad-Report_New.pdf, retrieved May 15, 2017.

Columbia University Center for Career Education, "2016 Graduating Student Survey Results," https://www.careereducation.columbia.edu/sites/default/files/2016 GSS—CC %26 SEAS-UG.pdf, retrieved May 15, 2017.

Johns Hopkins University Student Affairs, "Post Graduate Survey Class of 2013 Highlights," https://studentaffairs.jhu.edu/careers/wp-content/uploads/sites/7/2016/03/JHU-PGS-2013-Copy.pdf, retrieved May 15, 2017.

University of Chicago College Admissions, "Class of 2016 Outcomes Report," http://collegeadmissions.uchicago.edu/sites/default/files/uploads/pdfs/uchicago-class-of-2016-outcomes.pdf, retrieved May 15, 2017.

Georgetown Cawley Career Education Center, "Class of 2016 Class Summary," https://georgetown.app.box.com/s/ nzzjv0ogpr7uwplifb4w20j5a43jvp3a, retrieved May 15, 2017.

Duke University Student Affairs, "Class of 2011 Statistics," https:// studentaffairs.duke.edu/career/statistics-reports/career-center-senior -survey/class-2011-statistics, retrieved May 15, 2017.

The use of prescription drugs is at an all-time high among college students...: Isabel Kwai, "The Most Popular Office on Campus," *The Atlantic*, October 9, 2016.

In 2014, an American College Health Association survey...: American College Health Association, "National College Health Assessment, Spring 2014, Reference Group Executive Summary."

Gender imbalances on many campuses...: Lisa Wade, *American Hookup: The New Culture of Sex on Campus* (New York: W. W. Norton Company, 2017), p. 15.

...private company ownership is down more than 60 percent among 18- to 30-year-olds...: Ruth Simon and Caelainn Barr, "Endangered Species: Young U.S. Entrepreneurs. New Data Underscore Financial Challenges and Low Tolerance for Risk among Young Americans," *Wall Street Journal*, January 2, 2015.

"The message wasn't explicit...". J. D. Vance, *Hillbilly Elegy: A Memoir of a Family and Culture in Crisis* (New York: Harper Collins, 2016), pp. 56–57.

The meritocracy was never intended to be a real thing...: David Freedman, "The War on Stupid People," *The Atlantic*, July–August 2016.

"The way we treat stupid people in the future...": Yuval Harari, *Homo Deus: A Brief History of Tomorrow* (New York: HarperCollins, 2017), p. 100.

CHAPTER 10: MINDSETS OF SCARCITY AND ABUNDANCE

A UK study found that the most common shared trait across entrepreneurs...: David G. Blanchflower and Andrew J. Oswald, "What

Makes an Entrepreneur?" 1998, retrieved from http://www.andrewoswald
.com/docs/entrepre.pdf.

*A U.S. survey found that in 2014 over 80 percent of startups were initially
self-funded...*: Carly Okyle, "The Year in Startup Funding (Infographic),"
Entrepreneur, January 3, 2015.

*...the majority of high-growth entrepreneurs were white (84 percent) males
(72 percent...*: Jordan Weissman, "Entrepreneurship: The Ultimate White
Privilege?" *The Atlantic*, August 16, 2013.

*Barbara Corcoran and Daymond John both described growing up dyslexic
and being told that school wasn't going to be their route to success*: Kim
Lachance Shandrow, "How Being Dyslexic and 'Lousy in School' Made
Shark Tank Star Barbara Corcoran a Better Entrepreneur," *Entrepreneur*,
September 19, 2014.

*A study of tens of thousands of JPMorgan Chase customers saw average
monthly income volatility of 30–40 percent per month...*: Patricia Cohen,
"Steady Jobs, with Pay and Hours That Are Anything But," *New York Times*,
May 31, 2017.

The average worker dreads schedule volatility so much...: Alexandre Mas
and Amanda Pallais, "Valuing Alternative Work Arrangements," National
Bureau of Economic Research, September 2016.

Eldar Shafir...and Sendhil Mullainathan conducted a series of studies...:
Sendhil Mullainathan and Eldar Shafir, *Scarcity: Why Having Too Little Means
So Much* (New York: Times Books, 2013), pp. 49–56. Also see Amy Novotney,
"The Psychology of Scarcity," *Monitor on Psychology* 45, no. 2 (February 2014).

CHAPTER 11: GEOGRAPHY IS DESTINY

Many of the facts about Youngstown's rise and fall are from Sean Posey,
"America's Fastest Shrinking City: The Story of Youngstown, Ohio,"
Hampton Institute, June 18, 2013.

The history of Youngstown is from Sherry Lee Linkon and John Russo,
Steeltown U.S.A.: Work and Memory in Youngstown, Culture America
(Lawrence: University Press of Kansas, 2002), pp. 47–53.

The city was transformed by a psychological and cultural breakdown: Derek Thompson, "A World without Work," *The Atlantic*, July–August 2015.

"I thought we were rich": PBS News Hour, "How Rust Belt City Youngstown Plans to Overcome Decades Of Decline," https://www .youtube.com/watch?v=IKuGNt1w0tA.

"I started off working with a shovel and pick…": Chris Arnade, "White Flight Followed Factory Jobs out of Gary, Indiana. Black People Didn't Have a Choice," *The Guardian*, March 28, 2017.

"I really would like to move someplace more beautiful…": Chris Arnade, "White Flight Followed Factory Jobs out of Gary, Indiana. Black People Didn't Have a Choice," *The Guardian*, March 28, 2017.

"Between 1950 and 1980…patterns of social pathology emerged…": Howard Gillette, Jr., *Camden after the Fall: Decline and Renewal in a Post-Industrial City* (Philadelphia: University of Pennsylvania Press, 2006), pp. 12–13.

…"a major metropolitan area run by armed teenagers with no access to jobs or healthy food"…: Matt Taibbi, "Apocalypse, New Jersey: A Dispatch from America's Most Desperate Town," *Rolling Stone*, December 11, 2013.

…since 1970 the difference between the most and least educated U.S. cities has doubled…: Tyler Cowen, *Average Is Over: Powering America beyond the Age of the Great Stagnation* (New York: Penguin Books, 2013), pp. 172–173.

Fifty-nine percent of American counties saw more businesses close than open…: "Dynamism in Retreat: Consequences for Regions, Markets and Workers," Economic Innovation Group, February 2017.

California, New York, and Massachusetts accounted for 75 percent of venture capital in 2016…: Richard Florida, "A Closer Look at the Geography of Venture Capital in the U.S." CityLab, February 23, 2016.

A series of studies by the economists Raj Chetty and Nathaniel Hendren…: Raj Chetty and Nathaniel Hendren, "The Impacts of Neighborhoods on Intergenerational Mobility: Childhood Exposure Effects and County-Level Estimates," Equality of Opportunity, May 2015.

David Brooks described such towns vividly...: David Brooks, "What's the Matter with Republicans?" *New York Times*, July 4, 2017.

CHAPTER 12: MEN, WOMEN, AND CHILDREN

...when manufacturing work becomes less available...: David Autor, David Dorn, and Gordon Hanson, "When Work Disappears: Manufacturing Decline and the Falling Marriage-Market Value of Men," National Bureau of Economic Research, February 2017.

Average male wages [for working-class men] have declined since 1990 in real terms: Jared Bernstein, "Real Earnings, Real Anger," *Washington Post*, March 9, 2016.

A Pew research study showed that many men are foregoing or delaying marriage...: Kim Parker and Renee Stepler, "As U.S. Marriage Rate Hovers at 50 percent, Education Gap in Marital Status Widens," Pew Research Center, September 14, 2017. Also see Wendy Wang and Kim Parker, "Record Share of Americans Have Never Married," Pew Research Center, September 24, 2014.

...one in six men in America of prime age (25–54) are either unemployed or out of the workforce...: Derek Thompson, "The Missing Men," *The Atlantic*, June 27, 2016.

Young men without college degrees have replaced 75 percent of the time they used to spend...: Ana Swanson, "Study Finds Young Men Are Playing Video Games Instead of Getting Jobs," *Chicago Tribune*, September 23, 2016.

Women are now the clear majority of college graduates: Alex Williams, "The New Math on Campus," *New York Times*, February 5, 2010.

Marriage has declined for all classes in the past 40 years...: Anthony Cilluffo, "Share of Married Americans Is Falling, but They Still Pay Most of the Nation's Income Taxes," Pew Research Center, April 12, 2017.

Of the 11 million families with children under age 18 and no spouse present, 8.5 million are single mothers: "2016 Current Population Survey Annual Social and Economic Supplement," U.S. Census Bureau.

...growing up with stably married parents makes one more likely to succeed at school, but that an absent father had a bigger impact on boys...: William J. Doherty, Brian J. Willoughby, and Jason L. Wilde, "Is the Gender Gap in College Enrollment Influenced by Nonmarital Birth Rates and Father Absence?" *Family Relations*, September 24, 2015.

"As a child, I associated accomplishments in school with femininity...".: J. D. Vance, *Hillbilly Elegy: A Memoir of a Family and Culture in Crisis* (New York: Harper Collins, 2016), pp. 245–246.

...one 2015 U.S. Centers for Disease Control study finding as many as 14 percent of boys received a diagnosis: National Center of Health Statistics, Centers for Disease Control and Prevention, "Attention Deficit Hyperactivity Disorder (ADHD)," https://www.cdc.gov/nchs/fastats/adhd.htm.

70 percent of valedictorians were girls in 2012: Jon Birger, *Date-onomics: How Dating Became a Lopsided Numbers Game* (New York: Workman, 2015), p. 32.

...50 percent of Americans live within 18 miles of their mother...: Quoctrung Bui and Claire Cain Miller, "The Typical American Lives Only 18 Miles from Mom," *New York Times*, December 23, 2015.

CHAPTER 13: THE PERMANENT SHADOW CLASS: WHAT DISPLACEMENT LOOKS LIKE

"[W]e thought it must be wrong...we just couldn't believe that this could have happened...: Jessica Boddy, "The Forces Driving Middle-Aged White People's 'Deaths of Despair,'" National Public Radio, March 23, 2017.

Coroners' offices in Ohio have reported being overwhelmed...: Kimiko de Freytas-Tamura, "Amid Opioid Overdoses, Ohio Coroner's Office Runs Out of Room for Bodies," *New York Times*, February 2, 2017.

The five states with the highest rates of death linked to drug overdoses...: Josh Katz, "Drug Deaths in America Are Rising Faster Than Ever," *New York Times*, June 5, 2017. Also see Center for Behavioral Health Statistics and Quality, "2015 National Survey on Drug Use and Health: Detailed

Tables," Substance Abuse and Mental Health Services Administration, Rockville, MD, 2016.

Addiction is so widespread that in Cincinnati hospitals now require universal drug testing for pregnant mothers...: Laura Newman, "As Substance Abuse Rises, Hospitals Drug Test Mothers, Newborns," *Clinical Laboratory News*, March 1, 2016.

...Purdue Pharma, which was fined $635 million in 2007 for misbranding the drug...: Mike Mariani, "How the American Opiate Epidemic Was Started by One Pharmaceutical Company," *The Week*, March 4, 2015.

"[W]e know of no other medication routinely used for a nonfatal condition that kills patients so frequently": Sonia Moghe, Opioid History: From 'Wonder Drug' to Abuse Epidemic," CNN, October 14, 2016.

"We are seeing an unbelievably sad and extensive heroin epidemic...": "The Heroin Business Is Booming in America," *Bloomberg Businessweek*, May 11, 2017.

The lifetime value of a disability award is about $300K for the average recipient: Steve Kroft, "Disability, USA," CBS News, October 10, 2013.

About 40 percent of claims are ultimately approved...: "Annual Statistical Report on the Social Security Disability Insurance Program, 2015," U.S. Social Security Administration.

One law firm generated $70 million in revenue in one year alone...: Chana Joffe-Walt, "Unfit for Work: The Startling Rise of Disability in America," National Public Radio, http://apps.npr.org/unfit-for-work, retrieved November 8, 2017.

...Social Security Disability Insurance today essentially serves as unemployment insurance...: David H. Autor and Mark G. Duggan, "The Growth in the Social Security Disability Rolls: A Fiscal Crisis Unfolding," *Journal of Economic Perspectives*, Summer 2006.

"If the American public knew what was going on in our system, half would be outraged and the other half would apply for benefits.": Steve Kroft, "Disability, USA," CBS News, October 10, 2013.

In 2013, 56.5 percent of prime-age men 25–54 who were not in the workforce reported receiving disability payments: Nicholas Eberstadt, *Men without Work: America's Invisible Crisis* (West Conshohocken, PA: Templeton Press, 2016), p. 118.

CHAPTER 14: VIDEO GAMES AND THE (MALE) MEANING OF LIFE

...22 percent of men between the ages of 21 and 30 with less than a bachelor's degree reported not working at all in the previous year...: Ana Swanson, "Study Finds Young Men Are Playing Video Games Instead of Getting Jobs," *Chicago Tribune*, September 23, 2016.

...young men without college degrees have replaced 75 percent of the time...: Peter Suderman, "Young Men Are Playing Video Games Instead of Getting Jobs. That's OK. (For Now.)," *Reason*, July 2017.

More U.S. men aged 18–34 are now living with their parents...: Kim Parker and Renee Stepler, "As U.S. Marriage Rate Hovers at 50 Percent, Education Gap in Marital Status Widens," Pew Research Center, September 14, 2017.

The Annual Time Use survey in 2014 indicated high levels of time spent "attending gambling establishments"...: Nicholas Eberstadt, *Men without Work: America's Invisible Crisis* (West Conshohocken, PA: Templeton Press, 2016), p. 93.

CHAPTER 15: THE SHAPE WE'RE IN/DISINTEGRATION

Membership in organizations...has declined by between 25 to 50 percent since the 1960s: Robert D. Putnam, "The Strange Disappearance of Civic America," *American Prospect*, winter 1995.

...approximately 2,500 leftist bombings in America between 1971 and 1972...: Bryan Burrough, "The Bombings of America That We Forgot," *Time*, September 20, 2016.

...approximately 270 to 310 million firearms in the United States...: "A Minority of Americans Own Guns, but Just How Many Is Unclear," Pew Research Center, June 4, 2013.

...Peter Turchin proposes a structural-demographic theory of political instability...: Peter Turchin, *Ages of Discord: A Structural-Demographic Analysis of American History* (Chaplin, CT: Beresta Books, 2016), pp. 200–202.

Alec Ross... described the Freddie Gray riots in 2015 as partially a product of economic despair: Alec Ross, *The Industries of the Future* (New York: Simon and Schuster, 2015), p. 38.

...about one-third of Californians supported secession in a recent poll...: Sharon Bernstein, "More Californians Dreaming of a Country without Trump: Poll," Reuters, January 23, 2017.

CHAPTER 16: THE FREEDOM DIVIDEND

Peter Frase... points out that work encompasses three things...: Derek Thompson, "A World without Work," *The Atlantic*, July–August 2015.

Thomas Paine, 1796: Simon Birnbaum and Karl Widerquist, "History of Basic Income," Basic Income Earth Network, 1986.

Martin Luther King Jr., 1967: Martin Luther King Jr., "Final Words of Advice," Address made to the Tenth Anniversary Convention of the SCLC, Atlanta, on August 16, 1967.

Richard Nixon, August 1969: Richard Nixon, "324—Address to the Nation on Domestic Programs," American President Project, August 8, 1969.

Milton Friedman, 1980: "Brief History of Basic Income Ideas," Basic Income Earth Network, 1986.

Bernie Sanders, May 2014: Scott Santens, "On the Record: Bernie Sanders on Basic Income," *Medium*, January 29, 2016.

Stephen Hawking, July 2015: "Answers to Stephen Hawking's AMA Are Here," *Wired*, July 2015.

Barack Obama, June 2016: Chris Weller, "President Obama Hints at Supporting Unconditional Free Money Because of a Looming Robot Takeover," *Business Insider*, June 24, 2016.

Barack Obama, October 2016: Scott Dadich, "Barack Obama, Neural Nets, Self-Driving Cars, and the Future of the World," *Wired*, November 2016.

Warren Buffett and Bill Gates, January 2017: Charlie Rose, interview with Bill Gates and Warren Buffett, Columbia University, January 2017.

Elon Musk, February, 2017: Chris Weller, "Elon Musk Doubles Down on Universal Basic Income: 'It's Going to Be Necessary,'" *Business Insider*, February 13, 2017.

Mark Zuckerberg, May 2017: Mark Zuckerberg, commencement speech, Harvard University, May 2017.

…adopting it would permanently grow the economy by 12.56 to 13.10 percent…: Michalis Nikiforos, Marshall Steinbaum, and Gennaro Zezza, "Modeling the Macroeconomic Effects of a Universal Basic Income," Roosevelt Institute, August 29, 2017.

…technology companies are excellent at avoiding taxes: "Fortune 500 Companies Hold a Record $2.6 Trillion Offshore," Institute on Taxation and Economic Policy, March 2017.

"UBI…is not shaming…": https://www.facebook.com/basicincomequotes/videos/1365257523593155.

CHAPTER 17: UNIVERSAL BASIC INCOME IN THE REAL WORLD

In 1969, President Nixon proposed the Family Assistance Plan…: Lila MacLellan, "That Time When Dick Cheney and Donald Rumsfeld Ran a Universal Basic Income Experiment for Nixon," *Quartz*, March 13, 2017.

The New Jersey Graduated Work Incentive Experiment gave cash payments: Mike Albert and Kevin C. Brown, "Guaranteed Income's Moment in the Sun," *Remapping Debate*, April 24, 2013.

…the most rigorous and generous study in Denver and Seattle…: Gary Christophersen, *Final Report of the Seattle-Denver Income Maintenance Experiment* (Washington, DC.: U.S. Dept. of Health and Human Services, 1983).

"Politically, there was a concern...": Rutger Bregman, *Utopia for Realists: The Case for a Universal Basic Income, Open Borders, and a 15-hour Workweek* (Boston: Little, Brown and Company, 2016), p. 37.

Each Alaskan now receives a petroleum dividend...: Brian Merchant, "The Only State Where Everyone Gets Free Money," Motherboard Vice, September 4, 2015.

...the dividend has increased average infant birthweight...: Wankyo Chung, Hyungserk Ha, and Beomsoo Kim, "Money Transfer and Birth Weight: Evidence from the Alaska Permanent Fund Dividend," *Economic Inquiry* 54 (2013).

...helped keep rural Alaskans solvent: Scott Goldsmith, "The Alaska Permanent Fund Dividend: A Case Study in the Direct Distribution of Resource Rent," Alaska Permanent Fund Dividend Program, January 2011.

...one reason that Alaska has the second-lowest income inequality in the country: Rachel Waldholz, "Alaska's Annual Dividend Adds Up for Residents," Marketplace, March 16, 2016.

In 1995, a group of researchers began tracking the personalities of 1,420 low-income children...: Roberto A. Ferdman, "The Remarkable Thing That Happens to Poor Kids When You Give Their Parents a Little Money," *Washington Post*, October 8, 2015.

...GiveDirectly has raised more than $120 million...: Annie Lowrey, "The Future of Not Working," *New York Times*, February 26, 2017.

"GiveDirectly...has sent shockwaves through the charity sector...": Claire Provost, "Charity Begins on Your Phone: East Africans Buoyed by Novel Way of Giving," *The Guardian*, December 31, 2013.

Canada is giving 4,000 participants in Ontario grants of up to $12,570...: Ashifa Kassam, "Ontario Plans to Launch Universal Basic Income Trial Run This Summer," *The Guardian*, April 24, 2017.

Iran implemented a full-blown equivalent of UBI in 2011...: Jeff Ihaza, "Here's What Happened When Iran Introduced a Basic Income," *Outline*, May 31, 2017.

CHAPTER 18: TIME AS THE NEW MONEY

"A man . . . with no means of filling up time, is as miserable out of work as a dog on the chain": George Orwell, *Down and Out in Paris and London* (New York: Mariner Books, 1972), p. 129.

Teach for America spends approximately $51,000 per corps member . . .: Rachel M. Cohen, "The True Cost of Teach for America's Impact on Urban Schools," *American Prospect*, January 5, 2015.

The U.S. Military spends approximately $170,000 per soldier per year . . .: "Growth in DoD's Budget from 2000 to 2014," Congressional Budget Office, November 2014.

The Peace Corps has over 1,000 full-time employees supporting 7,200 volunteers . . .: "Performance and Accountability Report," Peace Corps, November 15, 2015.

During the Great Depression in the 1930s, the U.S. government hired 40,000 recreation officers and artists . . .: Susan Currell, *The March of Spare Time: The Problem and Promise of Leisure in the Great Depression* (Philadelphia: University of Pennsylvania Press, 2005), pp. 51–53.

. . . 315 members of the local time bank members have exchanged 64,000 hours of mutual work . . .: Time Banks Brattleboro Time Trade, Time Banks, accessed on September 8, 2017.

Amanda Witman, a 40-year-old single mother, wrote about her experience . . .: "Real Women's Stories: 'We Make Ends Meet without Money,'" AllYou.com.

Americans face at least three interlocking sets of problems . . .: Edgar Cahn and Jonathan Rowe, *Time Dollars: The New Currency That Enables Americans to Turn Their Hidden Resource—Time—into Personal Security and Community Renewal* (Emmaus, PA: Rodale Press, 1992).

CHAPTER 19: HUMAN CAPITALISM

The concept of GDP and economic progress didn't even exist until the Great Depression: The Federal Reserve of St. Louis, Discover Economic History,

National Income, 1929–32. Letter from the Acting Secretary of Commerce Transmitting in Response to Senate Resolution No. 220 (72D CONG.) *A Report on National Income, 1929–32* (Washington, DC: Government Printing Office, 1934).

Steve Ballmer set up a series of measurements and facts at www.USAFacts .org that is a treasure trove of social metrics and pulls from many public and private sources.

CHAPTER 20: THE STRONG STATE AND THE NEW CITIZENSHIP

When Harry Truman left the office of the presidency in 1953…: Jeff Jacoby, "Harry Truman's Obsolete Integrity," *New York Times*, March 2, 2007.

This practice started changing with Gerald Ford joining the boards…: Scott Wilson, "In Demand: Washington's Highest (and Lowest) Speaking Fees," ABC News, July 14, 2014.

Sheila Bair…, the former head of the Federal Deposit Insurance Corporation, lived through this conflict herself…: Ben Protess, "Slowing the Revolving Door between Public and Private Jobs," *New York Times*, November 11, 2013.

The family that owns Purdue Pharma…is now the 16th richest family in the country…: Alex Morrell, "The OxyContin Clan: The $14 Billion Newcomer to Forbes 2015 List of Richest U.S. Families," *Forbes*, July 1, 2015.

The big banks eventually settled with the Department of Justice for billions of dollars…: Kate Cox, "How Corporations Got the Same Rights as People (but Don't Ever Go to Jail)," *Consumerist.com*, September 12, 2014.

Elon Musk in 2017 called for proactive regulation of AI…: Samuel Gibbs, "Elon Musk: Regulate AI to Combat 'Existential Threat' before It's Too Late," *The Guardian*, July 17, 2017.

Tristan Harris…has written compellingly about how apps are designed to function like slot machines…: Tristan Harris, "How Technology Is Hijacking Your Mind—from a Magician and Google Design Ethicist," *Thrive Global*, May 18, 2016.

... *"the best minds of my generation are thinking about how to make people click ads"*: Drake Baer, "Why Data God Jeffrey Hammerbacher Left Facebook to Found Cloudera," *Fast Company,* April 18, 2013.

CHAPTER 21: HEALTH CARE IN A WORLD WITHOUT JOBS

Health care bills were the number one cause of personal bankruptcy in 2013...: Dan Mangan, "Medical Bills Are the Biggest Cause of US Bankruptcies: Study," CNBC.com, June 24, 2013.

...we are last among major industrialized nations in efficiency, equity, and health outcomes attributable to medical care...: Courtney Baird, "Top Healthcare Stories for 2016: Pay-for-Performance," Committee for Economic Development, March 8, 2016.

"Unless you are protected by Medicare, the health care market is not a market at all": Steven Brill, "Bitter Pill: Why Medical Bills Are Killing Us: How Outrageous Pricing and Egregious Profits Are Destroying Our Health Care," *Time*, March 4, 2013.

"We do waste money on insurance, but we also pay basically twice as much for everything": Joshua Holland, "Medicare-for-All Isn't the Solution for Universal Health Care," *The Nation*, August 2, 2017.

...doctors today see themselves not as "pillars of any community" but as "technicians on an assembly line"...: Meghan O'Rourke, "Doctors Tell All—and It's Bad," *The Atlantic*, November 2014.

A 2016 survey of American doctors by the Physicians Foundation...: "Survey: Many Doctors Looking to Leave Profession amid Burnout, Low Morale," Advisory Board, September 26, 2016.

The average educational debt load for a medical school graduate is $180,000...: Aaron E. Carroll, "A Doctor Shortage? Let's Take a Closer Look," *New York Times*, November 7, 2016.

About 65 million Americans live in what one expert called basically "a primary care desert": Emma Court, "America's Facing a Shortage of Primary-Care Doctors," MarketWatch, April 4, 2016.

The Association of American Medical Colleges estimated that the number of additional doctors necessary...: "The Complexities of Physician Supply and Demand: Projections from 2014 to 2025," Association of American Medical Colleges, April 5, 2016.

In one study, IBM's Watson made the same recommendation as human doctors did in 99 percent of 1,000 medical cases...: Dom Galeon, "IBM's Watson AI Recommends Same Treatment as Doctors in 99 percent of Cancer Cases," Futurism.com, October 28, 2016.

The best approach is what they do at the Cleveland Clinic...: Megan McArdle, "Can the Cleveland Clinic Save American Health Care?" *Daily Beast*, February 26, 2013.

The Southcentral Foundation...treats health problems and behavioral problems as tied together...: Joanne Silberner, "The Doctor Will Analyze You Now," *Politico*, August 9, 2017.

CHAPTER 22: BUILDING PEOPLE

"Character is the main object of education": David Brooks, "Becoming a Real Person," *New York Times*, September 8, 2014.

...William James wrote around the same time that character and moral significance are built...: David Brooks, "Becoming a Real Person," *New York Times*, September 8, 2014.

SAT scores have declined significantly in the last 10 years: Nick Anderson, "SAT Scores at Lowest Level in 10 Years, Fueling Worries about High Schools," *Washington Post*, September 3, 2015.

...smartphone use has caused a spike in depression and anxiety...: Jean M. Twenge, *iGen: Why Today's Super-Connected Kids Are Growing Up Less Rebellious, More Tolerant, Less Happy—and Completely Unprepared for Adulthood—and What That Means for the Rest of Us* (New York: Atria Books, 2017).

... "the worst use of software in [education] is in replacement of humans...": John Battelle, "Max Ventilla of AltSchool: The Full Shift Dialogs Transcript," NewCo Shift, July 13, 2016.

The United States is one of only four out of 196 countries in the world... that does not have federally mandated time off from work for new mothers: Matt Phillips, "Countries without Paid Maternity Leave: Swaziland, Lesotho, Papua New Guinea, and the United States of America," *Quartz*, January 15, 2014.

...Denmark gives parents 52 weeks of paid leave they can split between them...: Chris Weller, "These 10 Countries Have the Best Parental Leave Policies in the World," *Business Insider*, August 22, 2016.

Studies have shown that robust family leave policies improve children's health and heighten women's employment rates...: Barbara Gault et al., "Paid Parental Leave in the United States: What the Data Tell Us about Access, Usage, and Economic and Health Benefits," U.S. Department of Labor Women's Bureau, Institute for Women's Policy Research, January 23, 2014.

...11.4 million single mothers raising 17.2 million children in the United States...: "Table C2, Household Relationship and Living Arrangements of Children Under 18 Years, by Age and Sex: 2016," U.S. Census Bureau, 2017.

Communal living arrangements have been shown to increase social cohesion...: Saskia De Melker, "Cohousing Communities Help Prevent Social Isolation," *PBS News Hour*, February 12, 2017.

Only 6 percent of American high school students were enrolled in a vocational course of study in 2013...: Dana Goldstein, "Seeing Hope for Flagging Economy, West Virginia Revamps Vocational Track," *New York Times*, August 10, 2017.

A Georgetown center estimated that there are 30 million good-paying jobs that don't require a college degree...: Anthony P. Carnevale et al., "Good Jobs That Pay without a BA," Georgetown University Center on Education and the Workforce, 2017.

The most recent graduation rate for first-time, full-time undergraduate students...: "Undergraduate Retention and Graduation Rates," Condition of Education 2017. National Center for Education Statistics, April 2017.

The main reasons cited for dropping out are being unprepared for the rigors of academic work...: Lou Carlozo, "Why College Students Stop Short of a Degree," *Reuters*, March 27, 2012.

We are up to a record $1.4 trillion in educational debt that serves as an anchor...: Kerry Rivera, "The State of Student Loan Debt in 2017," Experian.com, August 23, 2017.

...college tuition has risen at several times the rate of inflation the past 20 years...: Steve Odland, "College Costs out of Control," *Forbes*, March 24, 2012.

Average college tuition has risen as much as 440 percent in the last 25 years: Lynn O'Shaughnessy, "Higher Education Bubble Will Burst," *U.S. News and World Report*, May 3, 2011.

...administrative positions at colleges and universities grew by 60 percent between 1993 and 2009...: John Hechinger, "The Troubling Dean-to-Professor Ratio," *Bloomberg Businessweek*, November 21, 2012.

...Yale spent more the previous year on private equity managers managing its endowment...: Victor Fleischer, "Stop Universities from Hoarding Money," *New York Times*, August 19, 2015.

...cost of taxpayer subsidies for a community college student as between $2,000 and $4,000 per student per year...: Jorge Klor de Alva and Mark Schneider, *Rich Schools, Poor Students: Tapping Large University Endowments to Improve Student Outcomes*, Nexus Research, April 2015.

In 1975, colleges employed one professional staffer...for every 50 students: Benjamin Ginsberg, "Administrators Ate My Tuition," *Washington Monthly*, September–October 2011.

The 90 coding boot camps across the country produced about 23,000 graduates in total...: Steve Lohr, "As Coding Boot Camps Close, the Field Faces a Reality Check," *New York Times*, August 24, 2017.

At Minerva, students take classes online, but they do so while living together in dorm-style housing: Claire Cain Miller, "Extreme Study Abroad: The World Is Their Campus," *New York Times*, October 30, 2015.

Teacher quality dramatically impacts student learning. One school in Manhattan, the Equity Project, pays teachers $125,000 a year on the same budget as a normal school by having fewer administrators and having teachers take on more responsibility instead. This approach is showing remarkable results: Frederick M. Hess, "Teacher Quality, Not Quantity," *National Review*, October 28, 2014.

Recent research from Stanford University found that one-on-one tutoring does not only better prepare children, but it also calms the fear circuitry in the brain: Patti Neighmond, "1 Tutor + 1 Student = Better Math Scores, Less Fear," National Public Radio, September 8, 2015.

Blue Engine recruits and places college graduates as full-time teaching assistants in high schools, leading to a student to teacher ratio of approximately 6 to 1 instead of the usual 26 to 1. Students receive rapid-fire feedback and weekly 'social cognition' coaching sessions: David Bornstein, "A Team Approach to Get Students College Ready," *New York Times*, May 13, 2017.

INDEX

Page references followed by *f* indicate tables, charts, or graphs.